MOTORCYCLE TOURING
An International Directory – 1991/92

A Whirlaway Book

Whitehorse Press, Boston

Copyright © 1991 by Kennedy Associates

All rights reserved. No part of this publication may be reproduced or transmitted in any form or by any means, electronic or mechanical, including photocopy, recording, or any information storage or retrieval system, without permission in writing from the publisher.

Cover photo courtesy of Edelweis Bike Travel. Photo was taken by Klaus Daams on the west side of Lago di Garda, in Italy.

A Whirlaway Book. Published in March 1991 by Whitehorse Press, 154 West Brookline Street, Boston, Massachusetts 02118, U.S.A.

Publisher: Daniel Kennedy
Editor: Susie deVille
Research Associate: Paul Lyons
Research Assistant: Max Canis

Whirlaway and Whitehorse Press are trademarks of Kennedy Associates.

ISBN 0-9621834-3-1

5 4 3 2 1

Printed in the United States of America

INTRODUCTION

Motorcycle Touring: An International Directory – 1991/92 is dedicated to our readers, those who are and those who are becoming touring enthusiasts. We want to play a part in getting you on the road more often and in more exciting places, on group tours, and on independent adventures. Our job, as we see it, is to make motorcycle touring more accessible to you.

As you will soon see, there is a lot of information in this book. The nature of travel tours is volatile; things are changing all the time. While we have tried to be complete and accurate, inevitably there will be omissions and errors of various kinds. Schedules and prices are current as we go to press but are subject to change at any time.

You should use this book to get an idea of the kind of trips offered in various parts of the world. When you have narrowed your interest down to a few tour operators or motorcycle rental agents, contact them for current information about dates, prices, and other details. This book is not intended to be a substitute for the information you'll receive from the businesses listed here, but rather as a guide to those you'll want to learn more about.

In presenting matters of price, we use the dollar sign ($) alone only for United States currency. For other countries' dollars, such as Australian dollars, we wrote AUS $35. We kept the same units of currency used by the respective tour operator: Deutsche Marks, New Zealand dollars, and so on. Because these currencies fluctuate relative to the U.S. dollar, we felt it was better not to convert them. Still, to give you some idea of the relative values (as of late January, 1991) here are the conversions for currencies you'll find in this book:

One U.S. dollar = AS 10.53 (Austrian schillings)
One U.S. dollar = AUS $1.28 (Australian dollars)
One U.S. dollar = B 25.15 (Thai baht)
One U.S. dollar = CAN $1.16 (Canadian dollars)
One U.S. dollar = DM 1.49 (German Deutsche Marks)
One U.S. dollar = f. 1.68 (Dutch florin)
One U.S. dollar = Fr 5.07 (French francs)
One U.S. dollar = NZ $1.66 (New Zealand dollars)
One U.S. dollar = £0.51 (British pounds)

One Austrian schilling = .09 U.S. dollars
One Australian dollar = .78 U.S. dollars
One Thai baht = .04 U.S. dollars
One Canadian dollar = .86 U.S. dollars
One German Deutsche Mark = .67 U.S. dollars
One Dutch florin = .60 U.S. dollars
One French franc = .20 U.S. dollars
One New Zealand dollar = .60 U.S. dollars
One British pound = 1.96 U.S. dollars

It is worth mentioning that many of the tour operators represented in this book are relatively small enterprises; they are dealing with a small number of tours and a small number of guests. One traveler more or less can make the difference between a tour being cancelled, being held, or being overbooked. They (and ultimately you) will benefit greatly by early contact to let them know of your interest in a particular tour. You should book early once you've made your decision. If you wait too long to contact them, a tour may be filled or canceled before you even get to them. They can be very flexible in their planning — scheduling overflow provisions or keeping a tour — if they just have a little advance warning from you.

Similarly, motorcycle rental agencies tend to be small and will benefit from early contact from you once you decide to rent a motorcycle for your vacation trip. Because they have only a limited number of machines available for rent you will have a better chance of getting the kind of motorcycle you want if you give the agency plenty of advance notice.

Some countries where you travel will require visas, so make sure you check with the tour operator for details. If a visa is necessary and you are unable to go to the representative consulate, allow four to six weeks for your application to be processed through the mail. Similarly, some countries will require vaccinations prior to entry, so again check with the tour operator. It is also a good idea to discuss your travel plans with your doctor so he or she may prescribe prophylactic pharmaceuticals (e.g., malaria pills) if they are necessary. Note: if the tour you select takes you to high altitudes (over 4,500 feet), discuss altitude motion sickness with your tour operator and your doctor. Some people are more susceptible than others and you should be aware of the symptoms so you can prevent injury to yourself and others.

If you are new to motorcycle touring or would like to learn more about it, an excellent book is available to help you: *Motorcycle Touring and Travel*, by Bill Stermer (Whitehorse Press, Boston). Bill's book contains an impressive assortment of information essential to the serious motorcycle traveler, including sections on clothing, packing, motorcycle accessories, safety, and many other topics.

In the two years since the last edition was published, I have spoken with many motorcycle travelers about their vacation plans and needs. In those conversations I have noticed a widely held misunderstanding about the nature of organized motorcycle tours. It concerns the degree of independence permissible on organized tours. Many motorcyclists are very independent people (isn't that why a lot of us ride?) and they rebel at the thought of going from point A to point B with a dozen other riders. Many of the tours in this book (but not all) are what I would call "loosely guided tours". On those tours, each day's activity is left to the discretion of each participant. Your main obligation each day is to make it to the hotel designated for the next night's stay. During the day you are free to explore, or take it easy, or ride 'til you drop. On these loosely guided tours, the tour operators see their role as *facilitator* to your enjoyment: they provide the motorcycle, the hotel arrangements, maps and directions, most meals, usually the flight arrangements, and other details. Your job is to have a good time, at your own pace and in your own way. The tour operator is there to give you advice if you need it and to otherwise make you unaware of the details of planning.

Other tours are more tightly controlled. Many of the off-road trips and trips through potentially difficult territory (e.g. China, the Sahara desert) require all riders to stay together during the day for reasons of safety or convenience. The role of the tour operator on these trips is more pervasive and the freedom of each participant more limited. As you read the tour descriptions in this book I think in most cases you'll be able to tell whether it is of the loosely guided or tightly controlled type.

This is the second edition of this directory; the first was published two years ago. Putting it together has given us a chance to speak with motorcycle tour operators and rental companies all over the world. In the context of the Persian Gulf crisis which has been developing over the past few months, it is very reassuring to speak with people from other countries who share a love for motorcycling and travel and with whom we can work and enjoy a common interest. I believe travel is good for the human spirit. It allows us to learn about other people and their culture, letting us see them as friends rather than aliens. My hope is that you will find this book valuable in planning your next motorcycling vacation, and that you will want to go to one of the many interesting places represented here, either with a tour group or on your own. Motorcycling is a wonderful way to see the world, to meet other people, and to have the vacation of a lifetime.

We need your help to make sure that every edition of this book is as complete and accurate as humanly possible. Perhaps you know of another motorcycle tour, a motorcycle rental agency not included in this edition, or another company specializing in motorcycle transport services. We would appreciate hearing about anything you think would be of value to future readers of this directory. We want feedback about the tours you have taken, to provide a better subjective gauge for future participants. Please send your comments — pro and con. Write to us or call us at:

Whitehorse Press
154 West Brookline Street
Boston, Massachusetts 02118
Phone: 800-842-7077 or 617-241-5241

CONTENTS

Tour Operators	7

Organized Tours	63
Canada & Alaska 65	
United States 77	
Mexico & Caribbean 103	
South America 129	
Great Britain 141	
Western Europe 149	
Eastern Europe 193	
Mediterranean Area 201	
Africa & Middle East 215	
Asia & Indonesia 233	
Australia 257	
New Zealand 287	

Motorcycle Rental Agencies	293
United States 295	
South America 309	
Great Britain 310	
Western Europe 316	
Mediterranean Area 328	
Africa & Middle East 330	
Australia 330	
New Zealand 335	

Motorcycle Transport Facilities	339

Rides and Rallies in the United States	343

International Weather Chart	352

Index	353

TOUR OPERATORS

Here are the people who make it happen; wonderful folks with drive and vision and a love of motorcycles, travel and people. They knit together motorcycle routes, travel arrangements and schedules, and handle endless details so their customers are free to enjoy unencumbered pleasures of the road.

Since the first edition of this book, the number of individuals or firms offering motorcycle touring services has increased about 50 percent. But during that same time the average number of tours offered by each tour company has declined, indicating a tendency of the operators toward specialization rather than offering a wide range of touring options.

In addition to companies offering pre-designed trips, you'll also find in this edition several people who offer custom tour packaging services. They will work with you to design just the trip you want, handling as much or as little of the details as you want.

Tour operators in the following section are listed alphabetically so you can find them easily. These descriptions are meant to be used along with outlines of the various tours in later sections. Once you find a tour that appeals to you, learn more about the tour operator in this section.

Alaska Motorcycle Tours, Inc.

ALASKA
MOTORCYCLE
TOURS

P.O. Box 622
Bothell, WA 98041-0622

Contact: Ms. Vonnie Dahl,
 Office Manager
Phone: 800-642-6877
 (within Washington state:
 206-487-3219)
FAX: Not available

Background:
Alaska Motorcycle Tours began in 1987 when Duke McDonnell, a motorcycle fan for 20 years, realized there was an opportunity to show touring enthusiasts a new destination. With involvement in the travel industry for 18 years and experience for riding, the two were combined to create a great tour through the "Great Land".

He wrote and designed their first brochure and mailed it to motorcycling enthusiasts all over the United States. In March of 1987, the reservations started coming in. To fill their need for an office manager with extensive Alaska experience, they hired Vonnie Dahl to maintain and service all of their clients. Then in May he hired an experienced escort as their tour guide.

Alaska Motorcycle Tours' first season in 1988 was a success. In 1989, previous riders returned to relive their great Alaska adventure. 1990 also proved to be a success and, as this is written, preparations are being made for the 1991 season. Alaska is a great land to see by motorcycle.

Services offered:
- Guided tours of Alaska
- Alaska Motorcycle Tours can also arrange ocean cruises from Vancouver to Anchorage, or Anchorage to Vancouver, through the Inside Passage.

American Motorcyclist Association

American Motorcyclist Association
P.O. Box 6114
Westerville, OH 43081-6114

Contact: Sandy Kimmel or
 Greg Harrison
Phone: 614-891-2425
FAX: 614-891-5012

Greg Harrison

Background:

As the Executive Editor of *American Motorcyclist* magazine for many years, Greg Harrison has ridden extensively in the United States and Europe while preparing touring and racing articles for the magazine.

Many readers of *American Motorcyclist* use the magazine as a planning guide for their own tours. After a series of articles on England, Scotland, and the magical Isle of Man appeared a number of years ago, there was so much demand for an organized tour that AMA EuroTours was founded.

The goal of the EuroTour program is to allow experienced AMA members/riders the opportunity to discover the British Isles on their own terms. All bike rentals, hotel reservations, airport transfers, ferry reservations and suggested routes are arranged beforehand. Tour members meet each night to discuss the following day's itinerary, as well as share their evening meal. Then they are free to leave when they want, ride independently or with others, and maintain their own schedules for riding and sightseeing.

Services offered:

- Guided tours of England, Wales, Scotland, the Isle of Skye, and the Isle of Man
- A tour in 1992 to southern England, Ireland, and Scotland to participate in the FIM world touring rally in Edinburgh and represent the United States
- Motorcycle rentals, in conjunction with the tours

American Sportbike Tours

80 Red Brook Road
Waquoit, MA 02536

Contact: Carl Alander
Phone: 508-548-8197

California agent: Contact: Kaz Nakata
5408 1/2 Franklin Ave.
Los Angeles, CA 90027
Phone: 213-467-5878 or
800-772-1142
FAX: 213-962-6501

Background:
Carl Alander has been riding motorcycles for 26 years and has extensive road race, touring, and motocross experience. Having attended every major motorcycle event in the country, Carl hasn't found a tour company that specifically tailors tours to motorcycle events or offers the type of motorcycles that he prefers to ride. American Sportbike Tours developed out of a desire to provide the type of service Carl feels is necessary.

Carl's partner, Kaz Nakata, came to the United States five years ago in order to start a motorcycle export business. He has been riding motorcycles for 15 years. He is enthusiastic about being a part of American Sportbike Tours because it will give him an opportunity to ride more and share his touring experiences and large collection of motorcycles with others. Kaz is fluent in Japanese, thereby bringing a special service to Japanese customers.

Because American Sportbike Tours is a start-up company, there will be limited tours offered in 1991; however, Carl and Kaz request that you write to either the address in Massachusetts or California and ask for information. More tours will be available in 1992.

Services offered:
- American Sportbike Tours will supply tickets and motorcycles (or transportation for your own motorcycle) for motorcycle events such as Daytona, Laguna Seca, Loudon Classic, World Superbike, Los Angeles Grand Prix, and Phoenix Formula One. They will also schedule accommodations that suit your personal taste and budget.
- Tours will be structured around racing events; events will be part of the tour, but not the only feature of the tour. They offer a variety of sportbikes and Japanese collector's models (over 40 in the fleet). Carl and Kaz ask that you write with your interest in a particular event; they will work with you to customize a tour for your specific needs.

Aushina Tours

Suite 1
244-246 William St.
Sydney, N.S.W. 2011
AUSTRALIA

Contact: Michael Wu
Phone: (61) 2-356-3822
FAX: (61) 2-356-3398

🧧 AuShina TOURS

Michael Wu

Background:
Michael Wu was raised and educated in China. Before migrating to Australia in 1980 he worked as a science translator in Beijing and as a university teacher and tourist interpreter in Guangzhou. He also worked as a hotel duty manager before starting Aushina Tours.

Michael began his career as a tour organizer in 1982 by taking Australians to see China's more popular attractions. Soon, however, he grew tired of covering the same ground over and over and in 1986, he gained approval to take his (mainly Australian) clientele on motorcycling trips to the more remote parts of China. The idea caught on and has now become an annual event.

Michael feels that, in spite of the current political situation in China, it has been easy to maintain personal contact with the Chinese and is important to continue doing so.

Michael often lectures on "China for Travelers" in Australia.

Services offered:
- Organized tours of Manchuria, Central and Eastern China, and Inner Mongolia
- Motorcycle rentals in association with tours
- Customized tours of China for groups larger than ten

Australian-American Mototours

Craig and Kerry Keown

RR 1 Box 38
Waitsfield, VT 05673
USA

Contact: Craig or Kerry Keown
Phone: 802-496-3837
FAX: 802-496-4123

A-A Mototours

Background:
For almost a decade Kerry Keown, the "Australian," and Craig Keown, the "American," have been dedicated to being the best, expert travel specialists for the Land Down Under. Spending three to five months a year there, combined with Kerry's unique knowledge from growing up on Australia's east coast, provides their guests with the opportunity for special, out-of-the-ordinary service and travel planning.

When they are not guiding ski tours in New Zealand and motorcycle adventures in Australia, they are at home in Vermont providing future guests and current South Pacific travelers with some of the most personable and knowledgeable service of its kind. Of course, you might also catch them in Vermont motorcycling in the summer and skiing in winter.

Their clientele has grown steadily and they now run four personally guided tours during Australia's springtime. For many reasons, this is the best time to travel "down under," off-season prices and the best weather to name two.

Craig and Kerry (with her delightful Aussie accent), are proud to be among Australia's most experienced hosts. As they themselves say, "the best thing about AA Mototours is free . . . the advice of experts".

Services offered:
- Scheduled, guided tours of Australia
- Customized tours for individuals or groups including a wide range of special interests
- Motorcycle rentals and purchase/resale arrangements
- Expert and experienced Australia and New Zealand travel arrangements including air, accommodation, and vehicle hire
- Free consultation and advice on travel arrangements. (Many of the Keowns' guests ask for travel arrangements outside the scope of the motorcycle tour. Because of the time required to get to and from Australia, many people like to extend their trip to include perhaps a trip to New Zealand. Consider a ski tour in August combined with a bike tour in September. They are very flexible and will help you plan the trip you want.)

TOUR OPERATORS 13

Australian Motorcycle Adventures

One Lee Place
Illawong, N.S.W. 2234
AUSTRALIA

Contact: Warren Lang
Phone: (61) 2-543-7022
FAX: (61) 2-543-7022

Booking agent:
General Travel America
700 Larkspur Landing Cir., Suite 126
Larkspur, CA 94939-1744

Warren Lang

Contact: Alyce Graham
Phone: (415) 925-1199
FAX: Not available

Background:
Warren Lang, 44, recently turned in his suit and tie for permanent riding gear. He sold his highly successful marketing company and decided to turn his love of motorcycling into a business, now in its fledgling year.

Warren has been riding motorcycles for 20 years and has enjoyed many facets of the sport such as touring, moto-cross, and circuit racing on bitumen tracks. He has also been involved with rider training programs in Australia where he lives.

Services offered:
- Guided tours of Australia's east coast
- Motorcycle rentals (late model Harley-Davidsons) for those participating in the tours

Australian Motorcycle Touring

135 Campbell Street
Collingwood
Victoria 3066
AUSTRALIA
Contact: Geoff Coat
Phone: (61) 3-416-3393
FAX: (61) 3-416-3262

Geoff Coat

Agent for United Kingdom:
Twickers World
22 Church Street
Twickenham TW1 3NW
ENGLAND
Phone: (44) 81-892-7606
FAX: (44) 81-892-8061

Agent for United States/ Canada:
Adventure Center
1311 63rd Street; Suite 200
Emeryville, CA 94608
Phone: 415-654-1879
FAX: 415-654-4200

Background:
Australian Motorcycle Touring is owned and operated by Geoff Coat, who accompanies every tour. Geoff, now in his 40s, retired from the Australian Army as a Major and then went on to become national sales manager for Mercedes Benz buses. Among other talents, Geoff is a qualified watchmaker, has a long-standing love of motorcycles, and is a first-rate motorcycle mechanic (a valuable talent to have in the Australian outback). He has been president of the BMW Motorcycle Club of Australia and has toured extensively in Europe, the United States and the United Kingdom. Geoff knows Australia well and he knows how to see the best of the country by motorcycle.

Services offered:
• Organized tours in Australia

Baja Expeditions

P.O. Box 4258
San Clemente, CA 92674-4258

Contact: David Spencer
Phone: 714-661-8879
FAX: Not available

Baja Expeditions

David Spencer

Background:
Dave Spencer began riding dirt bikes at the age of 13. For 21 years he has traveled the highways and byways of Southern California looking for challenging roads. As he says, "I have always had a passion for two-wheel vehicles, especially motorcycles. I can't think of anything that I enjoy doing more than exploring new trails."

When not taking people out on tours of Mexico, Dave is busy in his motorcycle and auto repair shop, which he has owned for ten years.

Services offered:
- Expert guided tours through Baja
- A chase vehicle to carry gasoline, back-up bikes, spare parts, and your luggage
- A shuttle van from San Diego to Ensenada and back
- Motorcycle rental

"Well, I promised I'd take a bath every day . . ."

Beach's Motorcycle Adventures, Ltd.

2763 West River Parkway
Grand Island, NY 14072-2087

Contact: Robert D. Beach
Elizabeth L. Beach
Rob Beach
Phone: 716-773-4960
FAX: 716-773-5227
Telex: 6854139 GIBCO UW

Bob and Elizabeth Beach

BEACH'S MOTORCYCLE ADVENTURES, LTD.

Background:
Since 1972 Bob and Elizabeth Beach have been conducting motorcycle tours through the European Alpine areas. In 1991 they will observe their 20th year of conducting these exciting motorcycle tours. Their son, Rob, is a valuable part of the organization and specializes in the development and operation of tours to new and exciting locations.

Today, Beach tours are a distillation of years of personal motorcycle riding experiences as well as extensive research and study. By seeking out the new, the old, the unusual and the out-of-the-way, Beach's Motorcycle Adventures is able to offer a unique view of some of the most interesting areas of the world. All Beach tours are personally conducted by Bob and Elizabeth Beach and/or their son, Rob.

The Beach family has always stressed the joy of individual exploration. By removing the obstacles and minimizing the problems, they provide an exceptional and memorable experience for the first-time visitor as well as for the experienced international tourer.

Each Beach tour provides the opportunity for a fantastic ride in the country visited. Each itinerary has been planned to take advantage of the most exciting roads and scenic features without the need to ride long hours or at excessive speeds. Although the tours are motorcycle oriented, rental automobiles are available and become a welcome addition to each group.

Large group riding is discouraged on Beach tours. Each member is free to ride at his or her own pace, visit spots which have a special interest, and dawdle as long as desired. There is sufficient free time each day for enjoyable riding, taking photographs, exploring, and relaxing. Each evening after dinner, details of the day's adventures are discussed and recommendations are made for the following day.

Bob has owned 61 motorcycles and has been an active motorcycle rider for 52 years. He was awarded the BMW Motorcycle Owners of America (BMWMOA) 250,000-mile Medallion and has completed more than 100,000 miles of European Alpine riding. He is a BMWMOA Ambassador, membership #91, and is past president of the BMW Riders of western New York.

Rob Beach teaches sport-bike riding and holds an Expert Road Racing license. He is the founder of the Rider Advanced Training School, and has instructed motorcyclists in the finer techniques of riding on race courses throughout the states. In 1991 he will return to the Nürburgring for the second time as a coach. This prestigious riding school is possibly the world's premier rider and driver training course. Participants on tours conducted by Rob may take advantage of this experience by attending riding seminars offered throughout each tour.

With more than 15 years of street riding, Rob has now passed the 100,000 mile mark. Both Bob and Rob are members of BMWMOA and BMW Riders Association.

Services offered:
- Scheduled motorcycle tours to: Great Britain (England, Scotland, and Wales); the Alps (Switzerland, Italy, Germany, Austria, and Liechtenstein); and New Zealand (North and South Islands)
- Purchase of new BMW motorcycles with delivery in Europe
- Motorcycle and automobile rentals
- Customized tours for special groups

Big Bike Tours

BigBikeTours
Reisen & Motorräder

Riedstrasse 1
D-7465 Geislingen
GERMANY

Contact: Werner Kiefer
Phone: (49) 7433-2491
FAX: (49) 7433-6421

Background:
Big Bike Tours began in 1988 as a tour through the United States for German clients wishing to buy a motorcycle. The inaugural group toured from Minneapolis to Dallas, and that tour is still being offered. In the fall of 1989 Big Bike Tours merged with the travel agency Geislinger Reiseburo to form a new company with better capabilities.

18 TOUR OPERATORS

Through careful negotiations with Delta and Lufthansa airlines, Big Bike Tours was able to offer, in the spring of 1990, "fly-and-ride" tours, which allowed riders to bring their motorcycle on the plane with them and ride away from the airport. They also began to add more tours to new places across the United States and the world.

Services offered:
- Group tours of the United States and Switzerland
- Motorcycle transportation for groups and individuals
- Purchase arrangements for Europeans who want to buy a new motorcycle for use during the tour and transport it home with them
- Organized tours, complete with hotel reservations and motorcycle arrangements, for groups and individuals who wish to travel on their own
- Special tours. The following programs are only scheduled for specific dates and are often in conjunction with motorcycle clubs and associations. You can join these tours either in conjunction with the purchase of a new motorcycle or by transporting your own bike. Dates for 1991 are given below; similar dates are expected to apply in 1992.

Daytona 1991: February/March 1991

Sturgis 1991: Individual organized tour for Harley-Davidson riders using their own bikes; July/August 1991

Harley Special: Group organized tour for Harley-Davidson riders using their own motorcycles. The group will pass through Philadelphia, New York, Milwaukee, Sturgis, and Dallas. The tour includes two factory visits to Harley-Davidson and is organized in cooperation with the Harley-Davidson Club of Germany; July/August 1991

Wing-Ding 1991: Individual organized tour for Gold Wing riders; May 1991

Gold Wing Special: Group organized tour for Gold Wing riders. The group will pass through Atlanta, the Appalachian Mountains, Marysville, Niagara Falls, and Boston. The tour includes a factory visit to Honda and is organized in cooperation with the Gold Wing Club of Germany; May 1991

Bike Tours Australia

Kurt Weidner

Wolfgang Lemke

Einsiedeleiweg 16
D-5942 Kirchhundem 4
GERMANY

Contact:
  Eveline Veenkamp
Phone: (49) 2764-7824
FAX: (49) 2764-7938

Background:
Eight years ago Kurt Weidner fell in love with Australia. He decided to combine his three passions, motorcycling, touring, and organizing in his profession. Today, Mr. Weidner's company, Bike Tours Australia, takes explorers all over his beloved Australia throughout the year.

As a traveler, Kurt knows how to see the country and its people best; as a motorcyclist, he knows how to make a journey easier for the rider without intruding on personal freedom. The theme of independence carries over to the trips. Camping out in the wilderness, cooking on the fire, and outdoor life are not always perfectly comfortable but are always unique experiences. Over the years, Kurt has developed a group of loyal riders. It was his customers who asked for tours of North America. Bike Tours Australia is run by Kurt's closest friends while he leads all the Australian tours. The booking office remains in Germany.

Services offered:
- Scheduled tours in Australia, Bali, northwestern United States, Canadian Rockies, and Alaska
- Customized tours in those same areas on special request
- Videos of North American trip (90 minutes, DM 15) and of Australian tours (180 minutes, DM 15) are available. For mail delivery, deposit the charge in advance in the company account number 3809653800 at the Volksbank in Littfeld, Branch Number: 46062106.
- Motorcycle buy-sellback plans in Australia

Bivak International

Sjon Troost

Nachtegaallaan 1
Postbus 388
3720 AJ Bilthoven
THE NETHERLANDS

Contact: Sjon Troost or Trudi van Bentum
Phone: (31) 30-292541
FAX: (31) 30-292474

BIVAK INTERNATIONAL

Background:
Bivak International is a small tour company specializing in tours in which the culture and nature of a country are highlighted. The goals of these tours are to introduce travelers to the circumstances and habits of the country they are visiting. Bivak believes the best way to meet native people is to partake in their way of living.

Bivak International was founded in 1982 by Sjon Troost. Sjon ran his company alone until 1988 when Trudi van Bentum joined the business. Trudi had previously been employed by the ANWB, which is the largest and oldest consumer tour organization in The Netherlands. Together they doubled the company's business and created a thriving organization, devoted to high quality tours.

Services offered:
- Guided motorcycle tour of Thailand
- Over 20 culturally oriented trips to various parts of the world, most not employing motorcycles

Bosenberg Motorcycle Excursions

Mainzerstrasse 54
D-6550 Bad Kreuznach
GERMANY

Bosenberg Motorcycle Excursions

Contact: Leon A. Heindel
Phone: (49) 671-67312
FAX: (49) 671-67153

U.S. agent:
Sunshine Travel
P.O. Box 3099
De Pere, WI 54115

Leon Heindel

Contact: Martha Nicholson
Phone: 800-950-1001
 or 414-336-1001 (in Wisconsin and Canada)

Background:
BME specializes in motorcycle tours in the heart of Europe. Each of their four different excursions offer a unique style and atmosphere. New and exciting touring opportunities highlight their 1991 riding season. The "iron curtain" is gone and you can now see the dynamic changes yourself while experiencing a great motorcycle vacation at the same time. Each day you set the pace. Explore on your own or join your excursion leader for a great day's ride.

The owner of BME, Leon A. Heindel, started to offer tours in 1988. The company was named after a hill near Bad Kreuznach that produces some of the best Nahe valley wines. Besides some great riding, excursion participants also have a chance to sample wines from the Bosen hill.

Every detail is taken care of for you once you arrive in Europe. With their small groups of seven to eight motorcycles you won't notice participating in a tour. Led by enthusiastic and bilingual native riders, their excursions offer personalized, exciting and care-free European touring. Carefully researched routes, with travel days of 125-175 miles and two or three days at the same location, offer you the best combination of "organized" touring and individual discovery. With four BMW models available, you can upgrade your mount to two sportier models or a tourer to suit your riding style.

After the riding portion of your excursion ends and you return to Bad Kreuznach, your adventure continues at a different pace and in a different time. After a leisurely Rhine river cruise, you return five centuries in time as you enter the Kauzenburg fortress overlooking the Nahe river and feast as knights and ladies at a medieval banquet. While minstrels play

22 TOUR OPERATORS

and court jesters entertain, you relive for a few hours all the chivalry and excitement of a forgotten time.

Services offered:
- Scheduled tours in the Rhine and Mosel valleys, Luxembourg, Alsace/France and the Black Forest; the Alps and Dolomites, Switzerland, Italy with Lake Garda, Austria with Tyrol, and Bavaria; Germany including Berlin and Bavaria; and the Bavaria and Bohemia kingdoms in Germany and Czechoslovakia
- Use of insured 1991 model BMW R80RT included in excursion price, or upgrade to K75RT, K100LT or K100RS (for additional cost)
- Rental car or van for accompanying family members and/or friends
- Best or lowest-cost airfare arrangements made by their representing travel agency or option to make your own air travel arrangements through your local agency
- Individual BMW rentals from a rental center near the Frankfurt International Airport, Germany

Chiang Mai Motorcycle Touring Club

David Unkovich

P.O. Box 97
P.O. Mae Ping
Chiang Mai 50001
THAILAND

Contact: David Unkovich
Phone: (66) 53-278518
FAX: (66) 53-212219
  (show "Attn: David Unkovich")

Background:
David Unkovich, an Australian by birth, first came to Thailand in 1978. He immediately liked the country and its gracious people. He especially liked the Golden Triangle region of Northern Thailand; its steep, winding, narrow roads were perfect for motorcycle riding. He eventually settled in Chiang Mai, Thailand's second largest city, where he now lives with his Thai wife and four-year-old son.

After a few years, David became quite familiar with the roads and trails around Chiang Mai that had previously been unmapped. Locals and tourists began seeking him out for information on the best riding areas and places of interest. He decided to write a book that would provide accurate and concise information for those motorcyclists who wanted to plan their trip themselves. The success of the book lead David to start his own touring company, which he now runs with several motorcyclist friends.

Services offered:
• Guided tours of Thailand
• Motorcycle rental to tour members

Comerford Tours

769 Washington St.
Brookline, MA 02146

Contact: Paul Comerford
Phone: 617-625-3885 or 800-962-9304
FAX: Not available

Background:
In 1988, Paul Comerford, founder of Comerford Tours, was out for a Sunday motorcycle drive in the beautiful countryside of his native Ireland. The idea of taking motorcycling enthusiasts through this beautiful land struck him and after 12 months research on this idea, he began his first tour. Since that time Paul has taken two tours on this trip and he is presently researching a new tour into New England and Canada.

Services offered:
• Guided motorcycle tours of Ireland and the United Kingdom
• Motorcycle rental to tour participants
• Travel agency
• Guided motorcycle tours of New England and Canada

Cycle-East Adventures

No. 1, North Bridge Road, #24-06
High Street Centre
Singapore 0617
REPUBLIC OF SINGAPORE

Contact: Rodney Yeo
Phone: (65) 338-1933 ext. 18
FAX: (65) 337-2337

Rodney Yeo

Background:
Cycle-East Adventures was established in 1990 by Captain Rodney Yeo and his wife, Katherine. After serving sixteen years in the army, Rodney, now in his mid-thirties, decided to pursue his love of motorcycling by opening his own motorcycle tour business. Rodney and Katherine have traveled extensively throughout Malaysia and Rodney says they know Malaysia "like the back of their hand." Rodney has owned Harley-Davidsons and Honda Gold Wings and has driven all kinds of motorcycles, including super-bikes. Cycle-East Adventures has conducted many tours for motorcycle enthusiasts within their area. They are endorsed by the Malaysian Tourism Development Corporation.

Services offered:
- Guided motorcycle tours of Singapore and Malaysia
- Motorcycle rentals to tour participants
- Motorcycle transport arrangements for those who want to bring their own motorcycle to Singapore
- Consultation to riders wishing to tour Malaysia and Singapore on their own

Desmond Adventures, Inc.

1280 South Williams Street
Denver, CO 80210

Contact: Thomas E. Desmond or
	Randall B. Harmon
Phone: 303-733-9248
FAX: 303-733-9601

Tom Desmond

DESMOND ADVENTURES INC

Background:
Tom Desmond began serious motorcycling in the late sixties. He spent time touring all over the United States and Canada on a variety of different motorcycles. After selling his business in 1978, he traveled extensively throughout the world and then moved to Europe in 1979 to see the Continent. He picked up a motorcycle in Europe in the spring of 1979. Feeling there was no motorcycling anywhere in the world that compared to the Alps, he decided to share his experiences with his motorcycling friends at home. In August 1979, he conducted his first tour of the Alps. Years of research have paid off. He takes great pride in showing his charges the most interesting spots to see and to ride. There are plenty of both in Europe and Tom seems to know most of them. In the 1988 season alone, some 350 people joined Tom for a spin through the Alps. They just keep coming back.

Recently, Tom and the AlpenTour™ have enjoyed an explosion of press coverage heaping praise on virtually every aspect of his operations, stressing his careful planning, professional execution, attention to detail, and thorough knowledge of the area. (See *Rider,* January 1988; *BMW Owners News,* June 1988; *Motorcyclist,* January 1989; *BMW Owners News,* February 1989; *Rider,* December 1989; *Road Rider,* January 1990; *Motorcyclist,* January 1990; and *Cycle World,* February 1990.)

Desmond Adventures always maintains a friendly, knowledgeable staff. Employing seasoned motorcyclists, both domestic and abroad, Desmond's tours and tour guides are capable of offering tips on riding techniques to the most ardent enthusiast. After every day's ride, tour participants will relax and settle down to an entertaining evening party fueled with tall tales and stories of motorcycling encounters. In just sixteen days lifelong friendships are formed among complete strangers as a result of tour group camaraderie.

Services offered:
- Scheduled motorcycle and automobile tours through Switzerland, Liechtenstein, Germany, Austria, Italy, Monaco, and France.
- Scheduled motorcycle tours through the Southwest United States (California, Arizona, Utah, and Nevada)
- Motorcycle shipping (see the section on Motorcycle Transport)
- Custom tours in Europe or America, for groups of eight or more, to your own specifications
- Motorcycle rental (see the section on Motorcycle Rental)

Dutchcountry Motorcycle Tours

Jim Drescher

P.O. Box 34
Smoketown, PA 17576

Contact: Jim Drescher
Phone: 717-394-2060
FAX: 717-397-5768

DUTCHCOUNTRY Motorcycle Tours

Background:
Dutchcountry Motorcycle Tours was established three years ago when Jim Drescher noticed that many people were arriving on motorcycles for his bus tours of Dutch country and then leaving them behind. He decided that since motorcyclists were not being served by the tour groups in his area he would create his own tour.

Jim was introduced to motorcycle riding by his brother when in his early twenties. He had given up motorcycling while he was raising his family, but about five years ago he started to get back into it. He became more active in various motorcycling organizations, such as the American Motorcycling Association and the Eastern Pennsylvania Chapter of the Retreads, a club for riders 40 years old and above. Two years ago he bought a Gold Wing. Before venturing into the motorcycle touring business, Jim worked as tour guide in Amish country and as a substitute teacher.

Services offered:
- Organized tour of Pennsylvania Dutch Country

Edelweiss Bike Travel

Werner Wachter and Edelweiss Bike Travel tour guides

EDELWEISS BIKE TRAVEL

Steinreichweg 1
A-6414 Mieming
AUSTRIA
Contact: Werner Wachter
Phone: (43) 05264-5690
FAX: (43) 05264-58533
Telex: 534158 (rkmiem)

U.S. agent:

Armonk Travel
146 Bedford Road
Armonk, NY 10504
Contact: Linda Rosenbaum
Phone: 800-255-7451 or 914-273-8880
FAX: 914-273-4438

Background:
Edelweiss Bike Travel was founded in 1980 by Werner Wachter, starting in the Alps, the natural Eldorado for motorcyclists in Europe. Edelweiss has expanded its touring program year after year. Since 1980 the tours have been very well received by thousands of motorcyclists from around the world. The company offers a great variety of motorcycling challenge and adventure, whether in Europe, Africa, Australia, Asia, or America. In 1991 Edelweiss is offering its tours in 15 different countries. In the past ten years motorcyclists from 33 countries have covered over 5 million riding miles on Edelweiss Tours.

The people from Edelweiss try to strike a balance on their tours, so you can be sure to get the best a country has to offer: the most exciting roads, the most impressive landscapes and, not least, that special intimate contact with the local people.

One of the major achievements of Edelweiss Bike Travel is the opening of the Soviet Union, the largest country in the world, to motorcyclists. In 1988 Wachter negotiated a contract with the Ministry for Tourism in Moscow, allowing motorcyclists for the first time to ride their bike to Moscow and many other parts of Russia, Ukraine, Belorussia, and the Baltic states.

But it still seems that the Alps are the most important destination for riders from around the world. In 1990 more than one thousand riders toured with Edelweiss Bike Travel on one of their scheduled tours. Most did their riding through the Alps. There, the surroundings and the atmosphere seem to form what is commonly known as a motorcycling paradise in Europe. Recently several articles have been published about Edelweiss' Alpine tours in: *Motorcyclist,* December 1990; *Rider,* January 1991; and *Cycle,* January 1991.

Edelweiss' latest offering for the American rider is the Best of the West Tour, a terrain where Edelweiss has been touring with motorcyclists from around the world for the past ten years.

Services offered:
- Scheduled tours of the American West, Germany, Austria, Switzerland, Italy, France, Isle of Man, Hungary, Finland, Soviet Union, and Australia.

European Adventures

2 The Circle
Bryn Newydd
Prestatyn, Clwyd LL19 9EU
UNITED KINGDOM

Contact: Mike or Renate Hosgood
Phone: (44) 74-585-3455
FAX: (44) 74-588-8919

Background:
Mike Hosgood has been riding motorcycles for the past 38 years, not only as a motorcycle enthusiast, but also as a competitor in motocross, grass tracks and road racing events. He has also toured Europe extensively in groups and on his own.

After completing military service, Mike opened his own motorcycle dealership which he ran for 28 years, most recently as a BMW dealer. Having now retired, Mike and his wife Renate, a native of Germany, have devoted their time to developing tours throughout Germany.

Mike believes that a personal touch is important to ensuring the enjoyment of his clients. He runs all tours himself and schedules only as many events as he can comfortably handle.

Services offered:
- Organized tours of Germany and Austria

TOUR OPERATORS 29

Explo-Tours

Josef Geltl (center), with guides Peter and Anneliese

Arnulfstrasse 134
8000 Munich 19
GERMANY

Contact: Josef Geltl
Phone: (49) 89-160789
FAX: (49) 89-161716
Telex: 1631 btxd/089161716 1+

Background:
Joseph Geltl, 38, originally planned to become a teacher of physics and geography. However, on summer holidays he began to explore the countries around the Mediterranean Sea including the Near East and Morocco. Morocco lead him to the Sahara desert where his real passion took hold. He combined his enthusiasm for motorcycling with his love of the desert and Africa. Fortunately and happily, he married a woman who shares his enthusiasm for Africa.

Ten years ago he founded Explo-Tours and began organizing motorcycle tours through Africa. Mr. Geltl's first clients were geography and geology student groups. His tours are designed for hardy adventurers with endurocycle experience.

Services offered:
- Scheduled enduro tours of Northern, Central, and Southern Africa
- Motorcycle rentals for members of tours
- In addition to the five tours described in this book, Explo-Tours can combine several of them to create very long trips — up to 13 weeks duration.

Freedom Tours

P.O. Box 1288
Longmont, CO 80501

Contact: Robert Kenny
Phone: 303-776-2860
FAX: Not available

Background:
Freedom Tours began in 1984 as a single tour for a group of motorcyclists from Springfield, Missouri. After five years of planning and leading this tour throughout Colorado, Robert Kenny decided to offer his services to the public.

Robert has lived in Colorado for twenty-eight years and has been riding motorcycles in the mountains since 1970. During the time spent touring the mountains, he has found scenic roads and other interesting areas that are not listed on maps or in guide books. He also knows where to find the best hotels and restaurants.

Services offered:
- Guided tours of Colorado
- Individual or small group tours

Great Motorcycle Adventures

8241 Heartfield Lane
Beaumont, TX 77706

Contact: Mr. Les French
Phone: 800-642-3933
   (within Texas: 409-866-7891)
FAX: 409-835-2214

Les "Gringo" French

Background:
"Gringo" has been exploring Mexico and motorcycling since he was 13 years old. Prior to forming Great Motorcycle Adventures, Gringo owned and operated an adventure tour company specializing in archaeological and photographic expeditions throughout Mexico and Central America. "I've been fortunate enough to have introduced hundreds of people to the beautiful and varied cultures of Mexico," Les says.

"Our guests are surprised to find that Mexico is not a big desert, but rather a wonderfully diverse country of snowcapped mountains, fertile valleys, vast savannas, breathtaking gorges, and lush tropical seashores hosting many different cultures," he says.

Les has spent a good part of his life having fun with adventure activities: he's a certified sky diver, a certified scuba diver, a certified airplane pilot, a certified boat captain (to 300 tons), an experienced motorcyclist (touring, hill climbing, trail riding, drag racing, and enduro racing), and auto enthusiast (drag racing, quarter midgets, and stock cars). And if that weren't enough, he also has spent a good deal of time studying Meso-American archaeology, specializing in the Mayan civilization. There's no shortage of conversation with Gringo around.

Services offered:
- Organized guided tours and trail rides through Mexico, Belize, Guatemala, and Honduras
- An important part of Great Motorcycle Adventures' business is arranging custom rides for groups. Call for details.
- Motorcycle rentals for his trail riding and touring guests
- Four-wheel Fly & Explore adventures

Jed Halpern's S.A.P. Tour

Pilatusstrasse 1
CH Dierikon - 6030
Lucerne
SWITZERLAND

Contact: Jed Halpern
Phone: (41) 4-324-3482
FAX: (41) 4-324-3212

Jed Halpern

Background:
Jed Halpern, organizer and founder of S.A.P. Tour, is an Englishman by birth. In 1977, after finishing his education in hotel and catering management in Manchester, England, he traveled to Frankfurt, Germany to gain more experience in his trade. After two years there he decided to move to Switzerland, where he has remained ever since.

In 1979, Jed purchased his first Gold Wing, a GL1000 K2. It was not long before he began participating in Gold Wing events throughout Europe.

With an average of 25,000 kilometers a year under his belt and a great love for Gold Wing touring, Jed decided to start his own tour of the Alps and Passes of Switzerland, which he considers to be "one of the ultimate bike-touring countries" of the world. The tour is now in its seventh year.

Services offered:
• Guided motorcycle tours of Switzerland's Alps and passes

Indsun Adventure Tours

Christophstr. 59
8920 Schongau
Oberbayern
GERMANY

Contact: Hans-Joachim Klein
Phone: (49) 8861-7628
FAX: c/o (49) 8861-2691

Hans-Joachim Klein

INDSUN adventure tours

Booking agent:

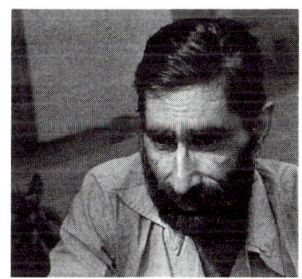

Indsun Adventure Tours
Rao Raja House
Naya Bas - Moti Dungri Road
Alwar - 301001
Rajasthan
INDIA

Contact: Himmat Singh
Phone: (91) 144-22211
    (before 10:00 a.m.)
FAX: Not available

Himmat Singh

Background:
Indsun Adventure Tours was incorporated in 1988 as an Indo-German joint venture to promote tours in India. Hans-Joachim Klein is one of the promoters of the company and he has lived in India for the past 12 years. He has toured India from Ladakh to Cape Comorin. Hans says, "There is only one way to experience India and that is on an Enfield motorcycle."

Services offered:
- Guided motorcycle and jeep tours in north and south India
- Indsun provides a service team that consists of a doctor or nurse and a mechanic and service vehicle for back-up assistance.
- Rafting and wind surfing excursions

Kalman International Motorcycle Touring

	534 Kelmore Street Moss Beach, CA 94038 Contact: David or Kathy Kalman Phone: 800-637-4337 or 415-728-3511 FAX: Same numbers as phone
Booking agent:	The Old Chapel North Street Leicester LE6 4EB ENGLAND Phone: (44) 530-811705 FAX: (44) 530-813410

Background:

David Kalman, 46, a native Californian and former executive in the computer industry, has over 30 years of motorcycle experience. His love of the sport and expertise in the western United States contribute to the adventure, excitement, and fun of his tours. His travels have taken him throughout Europe and Asia. Mr. Kalman is a member of numerous motorcycle organizations, including GWTA, GWRRA, BMWMOA and the Retreads.

Kathy Kalman has traveled extensively. She is curious about the unknown and has a knack for identifying and seeking out unusual sights and attractions as well as interesting merchants, overnight accommodations, cafes, diners, and restaurants.

According to the Kalmans, their mission is as follows: "Our intent is to offer the highest quality tours available for both the rider and his (her) passenger. Our desire is to allow the participants to let us do the worrying. We feel especially capable of doing this as we have both spent years in other industries and understand how to anticipate our customers' needs."

Services offered:
- Organized tours of western United States
- Motorcycle rentals for independent travelers (contact Kalman for details)

Lotus Consulting Services

1644 North Sedgewick St.
Chicago, IL 60614-5714

Contact: Burt Richmond
Phone: 312-951-0031
FAX: 312-951-7313

LOTUS

Burt Richmond

Background.
Burt Richmond's Lotus Consulting Services has been planning motorcycle trips for the past 12 years. It all began in 1979 when he planned a friend's honeymoon to Italy. Starting the newlyweds at the Ducati factory in Bologna, he directed them through Venice, the Alpina mountains, along the Ligurian coast and into Switzerland.

As an architect, Burt's career has enabled him to gain first-hand knowledge about many countries around the world. He served for six weeks as the guest lecturer of a graduate architecture course for the Central Committee of Education in China. On a subsequent trip to Asia he rented a motorcycle and traveled from the mountains of Kathmandu to the jungles of India where his motorcycle was carried across the Bagmatti river by an elephant.

Past tour locales have included Europe, Scandinavia, North Africa, select regions of the Soviet Union, New Zealand, China, Thailand, Nepal, Great Britain, western Canada, and the Rocky mountain region of the United States.

Burt Richmond's Lotus Consulting Services provides a unique service for the touring enthusiast. He designs tours that are tailored to the group's (or individual's) desired locale and time of year. Each tour blends the goals of the group with elements of culture, history, regional cooking, and adventure.

Burt designs trips that are simple or comprehensive, according to your wishes. They can be geared to your driving ability, experience, and personal agenda. Burt feels a group of six to eight riders and their passengers is an ideal size, but a honeymoon trip, with one motorcycle, can be accommodated just as easily. If circumstances allow, Burt might even be persuaded (for extra compensation) to join the group with his luggage van as tour director, interpreter, motorcycle mechanic, and official photographer.

For a design fee of typically $200 per person Burt will plan a ten- to fourteen-day foreign trip for eight to ten people that includes detailing scenic routes and points of interest, food, coordinating ferry schedules (e.g., overnight from Ancona, Italy to Split, Yugoslavia), lodging and individual motorcycle insurance. He can also arrange for shipping your motorcycle to and from your destination or renting you one for you to meet upon your arrival. All you need to do is instruct Burt about how much time you have to travel, the area in which you want to tour and which historic sights you would like to see.

Burt aims his service at busy people who have limited time to plan logistics, study maps, and execute the details of a complex trip. Past tour groups have usually been composed of senior executives who are accustomed to precise attention to detail.

Services offered:
- Custom tour design
- Motorcycle crating and shipping
- Support vehicle
- International motorcycle insurance
- Motorcycle rental or purchase

Motorcycle Adventures Australia

Lot 7 North Road
Pearcedale, Victoria 3912
AUSTRALIA

Contact: Jan and Terry Bryant
Phone: (61) 59 786 768
FAX: (61) 59 786 007

Jan and Terry Bryant

MOTORCYCLE ADVENTURES AUSTRALIA

Background:
Motorcycle Adventures Australia (formerly Top Gear Tours) is run by Terry and Jan Bryant who have 15 years experience in the motorcycle industry as Honda and Suzuki dealers in an outer Melbourne suburb. They have traveled the world extensively and inevitably got hooked on motorcycle touring. They now combine pleasure with business by running tours full-time. In the Australian summer, between December and April, they offer two different tours in Victoria and one in Tasmania. Between May and November, the tours switch to the outback of South Australia, western New South Wales and the Ayers Rock - Alice Springs area. These rides are all scheduled for the most ideal weather conditions for the year.

Terry is as close to the genuine Aussie as it is possible to find and he'll have riders saying "G'day" to strangers in nothing flat. Like all Aussies he's open and friendly, and treats everyone as an equal. He has a great love of the countryside and his knowledge of the highways and byways as well as the Australian bush is encyclopedic.

Services offered:
- Scheduled all-inclusive rides in Victoria, Tasmania and the outback. All rides include a light aircraft flight at the most scenic venues.
- Inquiries are welcomed from groups or clubs for tailored rides within Victoria, Tasmania, and the outback.

Meier's Weltreisen GmbH/Marlboro Reisen

Postfach 27 02 62
Monschauer Strasse 1
4000 Dusselforf 11
GERMANY

Contact: Elke Bodenburg
Phone: (49) 211-56020
FAX: (49) 211-5602147

Background:
Meier's Weltreisen, which celebrated its 10th aniversary in 1991, is one of Germany's largest wholesale tour operators. For the second season Meier's Weltreisen is operating the Marlboro Reisen, a program focusing on adventure travel across the United States and Canada. The Grand Circle tour is one the many other vacation tours that are offered through this program.

Services offered:
- Motorcycle tours of the United States
- Motorcycle rentals for members of tours
- Tours of the United States focusing on motorhome, horseback, bicycle and river raft

mhs Motorradtouren GmbH

Donnersbergerstr. 32
D-8000 Munich 19
GERMANY

Contact: Herbert Schellhorn
Phone: (49) 89/1684888
FAX: (49) 89/1665549

Herbert Schellhorn

mhs

Background:
mhs Motorradtouren was founded in 1987 by Herbert and Wolfgang Schellhorn. Wolfgang has been a Suzuki dealer for more than ten years in Wolfratshausen, near Munich.

Herbert is a car mechanic with experience also in motorcycle repairs. After his apprenticeship he studied business and engineering at the high school in Munich. Starting in 1984, in addition to his studies, Herbert worked as a tour guide for a large company organizing motorcycle trips. During that time he toured Austria, Switzerland, France, Italy, and Kenya. In 1987, he decided to start his own company. Based on his good reputation as a guide, many previous customers participated in the new mhs Motorradtouren trips. As a result of their careful preparation and follow-through, their guests keep coming back again and again.

They are very selective about their tour guides. Each must speak several languages, must be an experienced motorcyclist and mechanic, must be smart and polite, and must be an expert on the region of the particular tour involved.

mhs Motorradtouren's specialty is their coverage of the many interesting parts of Italy, France, Austria, Germany, Yugoslavia, Hungary, and South Africa. Mr. Schellhorn is a specialist in these areas. He not only knows the lands and their peoples, he knows the roads, the churches, the sights, hotels, restaurants, and a lot more.

Mr. Schellhorn takes pride in detailed preparation and organization of tours before departure: the insurance package, the excellent choice of routes, and of course the selection of knowledgeable and experienced leaders.

Additionally, mhs Motorradtouren has created a broad program for individual motorcycle travellers that includes their "Fly and Ride Around the World" program, rental bikes in various locations, and tour packages with booked hotels and train, air, or ship travel.

Services offered:
- Scheduled motorcycle tours to: the Alps, Italy, Austria, Germany, South Africa, Yugoslavia, and Hungary
- Motorcycle rentals to tour participants at several locations around the world
- Motorcycle rentals to independent travellers at several locations around the world
- Passenger Service. On all the tours which use an accompanying club bus (for transporting luggage), nine seats are available for companions who are not riding motorcycles and want to go along. It's comfortable for both of you, without additional charge on the passenger travel price.
- "Fly and Ride" program. A new and easy way to take your own motorcycle to one of 18 different cities on five continents. The procedure is easy: you bring your motorcycle to the airport one day prior to departure, put it onto a provided pallet, and the bike will travel on the same airplane in which you are flying. Tariffs are determined according to the German Holiday tariff on Lufthansa Airlines. Passengers pay the normal holiday rate (plus airport fees); the motorcycle tariff is equal to the tariff for one passenger, plus DM 395 (round trip).
- Tour packages for individuals that include booked hotels, maps, and descriptions for any of the following countries: Germany, France, Switzerland, Austria, Italy, Northern Yugoslavia, Kenya, and South Africa are available. The price is DM 40 to DM 60 plus DM 10 per day, plus DM 7 to DM 15 per booked hotel room. Each tour package is individually designed for each client.
- Customized motorcycle trips for companies, clubs, and associations from five to 50 persons
- Additional hotel and transportation reservations for tourers, before and after scheduled tours
- Various kinds of insurance packages
- Motorcycle Purchase Plan. Buy a new BMW (or a used one) in St. Louis and bring it back to Germany after your trip in the United States. mhs Motorradtouren will handle all the details, including: reservation of the bike, flight arrangements, insurance, air transportation of the bike to Germany, duty, taxes, and registration of the bike in Germany. Prices range from DM 14,000 to DM 25,000, all-inclusive. Reservations should be made early and must be accompanied by a deposit of DM 5,000. Balance is due within four weeks after all arrangements have been made.

Motorcycle Tours North

P.O. Box 143
Dawson Creek, B.C. V1G 4G3
CANADA

Contact: Claude Kidd
Phone: 604-782-6700
FAX: 604-782-9611

Claude Kidd

Background:
Claude Kidd, 52, is in his first season as a tour operator. He created his motorcycle touring business after the recent completion of the Alaska Highway. Claude is a farmer and rancher who has lived in British Columbia for the past 20 years. He is quite knowledgeable about the area and is well acquainted with the Alaska Highway. When not working on his farm and motorcycle tour business, Claude operates heavy machinery in the oil field construction industry.

Services offered:
- Guided motorcycle tour from Dawson Creek, British Columbia to Fairbanks, Alaska

Motorrad Expedition Sahara

Auf dem Romer 3
3576 Rauschenberg
GERMANY

Also: Street 9 - No. 61
Maadi, Cairo
EGYPT

Contact: Karim El-Mahdy
Phone: (20) 350-4406 in Egypt or (49) 6425 757 in Germany
FAX: Not available

Background:
Motorrad Expeditions is a German/Egyptian tour company founded in 1988 by Karim El-Mahdy, a 29-year-old dentist. Mr. El-Mahdy has lived in

Egypt for 16 years and has gained a great deal of experience riding in the desert, participating in the Pharaoh's Rally several times. Karim is ably assisted by Tarek El-Mahdy, a 26-year-old dentist, who follows the tour with equipment and supplies, and Judith Zborschil, 25, who attends the tour with food and logistical support. The organizers speak German, French, English, and Arabic.

Services offered:
- Guided motorcycle tours of Egypt and the Sahara
- Motorcycle rentals to tour members and those traveling independently

Motorrad-Reisen

Postfach 44 01 48
D-8000 Munich 44
GERMANY

Contact: Hermann Weil
Phone: (49) 89 39 57 68
FAX: (49) 89 34 48 32
Telex: 5218511

U.S. agent:	Motorrad-Reisen
P.O. Box 591
Oconomowoc, WI 53066

Contact: Jean Fish
Phone: 414-567-7548
FAX: 414-567-4775

Background:
Hermann Weil loves motorcycling and enjoys introducing people to natural and cultural resources — an unbeatable combination for the owner of a motorcycle touring agency. Even though the variety and scope of Motorrad-Reisen demands that Mr. Weil spends time off the road negotiating new programs, he still prefers tour guiding to any other activity.

Motorrad-Reisen (M-R) offers enough variety to suit the person who wants a few days of recreation in connection with a business trip, as well as a couple who plan an extended holiday. M-R specializes in a variety of tours illuminating the Alpine region and also offers other trips to the Caribbean and Czechoslovakia.

Tours feature relaxed riding with a bilingual guide. More experience, more adventure, and more fun are the leading principles of Mr. Weil's motorcycle tours. Guides are anxious to introduce aspects of the culture not available to most tourists and respond to individual requests. Safety is a primary concern for all M-R tours. All touring managers have attended several courses for security instructors and on first aid, and carry a two-way radio to help in the event of an emergency.

Each tour features cultural aspects. Cuisine and environment are selected with "heart and mind and are always in the traditions of the culture," according to Mr. Weil.

Services offered:
- Scheduled tours to Austria, the Alpine region, Germany, Italy, France, Switzerland, Caribbean, United States, and Czechoslavakia
- Customized tours out of Munich and in the United States
- Motorcycle rentals in conjunction with tours and for those who want to tour on their own are available. Rental includes collision insurance on the motorcycle ($400 deductible), riding suit, luggage case, spare parts.
- Purchase of BMW motorcycles for delivery in Munich
- Rental of accessories and cycle wear
- A full spectrum of travel services including arrangements for shipping motorcycles, booking flights, and making other land arrangements in conjunction with tours
- Package tours with prebooked hotels for independent travel

Motorrad Spaett, KG

Rüdesheimerstrasse 9
8000 Munich 21
GERMANY

Contact: Peter Spaett
or Tommy Wagner
Phone: (49) 89 57 93 70
FAX: (49) 89 57 017 69

Background:
Motorrad Spaett is one of the oldest and largest motorcycle dealers in Germany. The company was founded in 1951 by Josef Spaett, the father of Motorrad Spaett's chief, Peter. In the beginning it was a two-man company. Now, after 40 years, they have about 50 employees. In 1963 they sold their first new Honda, and in 1965 their first Yamaha. For a few years

Kawasaki and Suzuki were also listed in their program. Since 1969 they have imported motorcycles on their own. Today, they are the biggest shop in Bavaria, and their spare parts department is the biggest in Germany.

Peter, 48, runs the business now. He has visited the United States and Canada several times. He is married and has children interested in motorcycles. Peter is the father of three boys aged eleven to fifteen. He stays close to the office and is also an expert with motorcycle technicalities. He took part in the first motorcycle tour to China in 1983.

Services offered:
- Scheduled tours to Turkey since 1988
- Sales and service of new and used motorcycles, accessories, and clothing
- Motorcycle rentals

Motorsportvereniging Ophemert (MSV Ophemert)

Waalbandijk 1
NL-4061 AK Ophemert
THE NETHERLANDS

Contact: Alex Loef,
   Secretary of MSV Ophemert
Phone: (31) 3445-1660 or (31) 3445-1598
FAX: Not available

Background:
MSV Ophemert was started by Willem Zoet in 1975 as a club to support road racing from the town of Ophemert. In 1981 the interests of the club turned more to motorcycle touring. The first Dikes tour was organized at that time. Now in its 11th year, the Dikes tour is the main international event sponsored by the club, although its 60 members do organize other local events.

Alex Loef, secretary of MSV Ophemert for the past 11 years, is an active motorcyclist, logging some 50,000 km each year. He has ridden his BMW K100RT over 240,000 km since he bought it five years ago.

Services offered:
- One-day tour of the dikes in Holland.

44 TOUR OPERATORS

Overland Tours

Bruce Peeples and friend

P.O. Box 186
Poncha Springs, CO 81242

Contact: Bruce Peeples
Phone: 719-539-6032
   or 800-395-0407
FAX: 719-539-4954

Background:
Bruce Peeples, owner and operator of Overland Tours, has been riding motorcycles for over 30 years. For years Bruce and his wife Karen have been organizing motorcycle tours for their friends. The demand for their expertise on traveling through Mexico's Chaco Canyon and Colorado grew until Bruce decided to start his own motorcyle touring company. Overland Tours is now (1991) in its sixth year. Bruce belongs to the BMW Motorcycle Owners Association and is a life-long member of the Colorado Association of Motorcyclists (CAM). Bruce and Karen own a 30-horse ranch and also operate a ranch supply store.

Services offered:
- Guided motorcycle tours of Copper Canyon, Mexico
- Customized group tours of New Mexico and Colorado available on request.
- Group camping trips to Chaco Canyon, New Mexico

Pacific Northwest Motorcycle Adventures

P.O. Box 881
Gig Harbor, WA 98335

Contact: Stephen May
Phone: 206-389-1120
FAX: 206-646-4766

Steve May

Background:
Pacific Northwest Motorcycle Tours was conceived in the mid-1970s as a premier trail bike tour. Over the years it has evolved to include street, dual-sport, and enduro/off-road riders, too. Their objective is to provide each rider with a unique sampling of life in the Pacific Northwest, while treating participants to deluxe accommodations and food. They do all the work so their guests can go out and play, every day!

Tour operator Stephen May has over 25 years of street and off-road riding experience and is a motocross and cross country racing champion. He has trained thousands of motorcycle riders, novice to pro, in trail, track, and street riding, and is an award-winning and certified Street and Trail Training Instructor.

Stephen is ably assisted by Brad Ortega, who was instrumental in the creation of "Ready to Ride", the United States' award-winning urban off-road vehicle program, and by Marv McCamey (a.k.a. "The Old Man of the Mountains") who is the resident historian of the Pacific Northwest and a well-seasoned street and trail rider. They are supported by a staff of tour assistants, mechanics, and support personnel to make sure you have the time of your life. All tour members are Motorcycle Safety Foundation (MSF)-certified instructors.

Services offered:
- Custom designed tours of Washington state and the Pacific Northwest
- Motorcycles available to tour participants
- Complimentary video and brochures available

Pancho Villa Moto-Tours

9437 E.B. Taulbee
El Paso, TX 79924

Contact: Skip Mascorro
Phone: 915-757-3032
  or 800-233-0564
FAX: 915-751-4537

Skip Mascorro

Background:

Pancho Villa Moto-Tours (PVMT) began modestly in 1981 when Skip Mascorro ran his first motorcycle tour. At that time, he was president of Caravanas Voyagers, a large recreational vehicle travel firm running as many as 60 caravans to Mexico each season. After that first trip in 1981, motorcycle touring began to occupy more and more of Skip's time and eventually he left Caravanas to spend full time on motorcycling.

Today, Pancho Villa Moto-Tours runs a wide variety of tours south of the border, in New Zealand, and in the United States, including a number of customized tours for motorcycling clubs. Skip's tours have generated tremendous loyalty, bringing many riders back four or more times to travel with him. By all accounts, Skip is a colorful character and a delight to ride with.

Services offered:
- Scheduled tours to Mexico, Costa Rica, Panama, New Zealand, and Southwest United States
- Customized tours specially designed for dealers, riding clubs and touring organizations
- Motorcycle rentals for participants of any PVMT Mexico or U.S. tour
- Motorcycle rentals, insurance, for individual travelers
- Slide presentations for clubs, rallies, and motorcycle functions
- Mexico motorcycle insurance for tour participants
- Preparation of necessary visas and vehicle documents for entry to Mexico interior

Prima Klima Reisen GmbH

Hohenstaufenstrasse 69
1000 Berlin 30
GERMANY

Contact: Peter Schmidt or Klaus Brass
Phone: (49) 30 216 10 82/83
FAX: (49) 30 216 10 80
Telex: 186381 pkr d

Peter Schmidt

Background:
Prima Klima Reisen (PKR) was founded by four friends in 1983. They started as nonprofessional adventurers, individual travelers, coach drivers, and sport trainers. In the intervening years, their business has grown so that PKR now owns seven tour buses, with which they offer various trips through Europe for young people. They also rent luxury tour buses for traveling bands and movie production crews.

Their specialty is individualized tours, such as enduro tours in Cyprus, bus trips through India, and jeep trips through Venezuela and Morocco. They also are planning a tour through India with 1950s style Royal Enfield Silver Bullet 350cc bikes (made in India).

Peter Schmidt, responsible guide for the Cyprus motorcycle program, has been with PKR since 1985. He studied education, psychology, and art at the Free University of Berlin and has worked several years as a press photographer, coach driver, and tour guide in many European countries.

Services offered:
- Scheduled motorcycle tours to Cyprus and India
- Surfboard and equipment rental, all watersports (diving, water skiing)
- Self-catering guest houses
- Informal hotels
- Motorcycle rentals
- Coach tours through Europe and India
- Jeep tours through Venezuela and Morocco
- Guided walks
- Mountain bike tours and rentals in Cyprus

Rocky Mountain Moto Tours Ltd.

Box 7152 Stn. E
Calgary, Alberta T3C 3M1
CANADA

Contact: Nicholas Moar
Phone: 403-244-6939
FAX: 403-229-2788
Telex: 03-821172

Dave Blackwood and Nick Moar

Rocky Mountain Moto Tours Ltd.

Background:
Rocky Mountain Moto Tours began in 1987 as most adventure companies start: Nick Moar and David Blackwood enjoyed motorcycling so much, they decided to commit themselves to it one hundred percent. Not just for their guests' enjoyment, they do this for their own pleasure as well.

Nick Moar spent most of the seventies motorcycling around Australia and North America. If there was a back way to get there, he found it. After completing his education, Nick worked for a helicopter skiing company in the rugged mountains of British Columbia. It was there he realized how much people from other places wanted to experience the rugged and unspoiled beauty of western Canada.

Lifelong friend David Blackwood was a fellow motorcycle enthusiast. He found time to head up monthly tours of the northwestern United States and Canada while following the grand prix motorcycling circuit. They formed a natural partnership.

They cater to an international clientele and riders of various styles and ages. Their adventure holidays explore some of the most diverse geography in North America.

Services offered:
- Scheduled, all-inclusive seven-day tours of Alberta and British Columbia

Rocky Mountain Motorcycle Touring

Box 173
Gabriola Island, B.C. V0R 1X0
CANADA

Contact: Andrew Turner
Phone: 604-247-9281
FAX: Not available

Andrew Turner on his hand-built Kawasaki 750

Background:
Andrew Turner, Lorne Vogt, and Colin Cook, who have ridden motorcycles since being of legal age, established Rocky Mountain Motorcycle Touring in 1988. All three men are hobby mechanics and builders of motorcycles, but only one, Colin Cook, a full-time motorcycle dealer, has made motorcycles his career. Andrew Turner is a surveyor who has worked in British Columbia for the past 23 years. Lorne Vogt is a computer scientist who specializes in geographic information systems.

Services offered:
- Guided tours of Vancouver Island and British Columbia
- Export of motorcycles after completion of tours

Sahara Cross

St. Wolfgangstrasse 10
7910 Neu-Ulm 4
GERMANY

Contact: Jürgen Greif
Phone: (49) 73 7 31445
FAX: (49) 73 1 77627

Jürgen Greif

Background:
Jürgen Greif, the founder of Sahara Cross, traveled to Morocco during the summer of 1978 and fell in love with the country. To fulfill his desire to learn more about that part of the world, Jürgen and his wife returned later and traveled for a full year across Kenya, Egypt, and the Sudan. On that trip, he learned much about the country, where to go, and things to do. He

decided then that he wanted to share his experience with other adventure travelers. A passionate motorcyclist, Jürgen began formulating plans for a motorcycle touring company. He observed there were a number of other motorcycle touring companies with whom he would be competing. So, to distinguish his tours, he decided to focus on the Sahara, an area he knows and loves.

Since the inception of Sahara Cross in 1985, he has offered six tours each year, with never a serious accident or negative incident. In spite of his attention to safety, his tours maintain an element of adventure, often trying new routes and destinations.

Services offered:
- Organized tours to Egypt
- Organized tours to the Sinai

Sarroy Enterprises

P.O. Box 660
Capalaba, Queensland
AUSTRALIA 4157

Contact: George Cunningham
Phone: (61) 7-207-4267
FAX: (61) 7-245-6184

George Cunningham and guest

Background:
Sarroy Enterprises was formed in January 1989 by David Wells and George and Linda Cunningham after six months of research on motorcycle tours in Queensland.

Between the three of them there is about 35 years of motorcycle driving experience. The majority of that time has been spent touring Queensland. Each has a broad knowledge of the area.

George and Linda have been married for 14 years. They have known and worked with David for 12 years.

Services offered:
- Three-, five-, and seven-day guided tours of Queensland, Australia
- Motorcycle rental (Harley-Davidsons) to tour participants
- Motorcycle rentals available to general public

TOUR OPERATORS 51

Smoky Mountain Motorcycle Vacations

200 Upper Herron Cove Road
Weaverville, NC 28787

Contact: Gary Dagiel
Phone: 704-658-0239
  (weekday evenings)
FAX: Not available

Smoky Mountain Motorcycle Adventures

Gary Dagiel

Background:
Gary Dagiel, his wife and two children live in a house over 100 years old that they have renovated, privately nestled in the Blue Ridge Mountains just outside Asheville, North Carolina. They consider it paradise.

The inspiration for Smoky Mountain Motorcycle Vacations came during a "spirit-cleansing sunset ride" in 1987. Since then, Gary has been helping his guests enjoy some of motorcycling's "sweetest" days.

Gary has been an avid rider for over 20 years and paid for college by working as a motorcycle mechanic. His love of the breathtaking scenery, the history, and the world-class riding offered by these mountains is contagious.

Services offered:
• Guided tour of the Smoky Mountains

Sunset Off-Road

P.O. Box 1388
Manhattan Beach, CA 90266

Contact: Francois Deroeux
Phone: 213-676-2621
FAX: 213-676-2621

SUNSET OFF-ROAD

Francois Deroeux

Background:
At age 26, Francois Deroeux has an extensive motorcycle racing background. In France he competed for seven years in enduro and four-

wheel-drive races. In 1987 he decided to visit California and enter in the district 37 and SCORE desert races. He fell in love with the California deserts and has remained there since.

Although he no longer competes in races, he still spends a lot of his time riding in the desert.

He welcomes contact from Europeans interested in visiting North America.

Services offered:
- Sunset Off-Road provides customized motorcycle tours of Californian desert and mountains. Tour length, dates, highlights, and price are all determined by your schedule and how far you want to ride. All tours cover beautiful scenery and use dependable street, dirt, and dual-sport motorcycles.
- Four-wheel-drive tours of southern California
- Liaison for U.S. businesses and racers who want to know more about advertising, competitions, tourism, and the motorcycling industry in France and vice versa

Team Aventura

Karlsebene 2
8924 Steingaden
GERMANY

Contact: Christoph del Bondio
Phone: (49) 8862-6161
FAX: Not available

Background:
Team Aventura is a new touring organization, founded in 1987 by Christoph del Bondio. Mr. del Bondio organizes tours to the Sahara, Peru, Brazil, Bolivia, and Italy, all on rented motorcycles. Team Aventura operates some tours in cooperation with Suzuki in Europe, taking dual-purpose bikes into remote regions.

We received limited information from Team Aventura about their tours, and it was too late in the publishing process to refine it for this book. (The same thing happened with our previous edition.) We must therefore refer readers to Team Aventura for more details and hope you get better response than we did.

Te Waipounamu Motorcycle Tours

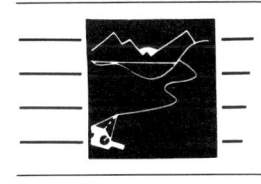

	P.O. Box 673 Christchurch, NEW ZEALAND Contact: John Rains Phone: (64) 3 523 541 FAX: (64) 3 652 155
Booking agent:	Beach's Motorcycle Adventures 2703 West River Parkway Grand Island, NY 14072-2087 USA Phone: 716-773-4960 FAX: 716-773-5227
Booking agent:	Schnieder Reisen Schomburgstrasse 120 2000 Hamburg 50, GERMANY Phone: (49) 403 802 0633 FAX: (49) 403 88965
Booking agent:	Volker Lenzner TransCyclist International CPO Box 2064 Tokyo, 100-91, JAPAN Phone: (81) 3-402-5385 FAX: (81) 3-402-5358

Background:
John and Maria Rains both speak the native language of Maori; between them they have "university degrees in New Zealand flora and fauna". Gaining vast experience motorcycling, they have lived in every corner of New Zealand and enjoy showing visitors their beautiful country.

In 1985 John and Maria established Te Waipounamu, named after the Maori word for the Southern Island of New Zealand. Translated, it means "greenstone water", and to the Maori it was the most valuable object they possessed. John and Maria feel the same way about their island home.

It is a constant source of amusement to his guests that John is always running into someone he knows, or vice versa, wherever he goes in New Zealand.

They provide friendly assistance to their groups and individual travelers.

Services offered:
- Guided tours of New Zealand
- Motorcycle rentals, in conjunction with guided tours and also for independent use
- Rental of motorcycling helmets, gloves, and rain suits

Tours, S.R.L.

VENEZUELA EN MOTOCICLETA
Venezuela on bike

Edif. Res. Los Sauces
Entrada A, Piso 8, Apto. 1
Valencia
VENEZUELA

Contact: Werner Glode
Phone: (58) 41-213007
FAX: (58) 41-342950
Telex: (58) 41-45116

U.S. reference: Karl Raedisch (home)
Phone: 813-624-6994

Background:

Tours, S.R.L. was established in 1983 by Werner Glode and his two sons with the objective of showing fabulous Venezuela to motorcyclists. Mr. Glode moved to Venezuela in 1954 and set up a private accounting practice there. He first got interested in motorcycles about ten years ago, when one of his potential clients gave him a BMW 60/5 with 1800 km on it as a gift. His three sons immediately supported his interest and explored the many great motorcycle treks in Venezuela with him. His middle son Martin, 26, recently graduated from the University of Carabobo with their first group of bilingual tourist guides.

Because the tours are an extension of their own hobby, riding and touring, the Glodes restrict each tour to a maximum of six motorcycles. Mr. Glode says that accompanying visitors is a hobby for him and claims not to be a professional tour operator.

Services offered:

- Scheduled tours to Venezuela
- Customized tours: upon request during their rainy season (May through September), into areas not covered by their formal tour programs.
- Motorcycle rentals to those riders wishing to tour on their own; full-value security deposit is required. For all standard and customized tours a security deposit of $500 is required.

Trail Bike Tours

134 Tunstall Road
Donvale, Victoria 3111
AUSTRALIA

Contact: Klaus or Barbara Mueller
Phone: (61) 3-842-4831
FAX: (61) 3-874-8277

Background:
Trail Bike Tours was founded in 1985 by Klaus Mueller. Klaus, 49, has over 25 years of motorcycle experience, mechanical and first aid training, and is considered an expert enduro rider. He is especially knowledgeable about the trails and paths of Victoria where he lives, for many of the routes that he uses are not found on maps. Klaus is also a contributing editor to *Australian Motorcycle News* magazine. Trail Bike Tours is a member of the Victorian Tour Operators Association.

Klaus Mueller

Services offered:
- Seven-day guided motorcycle tours of the Australian desert and high country
- Two-, three-, and five-days tours of the mountains of Victoria
- Motorcycle rental to tour participants

Trans America Tours

	Sophienstrasse 13 D-2400 Lubeck 1 GERMANY Contact: Peter Apel Phone: (49) 451-797203 FAX: (49) 451-704907
Brazilian office:	Rua Alfa 400 13.500 Rio Claro SP BRAZIL Contact: Bernd & Helmut Holzberger Phone: (55) 195-340533 FAX: (55) 195-242096

Background:
Trans America Tours was established in 1990 by Peter Apel and Bernd and Helmut Holzberger. Peter met the Holzberger brothers after traveling on motorcycle for four years from Alaska to Patagonia. His 100,000-mile journey left his BMW in need of restoration so he left it at the Holzbergers' shop in Brazil for repair.

The Holzbergers moved to Brazil from Germany in 1977. In Germany, Bernd and Helmut had always driven BMW motorcycles, but in Brazil they found difficulty importing their motorcycles and finding parts and service. The Holzbergers decided to create their own service center and manufacture their own parts. This endeavor led to the formation of a motorcycle manufacturing company, which produced its first two motorcycles in 1984. Their firm, Brazilian Motorcycle Company, now produces a motorcycle (BMC R 100 GS) that is a replica of one of the strongest enduro motorcycles in the world, the BMW R 100 GS Paris-Dakar. Trans America Tours uses BMC motorcycles in its tours of Brazil.

Services offered:
- Guided motorcycle tours of Brazil
- Motorcycle rental to tour participants
- Five-day tour, without motorcycle, of the Iguacu waterfalls and Paraguay
- Information and tips on traveling in South America, technical assistance, motorcycle repair shops, etc., for individual travelers

TransCyclist International

CPO Box 2064
Tokyo, 100-91
JAPAN

Contact: Volker Lenzner
Phone: (81) 3-3402-5385
FAX: (81) 3-3402-5358

Volker Lenzner

Background:
Headquartered in Tokyo, TransCyclist International (TC) started in 1979 as a mail box touring club for the exchange of information and mutual aid among long distance motorcycle travelers. It is a nonprofit motor travel organization based on the international motorcycle traveling experience of its founder, Volker Lenzner. TC strives to encourage better mutual understanding among people of the world through travel, with motorcycle travel being the form allowing the greatest freedom of expression. Volker Lenzner is a West German who has worked and traveled in West Germany, South Africa, Australia, the Pacific, and Japan.

Services offered:
- TransCyclist offers organized, guided, adventure tours, usually involving other outdoor activities (river rafting, horseback riding, etc.) to Australia, Canada, China, Japan, New Zealand, Venezuela, South Africa, Italy, West Germany, North Africa, Brazil, Peru, and the United States.
- TC arranges trips to international rallies (e.g., Paris-Dakar, Barstow-Vegas Rally) and racing events (e.g., Isle of Man, Laguna-Seca) often coupled with tours of the region. Inquire of TC for details.
- Arrangements for motorcycle rentals, buy-sellbacks, purchases, shipping, and exchanges
- Bike travel documentation workshops, contests (photo, video, report)
- Yearbook and newsletter
- Club aid and emergency rescue for long-distance motorcycle travelers
- International Club Shop for the exchange (or purchase) of rare models, parts, etc. through TC's worldwide network

Special Note: TC's departments of independent motorcycle travel and guided leisure tours operate independently of one another; however, all tour customers are automatically entitled to full membership/insider-status in the TC organization and to benefits from its worldwide programs. When requesting information, TC asks that you send a self-addressed envelope and one international reply coupon (available from the post office).

Travel Star

1725 C.R. 951; Suite 101
Naples, FL 33999

Contact: Randy Warren
Phone: 800-541-1223 or 813-455-5140
FAX: 813-455-5149

Background:
Travel Star began out of necessity and frustration. Co-owners Randy Warren and Suki O'Brien had a difficult time trying to find competent travel agents to handle their motorcycle-related travel plans. They began making their own travel arrangments and noticed a considerable difference in the prices. They decided to open their own travel company and began marketing their services to the motorcycle industry.

Before starting their business, Randy and Suki both worked in the motorcycle industry aftermarket. Also, Randy worked on a pit crew at the Daytona 200 and in 1983 was an announcer for the Loudon Classic.

Services offered:
Travel Star is a full-service travel agency that specializes in arranging travel plans for motorcycle events. Travel Star provides travel plans for major motorcycle events such as the U.S. Grand Prix, Daytona Bike Week, and the Black Hills Motorcycle Classic, and is the official travel agent for Brainerd International Raceway (World Superbike - U.S. round), Western Eastern Roadracers Association (W.E.R.A.), International Drag Bike Association (I.D.B.A.), and *Easyriders* magazine. Also, many of America's prominent road racers and teams use Travel Star for their race travel.

Travel Star's U.S. tours are customized to the needs of its clients. Although tours revolve around common dates, customers arrive and depart according to their own schedule and utilize accommodations that suit their own personal taste and budget.

International tours, however, are a bit more structured. Departure dates and choice of accommodations are limited.

Von Thielmann Tours

P.O. Box 87764
San Diego, CA 92138

Contact: Gina Guzzardo
Phone: 619-463-7788 or 619-234-1558
FAX: 619-234-1458

Michael von Thielmann

VON THIELMANN TOURS

Background:
Von Thielmann Tours was established in 1957. Originally founded in Munich, Germany, the headquarters of the tour company is now in San Diego, California.

Even though Von Thielmann Tours organizes and offers various types of special interest tours, including a complete travel service, their specialty has always been motorcycle tours.

Von Thielmann Tours has successfully conducted motorcycle tours in more than thirty countries throughout the world. Many of the tours have been guided personally by the president of the company, Michael von Thielmann. In 1984, he was the world's first tour operator to receive official permission to operate motorcycle tours in the People's Republic of China on a regular basis. In 1988 the Soviet Union granted Mr. von Thielmann permission to bring motorcyclists to the Soviet Union. Since 1983, he has added tours of New Zealand to the program. European Alpine countries are included in the most popular tours, but specific destinations change from year to year because of the high number of tour repeaters who wish to travel new scenic areas when they return again and again.

Michael von Thielmann was born in Germany and raised in Munich, Bavaria, where he received his Master of Business Administration at the Munich University. Even though he now lives in California, he spends much of his time in Europe and other countries, preparing and organizing tours.

Services offered:
- Scheduled tours operate in various parts of Europe, in New Zealand, Thailand, People's Republic of China, Mexico, Jamaica, Argentina, and the United States.
- Customized tours. Special tours, for clubs as an example, can be arranged any time and for any budget.

60 TOUR OPERATORS

- Tour members join from many states and several countries; travel and flight arrangements are made accordingly.
- Video tape presentation of tours
- Motorcycle rentals are available for tour participants and also for those traveling on their own. (See section on Motorcycle Rentals.)
- Motorcycle shipping
- Motorcycle purchasing services:
   In Europe: European Delivery Program, tax free vehicles (BMW), and used vehicles (BMW and Japanese)
   In California: new and used motorcycles

Western States Motorcycle Tours

534 West Wilshire Dr.
Phoenix, Arizona 85003

Contact: Frank Del Monte
Phone: 602-258-9048
FAX: 602-274-2836

Frank Del Monte

Background:
Frank Del Monte, 47, has been riding motorcycles for 32 years. He has toured the United Sates extensively and has ridden in just about every state. He is a 15-year member of the American Motorcyclist Association, one of the original Road Rider representatives and the founder of the International Norton Owners Association, which now has over 7,000 members.

Frank has lived in the Southwest (both Arizona and Nevada) for over 17 years and has been conducting tours of Arizona, Colorado, Utah and Nevada on an informal basis for the past three years. He is now giving up his career as a computer software engineer to formalize the tours and turn them into a full-time business.

Services offered:
- Guided tours to the southwestern United States
- Will assist travelers who want to purchase a motorcycle for use in the Southwest and resell it after the trip, and will make arrangements for registration and insurance
- Will provide a trip itinerary and hotel reservations for those who want to travel on their own in the Southwest United States

Wild Bull Tours

P.O. Box 461
Nambour, Queensland 4560
AUSTRALIA

Contact: Mark Jones
Phone: (61) 74 453 822 or (61) 74 459 440
FAX: (61) 74 459 200

Background:
Wild Bull Tours was established in 1988 by Mark Jones, Mike Hamilton, and Ken Wilson. Mike and Mark each have more than 20 years of touring experience, both in Australia and Southeast Asia. Ken has been in the motorcycle industry for more than 15 years and is the owner of Griffin Honda/Yamaha, which provides motorcycles, servicing, and technical advice to Wild Bull Tours. The guides on Wild Bull Tours are all active dual-sports riders and have many thousands of miles of experience driving in the outback.

Services offered:
- Guided motorcycle tours of Queensland, Australia
- Motorcycle rental to tour participants (limited number of motorcycles available)

World Motorcycle Tours

14 Forest Avenue
Caldwell, NJ 07006

Contact: Warren Goodman
Phone: 201-226-9107 or 800-443-7519
FAX: 201-226-8106

Flori and Warren Goodman

Background:
As a reward for a couple of years of successful ski tours to Austria, Warren and Flori Goodman, along with their motorcycle, were shipped over to Germany courtesy of Lufthansa to retrace Warren's WWII route. After a successful and enjoyable experience Warren felt that if he could do it, anyone else could too; hence, the formation of World Motorcycle Tours in 1973.

Over the years the Goodmans have shipped many motorcycles, all *uncrated*, both for participation in their tours and for those going "on their own." They continue to offer their services to one and all for the transport of their own uncrated motorcycles with gateways at New York, Chicago, and Los Angeles. Warren is continually working on expanding the number of departure points.

The Goodmans' tours specialize in the Alpine regions and feature deluxe and first-class hotels of the European style that include meals to match. Now, after twenty years of Alpine touring, they have selected some of the most interesting spots available for their clients. They feel that their routings and accommodations should whet just about every touring appetite.

Services offered:
- Organized tours of the Alps
- Customized tours for groups and individuals
- Shipping motorcycles to Europe for tourists

ORGANIZED TOURS

See the world by motorcycle. This is the universe in its breadth and complexity. These tours cover the globe and offer incredible variety in length, level of difficulty, and level of luxury. There is a journey here for every taste and disposition — from a tour that includes some of Europe's four-star hotels to one that features hard riding and camping in the Sahara. You can catch a tour for any season or any location — if you hurry. There are no excuses to stay home.

To ensure maximum accuracy in what we published, the tour outlines that follow were checked with the tour operators before we went to press. However, as with any product, adjustments are made to motorcycle tours as the operators discover what works and what doesn't. For that and for many other reasons, you may find deviations between our outline and the tour as it is actually offered by the tour operator. When you find a tour that appeals to you it is important to contact the tour operator directly to get the latest information about it.

ORGANIZED TOURS – CANADA & ALASKA

ALASKA Alaska

Tour operator:	Alaska Motorcycle Tours, Inc.
Length of tour:	Seven days, approximately 1,600 miles
Dates:	• Departs every Friday from June 14 through August 30, 1991
Trip begins and ends at:	Anchorage, Alaska

Highlights:
Stay in deluxe hotels each evening as you explore Alaska's wilderness by day. Start your journey with a drive to Homer, on the beautiful Kenai Peninsula, and continue on to Alyeska. You'll follow a spectacular route to Fairbanks in the heart of Alaska's gold rush country. Visit the Great One — at 20,320 feet, Mt. McKinley is North America's highest peak. Explore part of the two million acres of untouched wilderness that surrounds this magnificent mountain. Spend your final night in Anchorage, a city of 200,000. You'll appreciate the luxury of this personalized tour for six cyclists and their riders. Optional tours are offered in Anchorage, Fairbanks, and Denali National Park.

Price (includes motorcycle rental):
Two riders, double occupancy .... $1,300 per person

Price includes:
Six nights in luxury hotels, tour guide, baggage transfers, gratuities, motorcycle rental and fuel, and sightseeing where applicable

Motorcycle provisions:
1988 Honda Gold Wing with Corbin custom seats

Luggage provisions:
Motorcyclists will carry their own baggage. Extra luggage may be stored in Anchorage.

On the road: Alaska

ORGANIZED TOURS – CANADA & ALASKA 67

A photographer's dream (on the road to Fairbanks)

CANADA & ALASKA	Fairbanks to Vancouver
Tour operator:	Bike Tours Australia
Length of tour:	21 days
Dates:	• August 2 through August 22, 1992 • Next trip will be 1994
Trip begins:	Fairbanks, Alaska
Trip ends:	Vancouver, British Columbia

Highlights:
Watch eagles soar 20,320 feet to the snowcapped peak of Mount McKinley, North America's highest mountain. Look for grizzly bear and other spectacular wildlife in the frozen northwest wilderness. Spin through heavily glaciated mountains toward Anchorage on the Kenai Peninsula. Journey farther north across the Alcan Highway. Enter the Klondike, heart of gold rush country. From here, you'll loop southeast through Hazelton and Prince George. Pass Spatsizi Plateau and glimpse snowcapped Mount Edziza in the distance. Head down the Caribou Highway toward Vancouver.

Price (includes motorcycle rental):
- Single rider .... DM 3,650
- Motorcycle passenger .... DM 950
- Luggage van passenger .... DM 1,850
- Combination of two successive Bike Tours Australia tours .... DM 6,500

Price includes:
Camping equipment (except sleeping bag), transfer from airport to camp, campground fees, tents, and motorcycle rental, maintenance, and repairs

Not included in price:
Food, fuel (cost approximately $260 per tour per person), and all-risk insurance (voluntary), available for $35 (or $60 with no deductible) per week per motorcycle

Motorcycle provisions:
Yamaha XT 600 (latest model)

Luggage provisions:
A luggage van accompanies this tour.

Special notes:
The principal language of this tour is German. English can be spoken if necessary. This trip is timed to start just as the reverse trip ends; it takes a completely different route from Vancouver. For those travelers who want more of this beautiful countryside, plan to combine this tour and the reverse tour for a complete Vancouver-Fairbanks-Vancouver loop. May also be combined with Vancouver-San Francisco trips.

CANADA & ALASKA — Vancouver to Fairbanks

Tour operator:	Bike Tours Australia
Length of tour:	21 days
Dates:	• July 5 through July 25, 1992 • Next trip will be 1994
Trip begins:	Vancouver, British Columbia

ORGANIZED TOURS – CANADA & ALASKA 69

Trip ends:	Fairbanks, Alaska

Highlights:
Follow the sunrise toward spectacular Banff and Jasper National Parks in the rugged Canadian Rockies. Cruise through Dawson Creek where civilization ends and the wilderness begins. Head north on the famous Alcan Highway. At Whitehorse, Jack London's hometown, visit the pioneer museum. Pan for gold in northern streams. Enjoy the unspoiled pleasure of America's largest state.

Price (includes motorcycle rental):
- Single rider .... DM 3,650
- Motorcycle passenger .... DM   950
- Luggage van passenger .... DM 1,850
- Combination of two successive Bike Tours Australia tours .... DM 6,500

Price includes:
Camping equipment (except sleeping bag), transfer from airport to camp, campground fees, tents, and motorcycle rental, maintenance, and repairs

Not included in price:
Food, fuel (cost approximately $260 per tour per person), and all-risk insurance (voluntary), available for $35 (or $60 with no deductible) per week per motorcycle

Motorcycle provisions:
Yamaha XT 600 (latest model)

Luggage provisions:
A luggage van accompanies this tour.

Special notes:
The principal language of this tour is German. English can be spoken if necessary. The reverse direction of this trip is timed to start after this trip ends; it takes a completely different route back to Vancouver. For those travelers who want more of this beautiful countryside, plan to keep on going for another three weeks and take advantage of the combined Vancouver-Fairbanks-Vancouver loop.

CANADA & ALASKA

Great Northern Tour

Tour operator:	Motorcycle Tours North
Length of tour:	Nine days
Dates:	• June 17 through June 25, 1991 • June 29 through July 6, 1991 • July 15 through July 23, 1991 • July 29 through August 6, 1991 • August 12 through August 20, 1991
Trip begins and ends:	Dawson Creek, British Columbia

Highlights:
This tour will take you from Dawson Creek, British Columbia to Fairbanks, Alaska along the recently completed Alaska Highway. Tour operator Claude Kidd calls it "one of the man made wonders of the world." Come prepared to ride for you'll travel seven to eight hours a day across the Canadian wilderness and into Alaska. Visit Laird Hot Springs, an all season oasis, and the northern city of Whitehorse in the Yukon Territory. Spend two nights at the Cripple Creek Resort in Fairbanks, Alaska where you can try your luck panning for gold. Enjoy a salmon-bake supper or steak feed, take a cruise on a sternwheel riverboat, or attend one of the live evening shows at the Palace Saloon.

Price:
- Per person, double occupancy .... CAN $1,300
- A CAN $100 discount available to those who book their tour before February 28, 1991

Price includes:
Accommodations for eight nights in comfortable hotels or campsites, if preferred; all breakfasts and dinners; and scenic tour fees

Not included in price:
Fuel or lunch

Motorcycle provisions:
Each participant is responsible for providing his own motorcycle.

Luggage provisions:
Each participant is responsible for carrying his own luggage.

Special notes:
- A 25 percent deposit is required.
- Participants who wish to camp out should bring their own tent and sleeping bag. Other camping gear, such as cooking utensils, is not necessary.
- Each person should bring warm clothing, rain gear, and a bathing suit if he wants to bathe in hot springs.

ALBERTA & BRITISH COLUMBIA   The Best of the Canadian Rockies

Tour operator:	Rocky Mountain Moto Tours Ltd.
Length of tour:	Nine days, approximately 1,600 miles
Dates:	• June 21 through June 29, 1991 • July 20 through July 28, 1991 • August 8 through August 16, 1991 • 1992 dates available upon request after May 1, 1991
Trip begins and ends:	Calgary, Alberta

Highlights:
Leave the tamer life and plunge into the rugged, spacious landscape of Alberta. Skim through the foothills of the Rockies. Enter ranching country — the last frontier of the working cowboy.

You'll travel Alberta's foothills, the mountains of the Continental Range, the Rockies, the Purcells, the Bugaboos, the Columbia Icefields, Banff National Park, Waterton National Park, Kananaskis Provincial Park, plus hundreds of miles of the most exciting and remote wilderness routes you will ever experience. "Guaranteed," say the tour directors.

You'll be sharing these vistas mostly with wild animals and the new friends you'll meet on the tour.

Price (includes motorcycle rental):
- Double occupancy, per person . . . . .U.S. $1,399

Price includes:
Pickup at designated hotels on first morning of tour, the use of a fully-insured motorcycle, six nights deluxe and, if possible, unique accommodation (double occupancy), all breakfasts and lunches, and the services of an experienced tour guide

Motorcycle provisions:
Honda XL 600 dual-purpose motorcycle equipped with expedition racks

Luggage provisions:
Two saddlebags and tail bag are provided. Travel cases can be stored in Calgary if necessary.

Special notes:
On this tour, evenings are spent on remote guest ranches or in secluded mountain lodges. No fancy attire is required. Travel is mostly on isolated mountain trails and roads. Due to the vast uninhabited areas, you'll travel together for safety and comfort. Maximum tour size is six. Riding pace is moderate with little (zero) traffic.

Because of the type of riding and somewhat isolated accommodations on this tour, double room occupancy is encouraged. These tours are for single riders only, due to the kind of bikes used and the somewhat rugged roads traveled.

ALBERTA & BRITISH COLUMBIA — The Mountains of British Columbia

Tour operator: Rocky Mountain Moto Tours Ltd.

Time to smell the roses

Length of tour:	Seven days
Dates:	• June 7 through June 13, 1991 • September 10 through September 16, 1991 • 1992 dates available upon request after May 1, 1991
Trip begins and ends:	Calgary, Alberta

Highlights:
This is a stimulating mountain tour, including the Kananaski mountains, the Rocky mountains, the remote interior mountains of British Columbia including the Bugaboos, the Selkirks, and the Monashee mountain ranges. Tour the famous half-million-acre Douglas Lake Ranch, Lake Louise, the Glacier, Yoho, and Banff National Parks.

The September tour also features the British Columbia salmon run, one of the great natural phenomena as the salmon struggle 400 miles inland from the ocean to spawn in the mountain rivers.

You'll be sharing these vistas mostly with wild animals and the new friends you'll meet on the tour.

Price (includes motorcycle rental):
• Double occupancy, per person . . . . U.S. $1,099

Price includes:
Pickup at designated hotels on first morning of tour, the use of a fully insured motorcycle, six nights deluxe and, if possible, unique accommodation (double occupancy), all breakfasts and lunches, and the services of an experienced tour guide

Motorcycle provisions:
Honda XL 600 dual-purpose motorcycle equipped with expedition racks

Luggage provisions:
Two saddlebags and tail bag are provided. Travel cases can be stored in Calgary if necessary.

Special notes:
On all our tours, evenings are spent on remote guest ranches or in secluded mountain lodges. No fancy attire is required. Travel is mostly on isolated mountain trails and roads. Due to the vast uninhabited areas, you'll travel together for safety and comfort. Maximum tour size is six. Riding pace is moderate with little (zero) traffic.

Because of the type of riding and somewhat isolated accommodations on this tour, double room occupancy is encouraged. These tours are for single riders only, due to the kind of bikes used and the somewhat rugged roads traveled.

BRITISH COLUMBIA — Vancouver Island & Sunshine Coast

Tour operator:	Rocky Mountain Motorcycle Touring
Length of tour:	Seven days, approximately 1,000 miles
Dates:	• July 15 through July 22, 1991 • July 29 through August 5, 1991 • August 12 through August 19, 1991 • August 26 through September 2, 1991 • September 9 through September 16, 1991
Trip begins and ends:	All tours begin in Victoria, British Columbia and end in Vancouver, British Columbia.

Highlights:
New for 1991, this tour originates on Vancouver Island, blessed with some of the most curved, paved roads imaginable, scenery that defies description, beaches that stretch forever, and mountain vistas beyond compare. There are outdoor activites of all kinds, from scuba diving trips and killer whale watches to helicopter flights. Follow the tour across the island, over the Straight of Georgia, and down into Vancouver where it ends.

If you don't want to travel as part of a structured tour, set your own itinerary and take advantage of the support services that Rocky Mountain Motorcycle Touring can arrange for you. Lodging is your choice: tents, motels, or deluxe hotels.

Price:
At press time no prices were available. Contact RMMT.

Price includes:
Accommodations for seven nights, all meals, and fuel

Not included in price:
Health, travel, and accident insurance

Motorcycle provisions:
Participants may bring their own motorcycle or they may rent one.

Luggage provisions:
Participants are responsible for carrying their own luggage.

Special notes:
• Bookings must be accompanied by a CAN $500 deposit per person.
• Motorcycles rented for this tour may be purchased for export to the rider's home country or state.

CANADA	**Vancouver Road Rider**
Tour operator:	TransCyclist International
Length of tour:	Seven days, approximately 1,200 km
Dates:	Monthly during June and September (dates subject to booking requests and minimum six participants)
Trip begins and ends:	Vancouver, British Columbia

Highlights:
Join the "Three Coast Tour" on which the legend of the Canadian west coast comes to life as you ferry across to Vancouver Island. This is a land of soaring eagles where ancient Douglas fir trees tower in the landscape. Navigate along the old coach road down the Saanich Peninsula to Victoria, port town of old castles and gardens, totems, and old English tradition. Take a one-day coastal adventure galley cruise complete with fishing and diving adventures. Next, head up the island to Nanaimo, the Harbour City, and nearby Gabriola Island. The landscape shows evidence of island coal mines, native petroglyphs, and centuries of wind and waves. After leaving Nanaimo you will head toward the rugged coast with Tofino as an overnight stop. On your final day, journey to Comox and board another British Columbia ferry for a cruise to the town of Powell River on the Sunshine Coast.

Or, take the "Kettle Valley Tour" leaving early in the morning for the Seymour Mountains. See Vancouver at its scenic best. Visit Fort Langley Museum at Manning Lodge; take a ferry ride; stop at Kelona and Merritt. Travel along the mighty Fraser River through spectacular Fraser Canyon. Switch from motorcycle touring to exhilarating river rafting. Ride a famous tram across the river at Hell's Gate and return to Vancouver.

Price (includes motorcycle rental):
- Single rider, double occupancy $1,450
- Passenger (bike, van) double occupancy ....$ 985

Note: A $500 refundable insurance bond is required.

Price includes:
Accommodations for six nights, breakfasts and dinners, motorcycle rental, fuel and oil, third party insurance, ferries, camps, guide, route maps, tour briefings, one day free sightseeing in Vancouver, half-day shopping trip, and support van for larger groups. (Airport transfers can be arranged.)

Not included in price.
Lunch snacks and travel/accident insurance

Motorcycle provisions:
All Japanese makes — 400cc and up

Luggage provisions:
A support van for luggage and spares for larger groups is available. Travel lightly if member of a small group.

Special notes:
The Vancouver Road Rider offers tours to two discinct locations: the "Three Coast Tour" (coastline) and the "Kettle Valley Tour" (interior). International driver's license valid for motorcycle operation required by participants. Tour price is for a minimum of six participants and tour departure is subject to six minimum bookings. You are advised to book at least three months in advance (45-day booking deadline, full payment 30 days before tour departure). Cost adjustment will be made if you bring your own bike. In addition to these tours, a variation of short/long duration Freedom Rider USA Tours are offered. Send a self-addressed envelope and one international reply coupon (available from the post office) when inquiring about the tours.

. . . and we could put the main cabin near the boat launch and . . .
(photo courtesy of Rocky Mountain Moto Tours, Ltd.)

ORGANIZED TOURS – UNITED STATES

SOUTHWEST UNITED STATES — Best from the West Tour

Tour operator:	Big Bike Tours
Length of tour:	19 days
Dates:	• June 21 through July 9, 1991 • July 11 through July 30, 1991 • August 1 through August 20, 1991 • August 22 through September 10, 1991
Trip begins and ends:	Frankfurt, Germany

Highlights:

This tour incorporates the best places of the American Southwest. From the Grand Canyon to Monument Valley, from the gambler's paradise of Las Vegas to the beautiful hills of San Francisco. Experience the diverse riding terrain: from long stretches of highway that disappear into the horizon to the winding bends of Zion Canyon, Death Valley, and Yosemite National Park.

Your tour begins with a drive down the magnificent California coast from San Francisco to Los Angeles for a tour of Universal Film Studios and Disneyland. Next, you're off to San Diego where you will visit Seaworld and then cross the border into Mexico for a visit to Tijuana.

In Arizona a small charter plane will carry you over the awe-inspiring beauty of the Grand Canyon. A few days later a hot air balloon will lift you over the desert and return you to a champagne breakfast. You'll ride the Colorado river on a white water rafting trip through Bryce Canyon and then travel up to Las Vegas to do some gambling or see a show. Now is the opportunity to shop for a pair of cowboy boots or buy some jewelry from Indian craftsmen.

Ride through Death Valley, the lowest and hottest area in the United States, and Yosemite National Park. Then travel back to San Francisco, where you have a few days to explore the city's many attractions, such as Chinatown, Fisherman's Wharf, and Golden Gate Park, before departing for home.

Price:
With tour guide:
• Per person .... DM 6,990
• Per passenger .... DM 5,399
Without tour guide:
• Per person .... DM 5,790
• Per passenger .... DM 3,690

Price includes:
Airfare, accommodations (double occupancy) with breakfast, German tour guide, fuel, personal injury insurance, third-party motorcycle insurance, maps, taxis, transfers during the tour, reception and farewell party, return transportation for motorcycle and delivery in Germany (for motorcycles purchased in the United States), or transportation of your motorcycle to and from the United States (if you are bringing your own)

Price does not include:
Drinks, dinner, or entrance fees to attractions

Motorcycle provisions:
Big Bike Tours will arrange to have your motorcycle transported with you on your flight or will help you buy a new motorcycle in the United States and transport it back with you to Europe.

Luggage provisions:
Participants are responsible for carrying their own luggage.

Special notes:
Big Bike Tours will make arrangements for those groups or individuals who wish to follow the itinerary of this tour on their own. You have the option of bringing your own motorcycle with you, on the same flight, through Big Bike Tours' "fly-and-ride" program.

The tour guide speaks German and English.

Exploring the breathtaking American Southwest

MIDWESTERN UNITED STATES	**Mark Twain Tour**
Tour operator:	Big Bike Tours
Length of tour:	17 days
Dates:	• April 16 through May 2, 1991 • May 7 through May 23, 1991 • June 4 through June 20, 1991 • August 13 through August 29, 1991 • September 17 through October 3, 1991 • October 8 through October 24, 1991
Trip begins and ends:	Frankfurt, Germany

Highlights:

The Mark Twain Tour is a trip through the midwestern United States along the banks of the Mississippi river, then through the heartland of the United States. Begin your tour in Minneapolis and continue through La Crosse, Wisconsin to Kansas, the setting of many of Twain's books. Visit Hannibal, Twain's boyhood home and the setting of *Tom Sawyer* and *Huckleberry Finn*. You can see the homes of Tom, Huck, and Becky Thatcher, as well as the school house where their mischievous pranks occurred. Along the Mississippi you might even see an old paddle steamboat like the one Twain piloted.

The tour then proceeds down Highway 19 and winds its way through the forests of Missouri to the north of Arkansas. Many previous participants have found this part of the tour to be a great driving pleasure. The roads hug the hills and curves, and at one point there is a three-mile stretch that is a continuous wave of small hills and valleys. Many riders can't resist turning around and riding over this again.

The tour continues on to Hermann, a town steeped in German culture. There is plenty of wine and German sausages, and if you're lucky there might even be a festival going on. The tour then moves through the dusty and wind-swept plains of Oklahoma and on to Dallas, Texas where the ground portion of the tour ends.

Price:
With tour group:
• Per person .... DM 6,490
• Per passenger .... DM 4,199
Without tour guide:
• Per person .... DM 5,290
• Per passenger .... DM 3,190

ORGANIZED TOURS – UNITED STATES

Price includes:
Airfare, accommodations (double occupancy) with breakfast, German tour guide, fuel, personal injury insurance, third-party motorcycle insurance, maps, taxis, transfers during the tour, reception and farewell party, return transportation for motorcycle and delivery in Germany (for motorcycles purchased in the United States), or transportation of your motorcycle to and from the United States (if you are bringing your own)

Price does not include:
Drinks, dinner, or entrance fees to attractions

Motorcycle provisions:
Big Bike Tours will arrange to have your motorcycle transported with you on your flight or will help you buy a new motorcycle in the United States and transport it back with you to Europe.

Luggage provisions:
Participants are responsible for carrying their own luggage.

Special notes:
Big Bike Tours will make arrangements for those groups or individuals who wish to follow the itinerary of this tour on their own. You have the option of bringing your own motorcycle with you, on the same flight, through Big Bike Tours' "fly-and-ride" program.
The tour guide speaks German and English.

UNITED STATES & CANADA	**San Francisco to Vancouver & Vancouver to San Francisco**
Tour operator:	Bike Tours Australia
Length of tour:	21 days
Dates:	*San Francisco to Vancouver* • June 7 through June 27, 1992 *Vancouver to San Francisco* • August 30 through September 19, 1992 • Next trips will be 1994
Trip begins and ends:	San Francisco to Vancouver or Vancouver to San Francisco

Dining with the locals

Highlights:
Sweep from beautiful San Francisco Bay up to Tioga Pass on into Death Valley. Capture the full flavor of the American West. Visit the high-stake gambling tables of Las Vegas. See the red sandstone miracle of the Grand Canyon. Cross Wyoming and head toward Yellowstone National Park through the rugged Rocky Mountains and the continental divide. Ride hard and fast across the dry plateaus of east Washington, over the heavily forested Cascade Range, toward the Pacific Ocean and your final stop in Vancouver.

Price (includes motorcycle rental):
- Single rider .... DM 3,650
- Motorcycle passenger .... DM   950
- Luggage van passenger .... DM 1,850
- Combination of two successive Bike Tours Australia tours .... DM 6,500
  (see organized tours of Canada/Alaska)

Price includes:
Camping equipment (except sleeping bag), transfer from airport to camp, campground fees, tents, and motorcycle rental, maintenance, and repairs

Not included in price:
Food, fuel (cost approximately $260 per tour per person), and all-risk insurance (voluntary), available for $35 (or $60 with no deductible) per week per motorcycle

Motorcycle provisions:
Yamaha XT 600 (latest model)

Luggage provisions:
A luggage van accompanies this tour.

Special notes:
The principal language of this tour is German. English is also spoken.

SOUTHWEST UNITED STATES — WildWestTour

Tour operator:	Desmond Adventures, Inc.
Length of tour:	15 days
Dates:	*1991* • April 13 through April 28 • May 4 through May 19 • October 26 through November 10 • November 16 through December 1 *1992* • March 21 through April 5 • April 11 through April 26 • May 2 through May 17 • September 26 through October 11 • October 17 through November 1 • November 7 through November 22
Trip begins and ends:	Los Angeles

Highlights:
On this special motorcycling vacation, tour participants have a chance to take in the most spectacular portions of the Southwest United States. Especially attractive to motorcyclists from the East, tour participants can make use of Desmond's motorcycle shipping service to spare themselves the long trek across the United States to begin the tour.

A unique departure from standard motorcycle tours, Desmond Adventures has thoughtfully arranged a houseboat excursion to explore the unique canyons and sights of Lake Powell, Utah. While at Lake Powell, tour participants may choose to explore on their own with a Jet Ski built for two, a version of motorcycling on the water. Other fine opportunities await WildWestTour participants: gambling in Las Vegas, ballooning over Napa Valley, wine tasting in the wine country, seafood sampling in San Francisco by trolley car, and more. Moreover, participants will have a chance to witness for themselves the results of the enormous migration following the 1849 gold rush. It is amazing to reflect on how people sacrificed their newly established roots in the East for a remote chance at prosperity, only a little more than 100 years ago.

Price (does not include motorcycle rental):
• Driver, double occupancy $2,695
• Passenger, double occupancy $2,495
• Supplement for single room occupancy ....$ 390

Room to breathe and sense the size of things

Price includes:
Hotel accommodations each night, with continental breakfast; dinner each evening, except where the tour stays more than one night at the same location; WildWestTour maps and itineraries; luggage van and transfers; tour guides; and support staff

Motorcycle provisions:
A variety of motorcycles are available for rent on this tour. Specific model information is available four weeks prior to the tour dates. Rental includes liability and collision insurance. For those who wish to use their own motorcycle, Desmond offers its motorcycle shipping service to transport your motorcycle to Los Angeles. Contact Desmond Adventures for a quote, including transport insurance.

Luggage provisions:
A van accompanies each tour to carry luggage. Luggage is picked up from your hotel room as you leave a hotel, and delivered to your room at the destination.

Special notes:
Desmond Adventures can make all air reservations for you, at competitive rates.

Golden Gate Bridge, San Francisco

PENNSYLVANIA	**Pennsylvania Dutch Country**
Tour operator:	Dutchcountry Motorcycle Tours
Length of tour:	Four to eight hours
Dates:	Any day, providing good weather
Trip begins and ends:	Smoketown, PA

Highlights:
With prior confirmation, riders can choose from one of the following tour packages which all have an option of lunch, dinner, or tour only:
  Package A - Farmland Tour: Learn about the Amish, Mennonites and others. Visit an Amish farm and home. See Amish crafts, roadside stands, windmills, watermills, and schools.
  Package B - Historic Tour: Learn about Lancaster County history and culture. Visit Wheatland, Ephrata Cloister, Hans Herr House, and the world's largest pretzel factory, plus other possibilities or substitutions.
  Package C - Covered Bridge Tour: Ride through picturesque Lancaster County and its covered bridges. Enjoy a slow-paced getaway into the beautiful countryside and explore the many farm and pastures. You'll even stop for a picnic along the way.
  Package D - Rider's Choice: Design your own tour, your own specifications
  Package M - Coal Mine Tour: Enjoy a pleasant ride on the back roads of the Anthracite coal region of Pennsylvania. Your main stop will be at the Anthracite Museum in Ashland. Drive deep into a mine on coal cars and see the working conditions of coal miners during the days of the coal barons.

Price:
Guided tour, $8.00 per motorcycle for packages A, B, C, D and $26.00 per motorcycle for Anthracite coal mine tour. Price does not include meals nor admission to attractions or sites. All tours have option for a home cooked breakfast, lunch or dinner, ranging in price from $5.00 to $12.00 (meal prices subject to change).

Price includes:	Personally guided tour
Motorcycle provisions:	Riders must have their own motorcycles.
Luggage provisions:	Not applicable
Special notes:	Groups with fewer than ten motorcycles must pay a minimum base price of $80.00. Advanced registration is required.

SOUTHWEST UNITED STATES — Best of the West

Tour operator:	Edelweiss Bike Travel
Length of tour:	16 days, covering approximately 2,500 miles
Dates:	• May 10 through May 25, 1991 • May 31 through June 15, 1991 • June 28 through July 13, 1991 • July 19 through August 3, 1991 • August 9 through August 24, 1991 • August 30 through September 14, 1991
Trip begins and ends:	Los Angeles

Highlights:
Here is an ideal tour for those who would like to get to know the Wild West by motorcycle. The daily distances are not excessively long, the hotels are comfortable, the meals are substantial, and the natural beauty is overwhelming. There's also sufficient time for shopping and sightseeing. Suitable for single riders and couples alike. The roads are wide and in good condition. The easy way to see the West!

Start your trip by heading into the California desert from Los Angeles. You'll pass over the Coastal Mountains and through the small San Bernardino and Chocolate Mountains. As you turn north into Arizona the terrain changes and you'll travel over magnificent passes at altitudes up to 6,000 ft. Near Flagstaff Arizona you pick up the trail of the Colorado River and the phenomenal Grand Canyon. Vermilion Cliffs and Zion National Park are also on the itinerary as you wend your way to the gambling tables of Las Vegas. A night of glittering shows and casinos makes for a unique experience. The contrasts with Las Vegas will be stark as you travel across Death Valley and The Devil's Golf Course, 250 feet below sea level. To temper that experience you'll then pass through the snow-covered Into Mountains and Toiyabe National Forest, then cross the Sierra Nevada Mountains on the way to San Francisco. After a rest day, during which you can see Fisherman's Wharf, Alcatraz, the Golden Gate Bridge, Chinatown, and the cable cars, you turn south onto the legendary coastal Highway 1 and ride to San Simeon. There you can see the fabulous mansion built by William Hearst, the newspaper tycoon. The last leg of this trip will come too soon, as you ride back into Los Angeles for the return flight home.

Price (includes motorcycle rental):
• Single rider, double occupancy $2,945
• Motorcycle passenger, double occupancy $2,195

- Single room supplement ....$ 480
- Supplement for 750cc touring motorcycle ....$ 295
- Supplement for 1340cc U.S. touring "chopper" ....$ 745
- Supplement for 1400cc super touring motorcycle ....$ 395

Price includes:
Tour information package; transfers from and to Los Angeles airport; accommodations for 15 nights in comfortable hotels; two meals per day (normally breakfast and dinner); motorcycle rental, including insurance (750cc chopper, surcharge for other motorcycles); tour director; sightseeing and entry fees for National parks; and a tour gift

Motorcycle provisions:
Four types of motorcycles are available: a 750cc chopper for the solo rider, a comfortable 750cc touring motorcycle for two, a 1340cc touring chopper with soft saddlebags, and a 1400cc Super Touring motorcycle with lots of storage space for the pampered rider. All motorcycles except the 750cc chopper are available at a premium price.

Luggage provisions:
Each traveler is responsible for carrying his or her own luggage.

Special notes:
There is still snow on the roadsides on the May tour and it can be quite cool on high ground. In July it is extremely hot in Las Vegas and in Death Valley. Travelling begins very early each morning on that tour.

Hi, Mom

The majestic Rocky Mountains

COLORADO	**Colorado**
Tour operator:	Freedom Tours
Length of tour:	Six days, covering approximately 1,400 miles
Dates:	• June 24 through June 29, 1991 • July 1 through July 6, 1991 • July 22 through July 27, 1991 • August 19 through August 24, 1991 • August 26 through August 31, 1991 The dates for 1992 have not yet been set, but will include the week before Wing Ding, the week before Americade West, and three to five others.
Trip begins and ends:	Longmont, Colorado

Highlights:
The Freedom Tour takes you on a 1,400 mile journey through the majestic Rocky Mountains. Each day begins over a hearty breakfast where you'll review the day's itinerary and alternate routes. Join the group in its planned route or take off on one of the alternate routes by yourself and meet the group later. Watch Big Horn sheep play on the rock, enjoy an Indian art show, swim in a glacier-fed stream, or just soak in the clean air and natural beauty of the Rocky Mountains. Visit historic mining areas, scenic side roads, Aspen, Steamboat Springs, and numerous mountain passes.

Price:
- Per person .... $ 795
- Per couple $1,395

Price includes:
Accommodations for six nights in premium hotels, all breakfasts and dinners, tour guide, and maps

Not included in price:
Motorcycle rental, fuel, lunch, motorcycle repairs, and personal expenses

Motorcycle provisions:
Participants are responsible for providing their own motorcycle except Harley-Davidson Owners Group members. Freedom Tours will help H.O.G. members to ship and pick up their motorcycle or arrange for a rental motorcycle.

Luggage provisions:
A service van for excess luggage is available to groups only. Riders must otherwise carry their own luggage.

SOUTHWEST UNITED STATES — Ride the West

Tour operator:	Kalman International Motorcycle Touring
Length of tour:	One week or two weeks
Dates:	*One-week tours* • May 4 through May 12, 1991 • June 29 through July 7, 1991 • August 17 through August 25, 1991 • September 21 through September 29, 1991 • October 5 through October 13, 1991 • October 26 through November 3, 1991 • November 9 through November 17, 1991 *Two-week tours* • April 6 through April 21, 1991 • June 1 through June 16, 1991 • July 20 through August 4, 1991 • August 31 through September 15, 1991

Trip begins and ends:	San Francisco

Highlights:
No two tours are the same. The Kalmans take their guests through the most scenic areas of the west, riding luxury touring motorcycles and staying in comfortable and interesting hotels. Some of the Kalmans' favorite points include Las Vegas, Death Valley, Grand Canyon, Mojave Desert, Yosemite, Sierra Mountains, Monterey, and Big Sur.

Price (does not include motorcycle rental):
One-week tour
- Single rider, double occupancy $1,700
- Passenger, double occupancy $1,500
- Supplement for single room .... $ 250

Two-week tour
- Single rider, double occupancy $2,795
- Passenger, double occupancy $2,400
- Supplement for single room .... $ 450

Price includes:
Deluxe hotel accommodations for seven (or 15) nights, all breakfasts and dinners

Motorcycle provisions:
Kalman International owns seven Honda Gold Wings and three BMWs for rent to tour participants. The price for any motorcycle is $500 per week. You may also bring your own motorcycle. If needed, the Kalmans will assist you in making shipping arrangements. Motorcycle insurance for rental bikes is provided and included in the rental price. There is a $1000 deductible.

Luggage provisions:
A motorcycle trailer accompanies the two-week tours to carry a modest quantity of overflow luggage. You should be prepared to carry most of your luggage with you.

ORGANIZED TOURS – UNITED STATES 91

SOUTHWESTERN UNITED STATES	The Grand Circle
Tour operator:	Meier's Weltreisen
Length of tour:	14 days, covering approximately 2,800 miles
Departure dates:	*1991:* • March 15 • April 8 and 22 • May 6 and 20 • June 3 and 17 • July 1, 15 and 29 • August 12 and 26 • September 9 and 23 • October 7
Trip begins and ends:	Albuquerque, New Mexico

Highlights:
This tour makes a grand circle through the southwestern part of the United States, focusing on the history of the land — geographically and culturally — and the beautiful landscapes and national parks. After assembling in Albuquerque, you'll pass through Santa Fe, a charming town born of Spanish influence and possessing an active artist's colony. Ride into the rugged Sangre de Christo Mountains to the village of Taos for a visit to the famous Pueblos. Ride on through Durango, Silverton, and Cortez, towns that many years ago were bristling with silver mining. You'll pass through Monument Valley with its huge rock formations, a reminder of the great ocean that once covered the land. Bryce Canyon, Zion National Park, Death Valley, and the Grand Canyon are breathtaking attractions you must not miss along the way. Try your hand with lady luck as you spin the wheels in Las Vegas, a glittery gambler's paradise. The tour returns via Cameron, through Navajo country, past Canyon De Chelly and ends in Albuquerque.

Price (includes motorcycle rental):
• Single rider, double occupancy .... DM 2,448
• Share a motorcycle, double occupancy .... DM 1,579
• Supplement for single room occupancy .... DM   610

Price includes:
Accommodations for 14 nights in middle class hotels, insured Honda Shadow motorcycle (700cc to 900cc), transfers from/to Albuquerque airport, and information package

Not included in price:
Transportation to Albuquerque, Collision Damage Waiver (CDW), personal purchases, personal insurance, mileage over 2,800 miles, and additional hotel accommodations

Motorcycle provisions:
Included in the prices above is a Honda Shadow 700cc or 900cc motorcycle. At an additional cost you can reserve a Honda GoldWing (DM 651 extra) or a Harley-Davidson (Softtail, Classic, Electraglide) (DM 760 extra). You can also reserve a smaller motorcycle (500cc to 650cc Honda Shadow) for a slightly lower price; this motorcycle is suitable only for one rider (without pillion passenger).

Luggage:
Contact Meier's Weltreisen for details.

Special notes:
The common language of this tour is German. The guide is also fluent in English. Clients come from throughout Europe.

SOUTHWEST UNITED STATES
U.S.A. The Great American Dream: The New World

Tour operator:	Motorrad-Reisen
Length of tour:	14 days, approximately 995 miles
Dates:	• May 5 through May 18, 1991 • June 2 through June 15, 1991 • July 25 through August 7, 1991 • September 8 through September 21, 1991
Trip begins and ends:	Los Angeles

Highlights:
Enjoy almost 1,000 miles of American road. Drive from the freeways of Los Angeles to the glittering strip in Las Vegas. Bet your fortune on a roll of the dice in the casinos. Enjoy a dinner show. Hit the road again and head for the sands of Death Valley. See the vast beauty of Yosemite National Park. Thrill to the Grand Canyon, one of the natural wonders of the world. Ride over the Golden Gate to cosmopolitan San Francisco. Cruise down the Pacific coast to charming Monterey. Eat at truck stops and steak

houses on the way. Try sophisticated restaurants and San Francisco's Chinatown specialties. You'll sample the variety that is America.

Price (includes motorcycle rental):
- Rider and passenger, double occupancy $7,995
- Single rider, double occupancy $4,700
- Supplement for single room occupancy ....$ 840

Price includes:
All land arrangements, BMW motorcycle, bilingual (German and English) tour guide on motorcycle, board and lodging in twin bed rooms at familiar American hotels such as the Sheraton and Holiday Inn

Motorcycle provisions:
Rental of a BMW motorcycle is included in the tour price.

Luggage provisions:
Riders are responsible for carrying their own luggage.

NORTHWEST UNITED STATES — The Search for Bigfoot™

Tour operator:	Pacific Northwest Motorcycle Adventures
Length of tour:	Nine days, covering approximately 1,800 miles street riding and 800 miles of dual-sport/enduro riding

Dates:
- Tours operate every week in warm months, Saturday through Sunday.
- First tour of 1991 starts April 20 and the last tour starts September 21
- First tour of 1992 starts April 25 and the last tour starts September 26

Trip begins and ends:	Seattle, Washington

Highlights:
You'll capture Washington's diversity and beauty in these specially designed street, dual-sport, and enduro adventures. From the rain forests of the Olympics to the Columbia River, and from the rolling hills of the Palouse to the 200 foot sea stacks of the rugged Pacific Ocean coastline, Washington offers one of those rare places on earth that include seven of the eight world climactic regions. A kaleidoscope of majesty, wonder, and amazement awaits you. Travel from Mount Olympus to Hurricane Ridge.

Visit ghost towns, gold mines, and Mount Rainier with its 27 active glaciers. Sail the San Juan Islands aboard magical ferry boats.

According to the interests of each participant, side adventure trips provide an opportunity for hot air ballooning, golfing, deep sea fishing, a helicopter tour, and more.

Price:
Tour prices begin at $3,895, per person, depending on your choice of side trip adventures.

Price includes:
First class resort accommodations for eight nights, all breakfasts and dinners, motorcycle, fuel, a rider's skill clinic (MSF nationally certified), all parties, departure gifts, and personal video

Not included in price:
Airfare, lunches, beverages, or personal purchases

Motorcycle provisions:
- Street motorcycles: Honda 650 Hawk GT, 750 Night Hawk, GL1500, and a variety of Harley-Davidsons
- Trail Bikes: Honda XR 600, 200, 100, XRL 250, and Cub

Luggage provisions:
TraveLite™, a 40-foot custom motor coach is available to carry all luggage, from tank bags to golf clubs, and serves as completely staffed mobile maintenance center.

Special notes:
Limited space is available on each tour. All trips are custom designed to meet the specific desires and specifications of each participant. Price reflects selected components of options chosen.

Pacific Northwest Motorcycle Adventures has a fly and ride program in which they will purchase a Harley-Davidson for you, have it waiting for you when your get off the plane, and then ship it to your home, fully crated, after you have finished the tour.

UNITED STATES / SOUTHWEST — American Southwest

Tour operator:	Pancho Villa Moto-Tours
Length of tour:	13 days
Dates:	Contact Pancho Villa for dates
Trip begins and ends:	El Paso, Texas

Highlights:
Welcome to a very special part of America. A land void of big city hustle and bustle, full of wide open spaces, constantly contrasting scenery, and a mixture of cultures that even today maintains an attitude nurtured by a history of frontier survival. This is the great American Southwest.

Designed not only for the foreign visitor, it is a tour that will be enjoyed also by Americans with limited vacation time, who want to see this unique section of their country. Pancho Villa has routed this tour to avoid the tortuous desert heat when and where possible. It takes to the higher elevations by late afternoon and avoids such locales as Las Vegas and Death Valley. Plenty of time has been planned for individual pursuits and exploration.

This tour will take you to Ruidoso then along the Rio Grande to Albuquerque. Take to the mountains and visit Taos and an original adobe pueblo village still inhabited. Cross several mountains and pass through Silverton, Colorado, once a prosperous mining town. Onward through the mountains called Little Switzerland to Moab, filming site of countless western movies. The trip wouldn't be complete without a stop at Bryce and Zion National Parks, by some estimates the most beautiful in the country. Pass along the Grand Canyon for a close up view of this natural wonder. You'll probably be ready for the jacuzzi by the time you reach Sedona, Arizona, one of the nicest little towns in America and home of a growing artists' colony. The final leg takes you into the old west, through Tombstone, Arizona and the OK Corral. There is time enough to pick up some fine turquoise and silver jewelry before heading back to El Paso.

Price (does not include motorcycle rental):
- Per person, double occupancy $1,395
- Supplement for single room occupancy ....$ 395

Price includes:
Deluxe hotel accommodations for 12 nights (double occupancy), at least 15 meals with tips, entrance to national parks, chase vehicle for groups of 12 persons or more, road maps and tour information, tour guide, and Pancho Villa tee shirt

ORGANIZED TOURS – UNITED STATES

Motorcycle provisions:
Travelers are invited to bring their own motorcycle or they may rent one from Pancho Villa Moto-Tours (PVMT) for the special price of $995. Available are Harley-Davidson, Honda, Yamaha, and BMW motorcycles. A $400 security deposit for the motorcycle is required if renting (refundable).

Luggage provisions:
Travelers should be prepared to carry their own luggage with them. A luggage van will accompany the tour if there are at least 12 participants.

SOUTHEAST UNITED STATES

Smoky Mountains

Tour operator:	Smoky Mountain Motorcycle Vacations
Length of tour:	Seven days, covering 700 to 1,000 miles
Dates:	*1991:* • Spring vacation - June 2 through June 8 • Summer vacation - July 14 through July 20 • Summer vacation - Aug. 4 through Aug. 10 • Fall vacation - Sept. 22 throughSept. 28 *1992:* • Spring vacation - June 7 through June 13 • Summer vacation - July 12 through July 18 • Summer vacation - Aug. 2 through Aug. 8 • Fall vacation - Sept. 20 through Sept. 26
Trip begins and ends:	Asheville, North Carolina

Highlights:
Smoky Mountain Motorcycle Vacations offers much more than just the best places to explore in the spectacular Blue Ridge and Great Smoky Mountains. They will help you find the best roads, and when and in which direction to ride them (these choices can make the difference between looking at a rock wall with the sun in your eyes or having a perfectly lighted mountain view). They'll help you arrive at a great place to explore just as you've had enough riding. They know which of a dozen available hikes is just right for you. You'll learn the perfect place for a picnic lunch a mile up an unmarked road. Best of all, they'll let you travel at your own pace, with the peace of mind that comes with knowing your best options.

Ride your heart out

You'll discover that you really don't have to go far, to be "far away". Let go of the hurry-hurry pace of modern life as you cool your feet in a babbling mountain stream. See for yourself why the Indians attached religious significance to certain peaks. Realize how far humanity has come, in such a short time, as you roll through a preserved 1850s pioneer community. Absorb the peace in one of the few remaining virgin forests.

Let's not forget over 600 miles (more if you like) of some of the sweetest riding you'll ever do. Follow empty, perfectly paved, two-lane roads over mountains wrapped in blue mists and covered with lush forests . . . nature at her best.

Price (does not include motorcycle rental):
- Single rider, double occupancy $569
- Passenger, double occupancy $519
- Supplement for single room occupancy $100

Price includes:
Accommodations for six nights, most breakfasts, six dinners, and a well-informed tour guide

Motorcycle provisions:
Travelers are expected to bring their own motorcycle. Storage is available for trailers and tow vehicles.

Luggage provisions:
You must carry your own luggage.

SOUTHWEST UNITED STATES — Freedom Rider U.S.A.

Tour operator:	TransCyclist International
Length of tour:	Seven days, covering approximately 2,000 km
Dates:	• Monthly during May and September (dates subject to booking requests and minimum six participants)
Trip begins and ends:	Los Angeles

Highlights:
The legend of the great American outdoors comes to life on TC's Freedom Rider U.S.A. Tour through California and Arizona. View spectacular mountain roads, stunning canyons, towering peaks, and wildly rushing rivers, or frontier towns steeped in the cultural heritage of the Old West. Join this California to Nevada adventure tour along the trails of the famous Barstow-Vegas desert rally. Try your luck in the gamblers' city of Las Vegas, where fortune waits at the wheels. Visit a deserted ghost town in Arizona's arid landscape. Pull up at the roadside and soak in the spectacular scenery from grand canyons down to the wide open prairie. This tour also includes visits to Zion National Park and Grand Canyon, before returning to Los Angeles.

Price (includes motorcycle rental):
- Single rider, double occupancy $1,800
- Passenger (pillion or van), double occupancy $1,000

Note: A $500 security deposit is required for the motorcycle (refundable).

Price includes:
All accommodations, breakfasts and dinners, motorcycle rental, third-party insurance, airport transfers, tour briefings, guide, and extras

Not included in price:
Gas/oil, lunch, and travel accident insurance

Motorcycle provisions:
Honda, Yamaha, and Kawasaki 250 to 650cc and up

Luggage provisions:
Support van for group of ten or more participants

Special notes:
International driver's license valid for motorcycle operation required by participants visiting the United States. Tour price is for a minimum of six participants and subject to change. Cost adjustment will be made if you bring your own bike. You are advised to make your booking well in advance (three months ahead). Send a self-addressed envelope and one international reply coupon (available from the post office) when inquiring about the tour.

SOUTHWEST UNITED STATES

The Indian Badlands Rider

Tour operator:	TransCyclist International
Length of tour:	Five days, six nights; on- and off-road; covering approximately 2,000 km
Dates:	• Monthly (specific dates subject to booking requests)
Trip begins and ends:	Albuquerque, New Mexico

Highlights:
On this unique adventure you will relive the old Wild West and explore the lifestyles, history, and culture of the first citizens of the United States, the American Indians. Ride through magical New Mexico and South Colorado mountains; take part for a day in the life of Farmington, New Mexico; Durango, Colorado; Chama, New Mexico; Taos, New Mexico — all rich in the cultural heritage of the old west, and still alive today. You'll see stunning canyons, towering peaks, and wildly rushing rivers. This is the homeland of the Apache, the Aztecs, Navajo, and others.

Price (includes motorcycle rental):
• Single rider, double occupancy $1,850
• Passenger (van), double occupancy $1,050
Note: A $500 insurance bond is requested when renting the motorcycle; it is refundable when the motorcycle is returned free of damage.

Price includes:
Deluxe accommodation for six nights, breakfasts and dinners (13 meals in all), rental of motorcycle with unlimited mileage and insurance, support vehicle for additional passengers and luggage, tour escort-guide, tour

briefings and information folder with maps, Albuquerque airport transfers, and admissions to national parks, Indian reservations, museums, etc.

Not included in price:
Lunch snacks, fuel, and travel/accident insurance

Motorcycle provisions:
Kawasaki 650 or other Japanese makes (no pillion riding)

Luggage provisions:
A support van will accompany the tour to carry luggage.

Special notes:
International driver's license valid for motorcycle operation required by participants other than U.S. residents. Prices are subject to change. You are advised to book at least three months in advance. The tour requires a minimum of six participants. Five passengers can be accommodated in the support van. Key events, such as the Albuquerque Balloon Festival and Indian Festival can offer additional value to tours if timed properly. This would result in slight increase to cover additional costs. Send a self-addressed envelope and one international reply coupon (available from the post office) when inquiring about the tours.

SOUTHWEST UNITED STATES

Southwest United States

Tour operator:	Von Thielmann Tours
Length of tour:	21 days
Dates:	• February 12 through March 4, 1991 • May 14 through June 3, 1991 • July 16 through August 5, 1991 • October 15 through November 4, 1991 • Similar dates in 1992 and 1993
Trip begins and ends:	Frankfurt or Munich, Germany and San Diego, California

Highlights:
See California, Arizona, Nevada, and Utah. Enjoy very scenic rides from San Diego via Palms Springs, Grand Canyon, Bryce Canyon, Las Vegas, Goldfield, Yosemite National Park, Lake Tahoe, Tahoe National Forest,

Muir Woods, and San Francisco. Ride California's most scenic road along the Pacific coast from Monterey to Santa Barbara.

Price (does not include motorcycle rental):
- Single rider, double occupancy $2,726
- Two people, double occupancy $5,452
- Single passenger, double occupancy $2,726
- Supplement for single room occupancy ....$ 590

Price includes:
Round trip airfare Frankfurt/Los Angeles/San Diego, hotel accommodations, transfers, several meals, tour guide, and road maps

Motorcycle provisions:
Rentals available (foreigners must have international driver's license). Rates are: $48 per day plus $7 per day for insurance, including unlimited miles.

Luggage provisions:
Luggage van with motorcycle trailer included in the tour price.

Options:
Tour members may join the group in San Diego. In this case, the tour prices are reduced by the transatlantic and domestic airfares.

SOUTHWEST UNITED STATES — The Grand Tour

Tour operator:	Western States Motorcycle Tours
Length of tour:	14 days
Dates:	August 4 through August 17, 1991
Trip begins and ends:	Phoenix, Arizona

Highlights:
The 14-day Grand Tour is 2,900 miles of unforgettable scenery. It starts with a tour of the northern half of Arizona. Here you will visit the cowboy towns of Wickenburg and Prescott and the ghost town of Jerome. You will then ride through the red rock of Sedona and the coolness of Oak Creek on your way to the Grand Canyon.

For a change of pace you'll take a ride on a narrow gauge steam train through the magnificent mountain scenery. Then, mount up and ride the million dollar highway between Durango and Ouray, a 73-mile motorcyclist's dream.

You'll cross the Continental Divide six times as you ride at altitudes up to 12,095 feet along the backbone of the Rocky Mountains. You'll see the famous Wolf Creek Pass and ride through Pagosa Springs. Returning to Durango, you'll rest a day with a raft trip down the Animas river.

As you return to Arizona, you'll stop at the Four Corners Monument, the only place in the United States where you can stand in four states at the same time. You'll also visit the oldest trading post in Arizona and enjoy the petrified forest before returning home.

Price:
- Per rider $2,300
- Per passenger .... $ 500
- 6.5 percent tax must be added to these figures

Price includes:
Motorcycle purchasing and selling fees (for those without motorcycles), 13 nights lodging, fees to all National Parks, the train ride, and raft trip

Motorcycle provisions:
Western States Motorcycle Tours cannot rent motorcycles. However, for a fee of $300 they will sell you a bike that is both registered and licensed, and then buy it back at the tour's end for an additional fee of $100. Fee is included in tour price.

Luggage provisions:
Riders are responsible for transporting their own luggage.

Packed and ready to ride . . .
(Photo courtesy of Sunset Off-Road)

ORGANIZED TOURS – MEXICO & CARIBBEAN

BAJA CALIFORNIA — Baja Expedition

Tour operator:	Baja Expeditions
Length of tour:	All trips are three days in length, arriving on Thursday evening and returning on Sunday evening.
Dates:	This tour is operated twice each month from January through June and October through December.
Trip begins and ends:	San Diego, California

Highlights:

Baja is primarily known for its rugged deserts. However, there is also a wide range of terrain and climates found there. In the northern section of Baja there are mountain ranges that reach as high as 10,000 feet. There the climate is usually cool to mild and, depending on the elevation, snow can be found.

The desert, which can become quite warm, is home to plants, such as the giant Cardon cactus and Yucca Valida, found nowhere else in the world.

If you've ever dreamed of riding in the "Baja 1000" this trip will offer you a taste of what it is like, for you'll use many of the trails actually used in the race.

The trip begins in Ensenada, which is 60 miles south of the U.S. border. From there you will ride high into the Sierra De Juarez mountain range, a land of tall pines and mountain streams. Proceeding south to Valle De Trinidad, you'll stop to have lunch at Mike's Sky Ranch. After lunch you'll head down San Matias Pass and into the rugged Baja desert. After crossing the Laguna Diablo Dry Lake, the tour will stop at San Felipe, your evening rest area.

On day two you'll head south into the Baja desert and travel to Puertocitos, a picturesque fishing village on the gulf of California. Here you'll have lunch and then head back up the coast, via the beach, to San Felipe.

The tour leaves San Felipe on day three and travels back through the Sierra De Juarez mountains and San Matias pass to Ensenada for the conclusion of the trip. A shuttle van returns you to San Diego.

Price:
- Rider, double occupancy, includes motorcycle rental $895
- Rider, double occupancy, without motorcycle rental $695
- Passenger, double occupancy, with or without motorcycle rental .. $250

Barreling through the pines near Ensanada

Price includes:
Shuttle van from San Diego to Ensenada (starting point of tour) and back, four nights lodging, all meals, liability insurance, gasoline, and motorcycle, if needed

Motorcycle provisions:
Participants may rent a Honda XR600 or XR250, or bring their own motorcycle. However, only motorcycles with four-stroke engines will be allowed on the tour. Two stroke engines do not have the fuel range needed.

Luggage provisions:
A support vehicle is available to carry your luggage.

Special notes:
Liability insurance is provided for the rental motorcycles, but not for personal injury. Individuals are responsible for any damage to their motorcycle. Note that 90 percent of this trip is off-road, although it is not extremely demanding or technically difficult.

MEXICO	**Copper Canyon Trail Ride**
Tour operator:	Great Motorcycle Adventures
Length of tour:	Seven days, six nights
Dates:	• March 24 through March 30, 1991 • June 16 through June 22, 1991 • September 1 through September 7, 1991 • November 24 through November 30, 1991 • December 22 through December 28, 1991 • April 12 through April 18, 1992 • June 21 through June 27, 1992 • November 22 through November 28, 1992
Trip begins and ends:	El Paso, Texas

Highlights:
Explore the heights of the fabulous Sierra Madre Mountains and the depths of the great Copper Canyon. Discover incomparable scenery with mile-high sheer cliffs and tumbling waterfalls. Climb to mountain peaks at a height of 12,000 feet. Wind down the trail in Copper Canyon on a magnificent seven-mile descent to the historical mining town of Batopilas. Turn back the clock for your two-day stay in this Spanish colonial town. In the belly of this magnificent canyon, you'll find primitive yet still inhabited Indian cave dwellings and abandoned gold and silver mines. Ride through pine groves in cool mountain air. Wind your way through palm and banana trees in the tropical heat of the Canyon. Run dirt trails or challenging two-tracks, if it suits your fancy.

Price (does not include motorcycle rental):
• Rider, double occupancy $875
• Nonriding guest, double occupancy $875

Price includes:
Accommodations for six nights in first class hotels (or best available accommodations in the more remote regions), all meals while in Mexico, bilingual tour guide, support vehicle, motorcycle fuel while in Mexico, and a souvenir shirt

Motorcycle provisions:
Motorcycle rentals are $445 for the entire trip. Great Motorcycle Adventures (GMA) requires a $100 damage deposit. This is refundable at the end of the trip provided the motorcycle is returned in good condition. GMA has a good selection of late model, well-maintained, four-stroke

ORGANIZED TOURS – MEXICO & CARIBBEAN 107

Pit stop in the Copper Canyon

motorcycles available in sizes from 200cc to 650cc. When you rent a bike from GMA they will perform all adjustments and repairs, including flats. Rental includes transportation for you and your rental motorcycle from the border to the trailhead in Mexico via one of their staff passenger vans.

Luggage provisions:
A van accompanies this trip to carry luggage.

Special notes:
Surcharge to transport nonriding guest from border departure point to trailhead hotel in Mexico, round trip, is $35. This fee is included in the price if you rent a motorcycle from Great Motorcycle Adventures.

MEXICO	**Monterrey Sierra Madre Road Tour**
Tour operator:	Great Motorcycle Adventures
Length of tour:	Five days, four nights
Dates:	• July 1 through July 5, 1991 • March 2 through March 6, 1992 • July 3 through July 7, 1992
Trip begins and ends:	Laredo, Texas

Highlights:
South of the Mexican-American border, you'll ride 200 miles to Ciudad Victoria at the base of the Sierra Madre Oriental Mountains. Fiesta under the stars at a first-class hotel complete with Mariachis and an authentic Mexican "parrilla" (barbeque). On the second day it's over the mountains and down into the sleepy mountain village of Arremberri. A fellow tour guide friend of Gringo owns a special little hotel here where you'll spend nights two and three. You'll see incredible waterfalls in this area.

Next, you'll head up to the old mining ghost town of Real de Catorce. You must traverse a 24-kilometer cobblestone road and 2000 meter mining tunnel to reach this town, which at one time had a population of over 40,000 people. You'll spend that evening in Matahuala. On the final day ride 100 miles north to the colonial silver city of Satillo for lunch and great shopping. Then it's back to Laredo by early evening.

This trip would be a wonderful introduction to riding in Mexico and includes scenic and curvy roads.

Price (does not include motorcycle rental):
- Rider, double occupancy $479
- Nonriding guest, double occupancy $425
- Two-up (both people), double occupancy $895

Price includes:
Accommodations for four nights in first-class hotels, all meals while in Mexico, bilingual tour guide, support vehicle, motorcycle fuel while in Mexico, and a souvenir shirt

Motorcycle provisions:
Great Motorcycle Adventures (GMA) recommends large-displacement dual-sport or touring bikes for this trip. Motorcycle rentals are $575 for the entire trip; a $100 damage deposit is required, refundable at the end of the trip provided the motorcycle is returned in good condition. GMA has a good selection of late model, well-maintained, four-stroke motorcycles available in sizes from 600cc upward. When you rent a bike from GMA they will perform all adjustments and repairs, including flats. Rental includes transportation for you and your rental motorcycle from the border to the trailhead in Mexico via one of their staff passenger vans.

Luggage provisions:
A late model van accompanies this trip to carry luggage, spares, and guests.

Special notes:
If one of the scheduled trips is inconvenient, Great Motorcycle Adventures can arrange this trip for your special group at any time throughout the year.

MEXICO	**Monterrey Trail Ride**
Tour operator:	Great Motorcycle Adventures
Length of tour:	Seven days, six nights
Dates:	• May 26 through June 1, 1991 • May 24 through May 30, 1992 • September 6 through September 12, 1992
Trip begins and ends:	Laredo, Texas

Highlights:
South of the Mexican-American border, you'll caravan to an old hacienda high in the Sierra Madre Oriental Mountains. Use this as your base for a week of exploration on the challenging trails of the eastern Sierra Madres. Explore fabulous Huasteca Canyon. Also, you'll pack out for a two-day trip to a ghost town high in the Sierras. Ride over 24 kilometers of cobblestone and through 2,000 meters of mine shaft tunnel to an abandoned mining town, once a boom town with 40,000 miners and its own mint. You'll find sun, adventure, and Latin hospitality in the rugged Mexican mountains.

Price (does not include motorcycle rental):
• Rider, double occupancy $875
• Nonriding guest, double occupancy $875

Price includes:
Accommodations for six nights in first-class hotels (or best available hotels in the more remote regions), all meals while in Mexico, bilingual tour guide, support vehicle, motorcycle fuel while in Mexico, and a souvenir shirt

Motorcycle provisions:
Motorcycle rentals are $445 for the entire trip. Great Motorcycle Adventures (GMA) requires a $100 damage deposit. This is refundable at the end of the trip provided the motorcycle is returned in good condition. GMA has a good selection of late model, well-maintained, four-stroke motorcycles available in sizes from 200cc to 650cc. When you rent a bike from GMA they will perform all adjustments and repairs, including flats. Rental includes transportation for you and your rental motorcycle from the border to the trailhead in Mexico via one of their staff passenger vans.

Luggage provisions:
A van accompanies this trip to carry luggage.

Special notes:
Surcharge to transport nonriding guest from border departure point to trailhead hotel in Mexico, round trip, is $35. This fee is included in the price if you rent a motorcycle from Great Motorcycle Adventures.

MEXICO	**Yucatan Peninsula Road Tour**
Tour operator:	Great Motorcycle Adventures
Length of tour:	18 days
Dates:	• February 2 through February 19, 1991 • October 6 through October 23, 1991 • October 12 through October 29, 1992
Trip begins and ends:	Laredo, Texas

Highlights:
The Yucatan Peninsula has some of the most incredible sights this hemisphere has to offer. This 3,500-mile, 18-day odyssey encompasses just about every kind of scenery, including winding mountain roads, ancient Mayan ruin sites with towering pyramids jutting high above lush tropical canopies, colonial cities, quaint Mayan villages, and the beautiful Caribbean beaches along the primitive coast of Quintana Roo.

You'll meet your riding companions in Laredo, Texas for this adventure and then ride down the east coast of Mexico to the Yucatan. There you'll do a 600-mile route to circumnavigate the Mayan pyramids. You'll visit the major ruin sites as well as some remote, little-known spots Les French has discovered in his many years of travel in this area. You'll travel from pine forested mountains to tropical jungles complete with fascinating wildlife, waterfalls, and bromiliads. Southern Mexico has some of the most spectacular flora and fauna in the world.

The tour stops for a couple of days on the Caribbean at a great hotel on the beach, with all the amenities travelers have come to expect. Scuba diving is available; you'll be next to the clearest water in the world, according to Jacques Cousteau.

You'll stay in first-class hotels during the entire trip (some of which are Club Meds at the major ruin sites). The Yucatan cuisine is wonderful and is a culinary adventure in itself.

The first few days of this trip will be 250-mile days. After that, the pace will slow down to give you time to really experience the Yucatan.

Checking equipment for the next leg; Copper Canyon

Price (does not include motorcycle rental):
- Rider, double occupancy $2,175
- Riding or nonriding passenger, double occupancy $1,975

Price includes:
All deluxe hotel accommodations (or the best available hotels in the more remote regions), all meals south of the border, insurance for your motorcycle, support vehicle, all motorcycle fuel while in Mexico, experienced bilingual tour guide (including "Gringo" himself)

Motorcycle provisions:
Large displacement touring motorcycles and 600cc or larger dual-sport bikes are recommended for this trip. You may bring your own motorcycle to the trail head, or rent a late model touring motorcycle from Great Motorcycle Adventures. Rental rates are $1,195 for the 18-day tour. The rental rates include all maintenance, repairs (provided they are not caused by negligence or abuse), insurance, and fuel. Great Motorcycle Adventures has a limited number of dual-purpose motorcycles available for this trip, so make your reservation early.

Luggage provisions:
A van accompanies this trip to carry luggage and spares. Nonriding guests are welcome and can ride in the van if they wish.

Special notes:
GMA offers a seven-day, six-night "Fly and Ride" option for people who want to see the Yucatan but who have only a little time available. You can join the tour at about mid-point, in Merida, pick up your waiting motorcycle, travel for a week with the rest of the group, and then leave again from Merida. Contact GMA for details.

MARTINIQUE	**Martinique**
Tour operator:	Motorrad-Reisen
Length of tour:	12 days
Dates:	*1991* • January 31 through February 11 • February 28 through March 11 • March 14 through March 25 • March 28 through April 3 • April 11 through April 22 • October 24 through November 4 • November 7 through November 18 • November 21 through December 2 • December 5 through December 16
Trip begins and ends:	Martinique

Highlights:
Enjoy excursions to all parts of this beautiful island. Multilingual guides will help you enjoy every moment. You'll enjoy a one-day cruise on a sailing ship on these incomparable blue waters and enjoy excellent sea foods, including a seaside barbeque.

Price (includes motorcycle; flight to Martinique not included):
• Driver, ... U.S. $3,300
• Passenger, ... U.S. $2,300

Price includes:
All land arrangements, bilingual (French and English) tour guide on motorcycle, board and lodging in twin bed rooms at comfortable inns, and rental motorcycle

Motorcycle provisions:
BMW R100 GS

Luggage provisions:
Contact agent.

MEXICO	**Copper Canyon Tour**
Tour operator:	Overland Tours
Length of tour:	Seven days
Dates:	• May 11 through May 17, 1991 • May 11 through May 17, 1992 (tentative)
Trip begins:	Juarez, Mexico
Trip ends:	Presidio, Texas

Highlights:
The Copper Canyon is one of the most spectacular vacation destinations in Mexico. The area includes rugged peaks, shining upland lakes, vast peach and apple orchards, and dense forests of Ponderosa pine. While the mountain peaks are snow covered in the winter, the canyon floor maintains a near subtropical climate. The area is inhabited by the Tarahumara Indian tribe, famed for its long distance runners.

The tour begins in Juarez, Mexico where you'll spend the night getting to know your hosts. The tour departs early the next day for a six-hour ride to Chihuahua. There you'll leave the bikes behind and board the Chihuahua Pacific railway, otherwise known as "The Train Ride in the Sky," and climb 8,000 feet into the Western Sierra Madres for a four hundred mile journey through the Copper Canyon. You'll stop at Posada Barrancas to spend the night in a rustic inn and relish the beauty of Copper Canyon.

You'll pass through quaint towns along the way, including Creel, a mining center, and Divisadero and Cherocahui, where a mission was founded in 1690. All of the towns are potential shopping sites and English is spoken widely. The following day you'll board a mid-day train back to Chihuahua.

Explore the city of Chihuahua on a morning tour, highlighted by a visit to "Quinta Luz", the former home of Mexico's revolutionary, Pancho Villa. The afternoon belongs to you to explore the city's shopping areas. Take part in a farewell dinner, featuring Tarahumara dancers, before departing the next morning for Presidio, Texas where the tour ends.

Price:
• Per person, single accommodations $592
• Per person, double accommodations $484
• Per person, triple accommodations $454

114 ORGANIZED TOURS – MEXICO & CARIBBEAN

Price includes:
Accommodations for six nights; three breakfasts, two lunches, and four dinners; train tickets; shuttle between hotel and train station; and Urique Canyon tour and Chihuahua city tour

Not included in price:
Tips or fuel

Motorcycle provisions:
No rental motorcycles are available. Participants are responsible for providing their own motorcycle.

Luggage provisions:
Participants are responsible for carrying their own luggage.

Special notes:
- Reservations are required in advance.
- $150 deposit per person is required.
- Mexico vehicle insurance is required; rates run about $4 to $6 per day.

Taking a break at Mike's Sky Rancho, Valle de Trinidad, Mexico
(Photo courtesy of Baja Expeditions)

ORGANIZED TOURS – MEXICO & CARIBBEAN

MEXICO	**Baja & Copper Canyon Tour**
Tour operator:	Pancho Villa Moto-Tours
Length of tour:	16 days
Dates:	• January 14 through January 29, 1991 • February 18 through March 5, 1991 • March 18 through April 2, 1991 • April 7 through April 22, 1991 • February 17 through March 3, 1992 • March 16 through March 31, 1992 • April 13 through April 28, 1992
Trip begins:	Nogales, Arizona
Trip ends:	San Diego, California

Highlights:
Even with the completion of the paved Highway 1 in the early 1970s, this 800-mile stretch of peninsula remains one of the last frontiers of the Americas. Heading south from Nogales this tour covers some of the most fascinating terrain in Mexico. Every day the sights will change, with rugged mountains, desert forests, and views of the Sea of Cortez and the Pacific Ocean. You'll also experience the electric night life of Mazatlan, and enjoy the spectacular train journey to the Copper Canyon region of the High Sierra Madres. In this remote mountain region, you'll see the lifestyle of the primitive Tarahumara Indian, an indigenous group known for their natural prowess and long distance runners. The train trip itself is exciting; you pass through a maze of tunnels, over, through, and across the most forbidding region of the Sierras. It took nearly 100 years to complete construction of the railroad and you will see why!

Price (does not include motorcycle rental):
• Single rider, double occupancy $1,595
• Two people (one bike) $3,190
• Surcharge, second bike ....$ 50
• Supplement for single room occupancy ....$ 600

Price includes:
Deluxe hotel accommodations for 15 nights (double occupancy); at least 12 meals; a bilingual tour escort; road logs, maps, and information; fiesta at the Playa Mazatlan Hotel; ferry cabin and transport for your motorcycle across the Sea of Cortez from the mainland to Baja; train tickets and trans-

fers for the train ride to the Copper Canyon; Pancho Villa tee shirt; and processing of all visas and vehicle permits

Motorcycle provisions:
Travelers are invited to bring their own motorcycle or they may rent one from Pancho Villa Moto-Tours (PVMT). Rental machines must be picked up and delivered at El Paso, Texas; delivery to other points available for a charge.

Luggage provisions:
Travelers should be prepared to carry their own luggage with them. Excess luggage and purchases may be stored in the follow-up vehicle on a space-available basis.

Special notes:
If there are eight or more motorcycles, a follow-up vehicle will travel with the group to assist in the event of mechanical failures.

MEXICO	**Baja Expedition**
Tour operator:	Pancho Villa Moto-Tours
Length of tour:	11 days
Dates:	• January 13 through January 24, 1991 • February 17 through February 28, 1991 • March 17 through March 28, 1991 • April 14 through April 25, 1991 • Mid-November, 1991 • January 12 through January 23, 1992 • February 16 through February 27, 1992 • March 15 through March 26, 1992 • April 12 through April 23, 1992 • November 22 through December 3, 1992
Trip begins and ends:	San Diego, California

Highlights:
The Baja is paved from top to tip; yet for those who would like to experience the remote pristine beaches, high mountains, and quaint out-of-the-way fishing villages, you must get off the pavement, and on the road to discovery!

If you have a dual-purpose touring machine then you are probably ready to seek out some destinations of adventure. Imagine riding down fifty miles of nearly virgin uninhabited beach. Where else can you do this? Dozens of plant and cactus varieties exist that you will not find anywhere else in the world. And, if you like seafood, wait until you order up the fresh catch of the day.

Not a tour for everyone, but if you have a bit of *vagabundo* in you, then you are ready for the Baja.

Price (does not include motorcycle rental):
- Single rider, double occupancy $1,495
- Supplement for single room occupancy ....$ 375

Price includes:
Best available hotel accommodations for ten nights (double occupancy), at least 15 meals, a bilingual tour escort, Pancho Villa tee shirt, and staff assistant in chase vehicle

Motorcycle provisions:
Travelers are invited to bring their own motorcycle or they may rent one from Pancho Villa Moto-Tours (PVMT). Rental bikes include the Kawasaki KLR 650 dual-purpose.

Luggage provisions:
Chase van accompanies the tour to carry luggage and provide maintenance support.

Special notes:
Two-up riding not permitted on this tour, but space may be available in the chase vehicle for non-riding participants, depending upon number in the group.

MEXICO	**Colonial Tour**
Tour operator:	Pancho Villa Moto-Tours
Length of tour:	Ten days; covers approximately 1,700 miles (longest day is 325 miles; shortest is 120 miles)
Dates:	• March 11 through March 20, 1991 • April 8 through April 17, 1991 • May 6 through May 15, 1991 • October 7 through October 16, 1991

ORGANIZED TOURS – MEXICO & CARIBBEAN

- November 18 through November 27, 1991
- December 19 through December 28, 1991 (Christmas Tour)
- March 9 through March 18, 1992
- April 6 through April 15, 1992
- May 4 through May 13, 1992

Trip begins:	McAllen, Texas
Trip ends:	Laredo, Texas

Highlights:
This has become one of the most popular trips offered by Pancho Villa Moto-Tours (PVMT). Combining a rich blend of history, scenic riding, culture diversities, and special activities, this tour offers you a chance to see Mexico as few Americans do. You will ride through the heart of the Bajio region, a territory so influenced by the Spanish and French that you'll think you're in Europe. Sharp Gothic lines blend with Moorish domes; walled fortresses give way to cobblestone walkways and sidewalk cafes. Out in the country, you're likely to see men working a field with a wooden plow pulled by a team of oxen. Add to this the flavor of native markets, the fiesta, the sights, sounds, and smells that are Mexico, and you'll have an unforgettable trip.

Price (does not include motorcycle rental):
- Single rider, double occupancy .... $ 889
- Two people (one or two bikes) $1,778
- Supplement for single room occupancy .... $ 325

Price includes:
Ten overnight stays (double occupancy); ten meals; a bilingual tour escort; road logs, maps, and information; guided tour of Guanajuato; Pancho Villa tee shirt; and processing of all visas and vehicle permits

Motorcycle provisions:
Travelers are invited to bring their own motorcycle or they may rent one from Pancho Villa Moto-Tours. Rental machines must be picked up and delivered at El Paso, Texas; delivery to McAllen and pickup from Laredo can be arranged by PVMT.

Luggage provisions:
Travelers should be prepared to carry their own luggage with them. Excess luggage and purchases may be stored in the follow-up vehicle on a space-available basis.

Special notes:
If there are eight or more motorcycles, a follow-up vehicle will travel with the group to assist in the event of mechanical failures.

COSTA RICA	**Costa Rica**
Tour operator:	Pancho Villa Moto-Tours
Length of tour:	15 days
Dates:	• January 12 through January 26, 1991 • January 28 through February 12, 1991 • February 15 through March 1, 1991 • March 2 through March 16, 1991 • March 18 through April 1, 1991 • January 11 through January 25, 1992 • January 27 through February 10, 1992 • February 14 through February 28, 1992 • May 7 through May 21, 1992
Trip begins and ends:	San Jose, Costa Rica

Highlights:
Costa Rica is one of the best kept secrets of the northern hemisphere. A land of tropical splendor, it can boast of 1,200 varieties of orchids, 800 species of birds, 150 species of edible fruit, more than 600 miles of beaches and remote coasts, a mountain 12,606 feet high, ten percent of ALL the butterflies in the world, and people known for their kindness and fierce pride in their country. It is one of the oldest democracies in the Americas, a country with more teachers than policemen, the second-highest literacy rate in the Americas, one of the lowest infant mortality rates in the world, and is home to over 25,000 Americans.

Your trip in Costa Rica will be made by dual-purpose motorcycle. Although most of the roads on the trip are paved, the lighter bikes will allow you more flexibility in getting to the more scenic locations. This is not a moto-cross or enduro tour, but one that riders will find comfortable and educational.

One of the highlights of this tour is a visit to the Panama Canal. Politically, Panama is now quite stable. Its government is actively taking measures to enhance the once-booming tourism trade.

Your guide for this tour will be Ed Culberson, one of the world's authorities on motorcycle travel in Central America and author of a fascinating book on that subject.

Price (includes motorcycle rental):
- Single rider, double occupancy $2,895
- Passenger, double occupancy $1,795
- Supplement for single room occupancy .... $ 475

Price includes:
Best available hotel accommodations for 14 nights (double occupancy); at least 16 meals; bilingual tour escort; road logs, maps, and information; city tour of San Jose; ferry transportation across the Gulf of Nicoya; comprehensive tour of the Panama Canal; entry fees to various parks and points of interest; airport transfers; and a tour gift

Motorcycle provisions:
Rental of a Kawasaki KLR 650 or similar motorcycle, with necessary insurance, is included with the tour price. A $400 security deposit for the motorcycle is required (refundable). Arrangements can be made to ship your own motorcycle for use on tour. Call for details.

Luggage provisions:
Each participant is expected to carry his own luggage. Pack lightly.

Special notes:
This tour will occasionally have you in more rustic accommodations, located in tropical settings, to allow you to experience the natural beauty for which Costa Rica is known. All accommodations will be comfortable, clean, and secure.

MEXICO, WEST COAST — **Mazatlan Winter Get-Away**

Tour operator:	Pancho Villa Moto-Tours
Length of tour:	12 days and 11 nights, covering approximately 1,750 miles
Dates:	• January 14 through January 25, 1991 • February 6 through February 17, 1991 • March 11 through March 22, 1991 • April 8 through April 19, 1991

- Late November
- January 13 through January 24, 1992
- February 5 through February 16, 1992
- March 9 through March 20, 1992
- April 6 through April 17, 1992
- November 16 through November 27, 1992

Trip begins and ends: Nogales, Arizona

Highlights:
Touring enthusiasts from the western United States will find this trip particularly convenient. The itinerary was designed to offer different accommodations and points of interest on each leg of the trip. No where is Mexico more colorful than Mazatlan. There vendors hawk their crafts and entertain you as well. There is much to do in Mazatlan, including a one of the most beautiful beaches in all of Mexico, and side tours to the jungle and mountains outside the town.

You will reach the Copper Canyon region in the high Sierra Madres via the Chihuahua al Pacifico Railway, the only way to get to this remote region. Here the Tarahumara live in caves clinging along the high cliffs of the barranca country. Stay overnight in a rustic lodge in the mountains, far from modern society.

Stop at colonial Alamos where you will stay in a two-century-old ex-convent and sample some of the warm hospitality for which Mexico is so well known.

Price (does not include motorcycle rental):
- Per person, double occupancy $1,295
- Supplement for single room occupancy ....$ 400

Price includes:
Deluxe lodging for 11 nights, no fewer than 12 meals, guided walking tour of colonial Alamos, train tickets and transfers to the Copper Canyon region of the Sierra Madres, processing of vehicle documents and visas, bilingual tour escort, currency exchange service, complete information packet, maps, and preparation materials

Not included in price:
Insurance is arranged but not included in the price.

Motorcycle provisions:
Motorcycles are available for rent starting from $45 (not including insurance) per day, plus any transport fees to and from El Paso, Texas. Call Pancho Villa Moto-Tours for inventory and details.

Luggage provisions:
Riders are to handle their own luggage. Space in the follow-up vehicle for excessive luggage on a space-availability basis. Information is provided concerning storage of trailers or other vehicles in Nogales while on tour.

MEXICO	**Pancho Villa Motorcycle Campaign**
Tour operator:	Pancho Villa Moto-Tours
Length of tour:	Seven days
Dates:	• April 20 through April 26, 1991 • May 25 through May 31, 1991 • June 22 through June 28, 1991 • July 6 through July 12, 1991 • August 31 through September 6, 1991 • April 18 through April 24, 1992 • May 23 through May 29, 1992 • June 20 through June 26, 1992 • July 4 through July 10, 1992 • August 29 through September 4, 1992
Trip begins and ends:	El Paso, Texas

Highlights:
No single figure in Mexican and border history is more controversial than Francisco "Pancho" Villa. To some he was a hooligan, but in the state of Chihuahua he is generally regarded as a "Robin Hood," taking from the rich and giving to the poor with his own special brand of justice. His military exploits during the Mexican Revolution of 1910 made him famous on both sides of the Rio Grande, and his campaigns with the ladies even more notorious. You will learn everything you wanted to know about Pancho on this tour.

The locale of the trip is the Copper Canyon region of Mexico, home of a primitive and much-studied tribe of Indians, the Tarahumara. They are foot runners with tremendous stamina who are now running a race to preserve their aboriginal lifestyle. The Copper Canyon area has been their refuge for hundreds of years.

Riding on this tour will take you from the desert to beautiful high mountains and cool mesas. Daily distances are minimal but with so much to do you'll never have a dull moment.

Price (does not include motorcycle rental):
- Single rider, double occupancy $595
- Supplement for single room occupancy $250

Price includes:
Deluxe hotel accommodations for six nights (double occupancy); at least eight meals; a bilingual tour escort; road logs, maps, and information; train tickets and transfers for the train ride to the Copper Canyon; walking tour of Chihuahua City and entrance fees; visit to the Mennonite Colony; Pancho Villa tee shirt; and processing of all visas and vehicle permits

Motorcycle provisions:
Travelers are invited to bring their own motorcycle or they may rent one from Pancho Villa Moto-Tours (PVMT). Rental machines must be picked up and delivered at El Paso, Texas.

Luggage provisions:
Travelers should be prepared to carry their own luggage with them.

MEXICO	**Sierra Madre Expedition**
Tour operator:	Pancho Villa Moto-Tours
Length of tour:	Eight days
Dates:	• September 16 through September 23, 1991 • October 7 through October 14, 1991 • November 10 through November 17, 1991 • September 14 through September 21, 1992 • October 5 through October 12, 1992 • November 8 through November 15, 1992
Trip begins and ends:	El Paso, Texas

Highlights:
This tour is for adventurers only — the "dual purpose" touring enthusiast. This term refers to the highway and off-road paths taken by this tour as you explore parts of Mexico well beyond the interstates. You'll need an appropriate motorcycle to enjoy this trip: one like the BMW G/S, the Kawasaki KLR 650, or the Cagiva Elefant, with extended fuel capacity, lighter weight and longer suspension travel. Your extra effort on this trip

will be rewarded by thrilling rides through breathtaking canyons with waterfalls cascading from shear cliffs, to remote villages accessible only by unpaved surfaces. You'll cross old wooden bridges and ford an occasional stream to reach the back country village of Batopilas, where you will see the Tarahumara Indian, a primitive group of people, many of whom still live in caves. Here, the men wear loin cloths, undaunted by modern custom. The Sierra Madres were long ago abandoned by Spanish explorers, but you'll see remnants of their influence in 17th century churches and follow their original trails. Here's an unusual chance to break away in a challenging and rewarding tour.

Price (does not include motorcycle rental):
- Single rider, double occupancy $995

Price includes:
Hotel accommodations for seven nights (double occupancy); at least 15 meals; a bilingual tour escort; road logs, maps, and information; city tour of Chihuahua; Pancho Villa tee shirt; and processing of all visas and vehicle permits

Motorcycle provisions:
Travelers are invited to bring their own dual-purpose motorcycle or they may rent one from Pancho Villa Moto-Tours.

Luggage provisions:
Travelers should be prepared to carry their own luggage with them. Excess luggage and purchases may be stored in the follow-up vehicle on a space-available basis.

Special Notes:
No open pipes are allowed. This is a motorcycle tour not a motocross race or trials competition. Riders are expected to display respect for the tranquility and environment of the Sierra Madres and the primitive inhabitants.

A followup vehicle will travel with the group to assist with emergency motorcycle repairs.

Non-riders: Limited space may be available in the followup vehicle for non-riding tour participants. Tour price is the same for vehicle passengers as for riding participants. Call for space availability.

ORGANIZED TOURS – MEXICO & CARIBBEAN 125

MEXICO	**Yucatan Tour**
Tour operator:	Pancho Villa Moto-Tours
Length of tour:	29 days; covers approximately 4,400 miles
Dates:	• February 25 through March 25, 1991 • February 24 through March 23, 1992
Trip begins:	Laredo, Texas
Trip ends:	McAllen, Texas

Highlights:
This is perhaps the ultimate motorcycle excursion to Mexico. You'll travel far south to the Yucatan Peninsula, through rain forests, jungle, high mountains, and low deserts. You'll see remnants from the lost Mayan civilization: ceremonial ball courts, advanced astronomical observatories, sacrificial wells, and fascinating temples rivaling the pyramids of Egypt. In addition to exploring the history and archaeology of the Mayans, you will also have plenty of time to enjoy the sunny beaches and blue waters of the Caribbean, the Gulf of Mexico, the Gulf of Campeche, and the Pacific on this tour. Perhaps the greatest reward though will be to get acquainted with the tribal peoples of Mexico, far from the influence of tourists. You will experience the lifestyle of Mexico's original native inhabitants. Here, you'll be called upon to adapt, so put on your explorer's hat.

Price (does not include motorcycle rental):
• Single rider, double occupancy $2,195
• Two people (one or two bikes) $3,595
• Supplement for single room occupancy ....$ 550

Price includes:
Deluxe hotel accommodations for 28 nights (double occupancy); at least 18 meals; a bilingual tour escort; road logs, maps, and information; guided tours of archaeological sites at Monte Alaban, Palenque, Chichen Itza, Tulum, and others; Light and Sound show at the temples of Uxmal; walking tour of the Spanish fortress of Ulula in Veracruz; excursion to Isla Mujeres in Cancun; city tour of colonial Oaxaca; Pancho Villa tee shirt; and processing of all visas and vehicle permits

Motorcycle provisions:
Travelers are invited to bring their own motorcycle or they may rent one from Pancho Villa Moto-Tours. Rental machines must be picked up and delivered at El Paso, Texas; delivery to Laredo and pickup from McAllen can be arranged by PVMT.

Luggage provisions:
Travelers should be prepared to carry their own luggage with them. Excess luggage and purchases may be stored in the follow-up vehicle on a space-available basis.

JAMAICA — Jamaica

Tour operator:	Von Thielmann Tours
Length of tour:	Nine days
Dates:	Every Saturday
Trip begins and ends:	Los Angeles or Miami

Highlights:
Fly and ride arrangements include all necessary reservations for this motorcycle tour for individuals. This tour is a circular trip of a beautiful Caribbean Island with the finest beaches and many things to see and to do.

Price (includes motorcycle rental):
- Single rider, double occupancy $1,355
- Two people, double occupancy $2,270
- Single passenger, double occupancy $1,185
- Supplement for single room occupancy .... $ 270

Price includes:
Airfare from Los Angeles, round trip; hotel accommodations; all breakfasts; transfers; and rental motorcycles and third party liability insurance.

Motorcycle provisions:
Rental motorcycle, approximately 200cc to 450cc, included.

Luggage provisions:
Suitcases may be stored at first hotel. Riders should bring their own tank bag, and travel light (warm weather). For groups of at least 15 passengers, a luggage bus with driver can be provided at approximately $75 per person.

MEXICO	**Mexico**
Tour operator:	Von Thielmann Tours
Length of tours:	15 days each
Dates:	• May 4 through May 18, 1991 • June 8 through June 22, 1991 • July 6 through July 20, 1991 • August 3 through August 17, 1991 • November 30 through December 14, 1991 • Similar dates in 1992 and 1993 • Special trips can be arranged for groups of 10 or more.
Trip begins and ends:	Tour I: begins in San Diego, California and ends in Tucson, Arizona Tour II: begins and ends in Guadalajara, Mexico

Highlights:
Tour I: Ride from San Diego to Cabo San Lucas at the tip of the Baja peninsula. Take the overnight ferry to the Gulf side and continue to the historic, colonial town of El Fuerte. Board the Copper Canyon train of the Chiahuahua Pacific Railway, which was completed in 1961 at a cost of over $100 million. It's the most dramatic railway in the western hemisphere, winding through 86 tunnels, crossing 37 bridges (one of them a third of a mile long) and spanning the continental divide three times.

Your overnight lodging is at a beautiful hotel on the breathtaking edge of the Canyon. Return to El Fuerte and ride to the historical town of Alamos. Returning north, your tour ends in Tucson, Arizona.

Tour II: For this tour you'll fly directly to Guadalajara in the state of Jalisco where you'll pick up a rental motorcycle. Your circular trip itinerary offers a unique combination of some of Mexico's historic and colonial cities. Travel along Mexico's beautiful coastal highway through the towns of Puerta Vallarta, Manzanillo, Playa Azul, and Zihuatanejo to the famous beach resort of Acapulco. Continue inland via Taxco, Morelia, Queretaro, Guanajuato and return, after an overnight stop at Lake Chapala, to Guadalajara. Returning passengers may add a stop-over in Mexico City or Cancun.

Price:
Available upon request

Price includes:
Tour I: hotel accommodations, passage on the ferry, several meals, luggage transportation in a support vehicle with motorcycle trailer, tour guide, and road maps

Tour II: round trip air fare to Guadalajara, hotel accommodations, several meals, luggage transportation in support vehicle, tour guide, and road maps

Motorcycle provisions:
You may bring your own motorcycle or rent one (rentals available in San Diego).

Luggage provisions:
Support vehicle (with motorcycle trailer) will carry luggage.

Fresh and ready to ride the "Baja Expedition," at Ojo Negros; near Ensanada, Mexico
(Photo courtesy of Baja Expeditions)

ORGANIZED TOURS – SOUTH AMERICA

VENEZUELA

Venezuela: The Northeast

Tour operator:	Tours, S.R.L.
Length of tour:	13 days, covering approximately 1,500 miles
Dates:	• October 13 through October 25, 1991 (Tour 1) • November 13 through November 25, 1991 (Tour 3)
Trip begins and ends:	Valencia, Venezuela

Highlights:
If you want to experience the blue waters of the Caribbean, sleepy fishing villages, and unusual sights, then this is the tour for you. You'll ride along the coast through tropical vegetation rich with bananas and papayas, eat fresh fish with the locals and, of course, have plenty of time to relax and swim. Also on the program are the world famous Guacharo caves, with their strange birds; Colonia Tovar, a village high in the Cordilleras founded by German settlers in 1843; and the National Park of Morrocoy, where exceptional bird watching is possible. You'll ride mostly on paved roads in good condition and mix hilly, winding, and flat roads, avoiding highways wherever possible. To take advantage of the short days in Venezuela (it gets dark about 6:30 p.m.) you'll get up early. The daily itinerary is tightly packed. Groups are limited to six motorcycles.

Price (includes motorcycle rental):
- Single rider, double occupancy, ...$2,275
- Passenger, double occupancy $1,140
- Supplement for single room occupancy ....$ 300

Price includes:
Insured motorcycle, hotel stays (double occupancy), a midday or evening meal each day, transport of luggage throughout the trip, an English- and German-speaking tour guide, and welcome and farewell parties

Motorcycle provisions:
BMW R100 S/RS

It's tough work but someone has to do it

Luggage provisions:
A van accompanies each tour to carry luggage, except if only one guest motorcycle is on tour.

Special notes:
You can combine Tour One with Tour Two for a three-week trip, or Tour Three with Tour Four for an exceptional four-week trip. See "Venezuela: The West and the Andes" and "Venezuela: The Andes."

VENEZUELA	**Venezuela: The Andes**
Tour operator:	Tours, S.R.L.
Length of tour:	Nine days, covering approximately 1,350 miles
Dates:	October 26 through November 3, 1991 (Tour 2)
Trip begins and ends:	Valencia, Venezuela

Highlights:
This tour is especially designed for riders who like to ride curves. The tour starts with a long leg toward the Andes through Barquisimeto to Carora. On the second day you'll hit the Andes and stay there for the rest of the tour, enjoying at least 300 miles of curves.

Traverse the highest paved road in all of South America. In Merida, take the opportunity to use the world's highest funicular railway. The tour ends after you pass through the Llanos (flats) where important cattle ranches are found.

Price (includes motorcycle rental):
- Single rider, double occupancy $1,450
- Passenger, double occupancy ....$ 785
- Supplement for single room occupancy ....$ 195

Price includes:
Insured motorcycle, hotel stays (double occupancy), a midday or evening meal each day, transport of luggage throughout the trip, an English- and German-speaking tour guide, and welcome and farewell parties

Motorcycle provisions:
BMW R100 S/RS

On Eagle Pass, the highest in South America (4,116 meters)

Luggage provisions:
A van accompanies each tour to carry luggage, except if only one guest motorcycle is on tour.

Special notes:
You can combine Tour Two with Tour Four for a three-week trip. See "Venezuela: The Northeast."

VENEZUELA	**Venezuela: The West and the Andes**
Tour operator:	Tours, S.R.L.
Length of tour:	13 days, covering approximately 1,500 miles
Dates:	November 27 through December 9, 1991 (Tour 4)
Trip begins and ends:	Valencia, Venezuela

Highlights:
Start this tour visiting the National Park of Morrocoy, where exceptional bird watching is possible, together with snorkeling and swimming in crystal clear water. You'll ride along the dunes of National Park Medanos de Coro, and walk around the old colonial town of Coro. Ride then to Maracaibo (the second most important city of the country) over the largest bridge in South America (eight kilometers). Down south as far as San Cristobal, the road runs through the most fertile part of Venezuela, center of Venezuela's important milk and beef production. In Merida, you have the opportunity to use the world's highest funicular and afterward, pass the highest paved road of all South America. Drive through the Llanos (flat lands) with their vast cattle herds and return to Valencia.

This tour is great for riders who like curves; you'll get 300 miles of them.

Price (includes motorcycle rental):
- Single rider, double occupancy $2,875
- Passenger, double occupancy $1,140
- Supplement for single room occupancy ....$ 300

Price includes:
Insured motorcycle, hotel stays (double occupancy), a midday or evening meal each day, transport of luggage throughout the trip, an English- and German-speaking tour guide, and welcome and farewell parties

Motorcycle provisions:
BMW R100 S/RS

Luggage provisions:
A van accompanies each tour to carry luggage, except if only one guest motorcycle is on tour.

Special notes:
You can combine Tour One with Tour Two for a three-week trip, or Tour Three with Tour Four for an exceptional four-week trip. See "Venezuela: The Northeast."

VENEZUELA — Venezuela: East, West and the Andes

Tour operator:	Tours, S.R.L.
Length of tour:	20 days, covering approximately 2,700 miles
Dates:	December 28, 1991 through January 17, 1992
Trip begins and ends:	Valencia, Venezuela

Highlights:
This tour covers essentially the Northeast and the West-Andes routes. It extends to the south, visiting Puerto Ordaz and Ciudad Bolivar, with a side trip to the second largest water-driven electrical power plant, Raul Leoni. Return through the Llanos states, Guarico and Apure, and afterward into the Andes. On this tour you'll get a fairly complete round trip of the country.

Price (includes motorcycle rental):
- Single rider, double occupancy $3,475
- Passenger, double occupancy $1,730
- Surcharge for single room occupancy .... $ 450

Price includes:
Insured motorcycle, hotel stays (double occupancy), a midday or evening meal each day, transport of luggage throughout the trip, an English- and German-speaking tour guide, and welcome and farewell parties

Motorcycle provisions:
BMW R100 S/RS

Luggage provisions:
A van accompanies each tour to carry luggage, except if only one guest motorcycle is on tour.

BRAZIL	**Tour Florianopolis**
Tour operator:	Trans America Tours
Length of tour:	16 days, covering approximately 2,250 miles (50 to 250 miles per day)
Dates:	Dates available during September to November and February to April upon request.
Trip begins and ends:	Rio Claro, Brazil

Highlights:
After a weekend stay in the countryside of Rio Claro, you begin your journey to Curitiba, the state capital of Parana, and then travel to the town of Ponta Grossa. Nearby is the Villa Velha National Park, with its red sandstone formations, lush green vegetation, and three water-filled craters called the Devil's Basin. Ride the elevator 150 feet down the crater's wall to reach the water's surface.

An old cobblestone road leads you from the dense jungle of the highlands, down along rivers and past waterfalls to the coastal village of Pontal Do Sul. After enjoying the beaches there, you head farther south and cross the bridge to the island of St. Catarina - Florianopolis.

On St. Catarina, more than 40 coves and bays await your discovery. White sand dunes and a lake at the heart of the island form a spectacular vista. From your oceanfront hotel, many small roads connect to other villages. Arts and crafts from all over South America are sold there. Enjoy a sailing trip through the area's islands aboard an old wooden schooner. Cross over the bridge to the city of Florianopolis to experience a variety of entertainment including Brazilian music, colorful folk and Samba shows, nightclubs, and theaters.

Overlooking the beach at Florianopolis

On the way back north the tour stops in Peruibe to visit to Jureia National Park and its beautiful waterfalls and flora. In Peruibe, watch the local fisherman bring in the day's catch and visit a craftsman who works on precious stones. Enjoy a seafood dinner at one of the area's many excellent beach restaurants. Next day, you'll head back to Rio Claro for a farewell party by the pool before departing for Sao Paulo.

Price:
Due to the volatile nature of the Brazilian cruzeiro, prices are available only by request.

Price includes:
Motorcycle rental, transfers to and from Sao Paulo airport, accommodations for 15 nights in selected hotels (double occupancy), two meals daily including nonalcoholic beverages, fuel and oil, all entrance fees, sailing trip, and welcoming and farewell parties

Not included in price:
Air fare and alcoholic beverages

Motorcycle provisions:
A Brazilian Motorcycle Company's BMC R 100 GS motorcycle, a replica of the BMW R 100 GS Paris-Dakar, is provided to each participant and comes equipped with tankbag and saddlebags.

Luggage provisions:
Each participant is responsible for carrying his own luggage. A service vehicle for passengers and extra luggage can be arranged if necessary.

Special notes:
Each tour is limited to nine motorcycles. The tour guides speak Portugese, English, and German.

A wet crossing in the Pantanal

BRAZIL — Tour Pantanal

Tour operator:	Trans America Tours
Length of tour:	18 days, covering approximately 2,500 miles (100 to 250 miles per day)
Dates:	Dates available in June, July, and August upon request
Trip begins and ends:	Campo Grande, Brazil

Highlights:
This adventure begins in Campo Grande, which lies at the border of the Pantanal. Excepting the Amazon Basin, the Pantanal represents the most important ecological system of South America. This 140,000-square-mile area, which stretches along the borders of Brazil, Paraguay, and Bolivia, is marked by alternately dry and rainy seasons. During the rainy season the Pantanal is flooded, but when it dries out in the summer the animals come out and gather around the waterholes. This is the time to view the numerous variety of animals that live in the Pantanal. Photography enthusiasts have a unique opportunity to capture the rain forest at the height of its splendor.

Price:
Due to the volatile nature of the Brazilian cruzeiro, prices are available only by request.

Price includes:
Motorcycle rental, transfer to and from Sao Paulo airport, accommodations for 17 nights in the best hotels available (quality varies according to area), two meals daily including nonalcoholic beverages, fuel and oil, all entrance fees, and farewell party

Not included in price:
Air fare and alcoholic beverages

Motorcycle provisions:
A Brazilian Motorcycle Company's, BMC R 100 GS motorcycle, a replica of the BMW R 100 GS Paris-Dakar, is provided to each to participant and comes equipped with tankbag and saddlebags.

Luggage provisions:
Each participant is responsible for carrying his own luggage. Service vehicle for extra luggage, such as photo equipment or passengers, can be arranged at an extra cost.

Special notes:
- The Tour Pantanal covers very rugged terrain under hot and dusty conditions and requires that riders have the physical stamina to endure the trip.
- No motorcycle passengers are allowed on this tour due to the off-road driving conditions.
- Trans America Tours recommends that you receive vaccination, for Yellow Fever, Hepatitis, and Malaria before participating in this tour.
- Members of this tour should be of good health and be willing to give a team effort to make it successful.
- Each tour is limited to nine motorcycles.
- The tour guides speak Portugese, English, and German.

BRAZIL	**Tour Parati**
Tour operator:	Trans America Tours
Length of tour:	16 days, covering approximately 2,250 miles (50 to 250 miles per day)
Dates:	Dates available during September to November and February to April upon request
Trip begins and ends:	Rio Claro, Brazil

Highlights:
The Parati Tour starts with a welcome party and a tour of the countryside around Rio Claro. You'll then depart through the lush green sugar cane fields and ride along the small rivers to Curitiba and its historical section of Santa Felicidade, famous for its excellent restaurants. Begin the next day with a drive along the Estrada Da Graciosa, a historic cobblestone road that leads to the small picturesque village of Morettes. This road then leads you through the dense jungle and up the coast to Peruibe, known for its long white beaches. Explore the hidden bays, famous waterfalls, and wonderful flowers and plants at nearby Jureia National Park.

Your next destination is the small island of Ilha Bela. From there you travel farther north to the historical town of Parati, where you'll spend a couple of days. The unique atmosphere of this preserved town, where cars are not allowed, fascinates every visitor. Beaches and bays lined with palm trees, narrow cobblestone roads, small shops and restaurants await you. Take a day trip into the hills around Parati or relax in the clear blue water of its beaches. Enjoy a one-day sailing trip around the islands on an old wooden schooner.

You'll spend one day and night in Rio De Janeiro, birthplace of the Samba. Visit the famous Copacabana Beach, and attend a colorful Samba show at night. Finally, return to Rio Claro for a day's rest at a country club and an evening farewell party before departing from Sao Paulo.

Price:
Due to the volatile nature of the Brazilian cruzeiro, prices are available only by request.

Price includes:
Motorcycle rental, transfers to and from Sao Paulo airport, accommodations for 15 nights in selected hotels (double occupancy), two meals daily including nonalcoholic beverages, fuel and oil, all entrance fees, sailing trip, and welcoming and farewell parties

A uniquely Brazilian form of wildlife

Not included in price.
Air fare or alcoholic beverages

Motorcycle provisions:
A Brazilian Motorcycle Company's BMC R 100 GS motorcycle, a replica of the BMW R 100 GS Paris-Dakar, is provided to each participant and comes equipped with tankbag and saddlebags.

Luggage provisions:
Each participant is responsible for carrying his own luggage. A service vehicle for passengers and extra luggage can be arranged if necessary.

Special notes:
Each tour is limited to nine motorcycles. The tour guides speak Portugese, English, and German.

ARGENTINA — Argentina

Tour operator:	Von Thielmann Tours
Length of tour:	20 days
Dates:	• November 1991 • February 1992 • Similar dates in subsequent years
Trip begins and ends:	Los Angeles

Highlights:
This tour will allow you to enjoy the following ever-changing scenery: dense forests, lakes and beaches, Los Cantaros Waterfalls, Pueblo National Park, Los Alercos National Park, Peninsula de Valdez, "Bird Island," and Bariloche, Buenos Aires.

Price (does not include motorcycle rental):
- Single rider, double occupancy $2,750
- Two people, double occupancy $5,500
- Single passenger, double occupancy $2,750
- Supplement for single room occupancy .... $ 680

Price includes:
Round trip airfare from Los Angeles, transfers, hotel accommodations, breakfast daily, plus many other meals, excursions and sightseeing, tour guide, and maps

Motorcycle provisions:
Rentals available

Luggage provisions:
Luggage will be carried in the support vehicle.

ORGANIZED TOURS – GREAT BRITAIN AND IRELAND

IRELAND	**AMA's EuroTour to Ireland and FIM Rally**
Tour operator:	American Motorcyclist Association
Length of tour:	22 days
Dates:	• July 15 through August 5, 1992 with extension possible for British Grand Prix
Trip begins and ends:	New York, Chicago, Los Angeles, or San Francisco.

Highlights:
Join Greg Harrison for a trip to the "other" England, the beautiful southern parts. Quiet seaside ports, the wind-swept moorlands of Devon and the haunting timelessness of Stonehenge are all along the route on this tour. You'll ferry across to the Emerald Isle for a week's worth of tiny back roads, thatched-roof villages, and Irish hospitality. Ireland is a motorcyclist's dream with breathtaking seascapes, castle ruins, and great roads. From Ireland, you'll ferry back across to Wales, then make your way north to Edinburgh, where you'll attend the Federation Internationale Motocycliste (FIM) Rally. You'll spend three days with thousands of other riders from around the world at the grandfather of all international touring events. You will represent the United States at this event. Later, you'll return to London for sightseeing and shopping before returning home. Meeting and riding with British motorcyclists is always a part of EuroTour.

Price:
Prices for the 1992 tour had not been established at press time. Contact AMA for details.

Motorcycle provisions:
A variety of midsized motorcycles will be available for rent. They are usually shaft-driven, water-cooled twins or fours fitted with a small fairing and luggage rack. Price depends upon exchange rate at the time of trip. AMA will arrange motorcycle or car rental and recommends that you rent a motorcycle rather than ship your own.

Special notes:
All participants must be AMA members.

ISLE OF MAN	**AMA's EuroTour to Isle of Man**
Tour operator:	American Motorcyclist Association
Length of tour:	22 days
Dates:	• 1991 tours are full as of press time • May 14 through June 4, 1992
Trip begins and ends:	New York, Chicago, Los Angeles, or San Francisco.

Highlights:
Join AMA members on a motorcycle adventure to England, Scotland, Wales, and of course the incredible Isle of Man for the TT. Explore the quaint villages and quiet country backroads of the English Cotswolds. Join 30,000 motorcyclists for a carnival of displays and activities at the Peterborough Rally, Europe's largest one-day motorcycling event. Twist and turn along the edge of the infamous and scenic Loch Ness as you explore the Scottish Highlands. Travel to the remote Isle of Skye for some of the most spectacular settings in the British Isles. Tackle the steepest roads of all in the magnificent Lake District, before bedding down in a 14th century coaching inn for the night. Take a late-night "ghost" tour amid the castles and keeps of Edinburgh, and visit the world's smallest Scotch distillery. Then, you'll take an ocean-going ship (with your motorcycle) to the Isle of Man and spend five days enjoying a motorcycle enthusiast's heaven on this beautiful isle during TT week. Finally, it's on to London where you will have time for shopping and sightseeing. Meeting and riding with British motorcyclists is always a part of EuroTour.

Price (does not include motorcycle rental):
Prices for the 1992 tour had not been established at press time. Price of the 1991 Isle of Man tour were (for single rider, double occupancy):
• New York departure $3,700
• Chicago $3,800
• Los Angeles $3,900
• San Francisco $3,900
• Supplement for single room occupancy ....$ 425

Price includes:
Round trip airfare, all hotels, full English breakfast and multicourse dinner each day, transfers, daily maps and routing, all ferries, plus admission to several attractions

144 ORGANIZED TOURS – GREAT BRITAIN & IRELAND

Motorcycle provisions:
A variety of midsized motorcycles are available for rent. They are usually shaft-driven, water-cooled twins or fours fitted with a small fairing and luggage rack. Price depends upon exchange rate at the time of trip. AMA will arrange motorcycle or car rental and recommends that you rent a motorcycle rather than ship your own. The price for a three-week motorcycle rental on the 1991 tour was $825, in addition to the price of the tour.

Special notes:
All participants must be AMA members.

ENGLAND & SCOTLAND

Beach's British Bat

Tour operator:	Beach's Motorcycle Adventures, Ltd.
Length of tour:	22 days
Dates:	• August 3 through August 24, 1991 • August 1 through August 22, 1992 • August 7 through August 28, 1993

Trip begins and ends:
Boston (other cities on request)

Highlights:
The Beach's British Bat is truly a trip through history. Start with a free day in London, and rest from the flight or see some of that great city's famous attractions: Trafalgar Square, the National Gallery, the Houses of Parliament, Big Ben, Buckingham Palace, and much more.

Head west, through Winchester and past Stonehenge. Visit the Welsh Folk Museum in St. Fagan's; meander through the Brecon Beacons, the Black Mountains, and on to the scenic luxury of Snowdonia Forest. Visit Chester, a city right out of the Middle Ages, with its enclosing ramparts still intact. Then it's on to the Lakes District, an area of picturesque villages and hamlets surrounding a variety of azure blue lakes.

Plenty of castles along the way

Get a taste of Scotland by riding through the emptiness of the Scottish highlands on your way to Glasgow, a well-populated center of industry. Overnight on the islands of Harris and Lewis in the Outer Hebrides. These islands are so isolated they rarely appear on any travel itinerary. All Beach tours strive to visit such unusual locations, allowing an in-depth look at the culture and history of each area.

The morning ferry returns to the mainland and this day's delightful ride may provide a glimpse of Nessie, the Loch Ness monster, as you pass by the mysterious lake whose name she bears. Then on to Edinburgh to enjoy the fascinating contrast between the Georgian architecture of New Town and the medieval buildings around the Royal Mile. Your arrival in Edinburgh coincides with the Tattoo. The image of the lone piper will remain with you forever. Two nights in Edinburgh, then it is time to push on to Tan Hill, the highest pub in Britain, where you can sample their local pub lunch. The trip terminates in London, with a free day to enjoy more of that wonderful city.

Price (does not include motorcycle rental):
- Tour, per person $3,800
- Supplement for single room occupancy .... $ 350

Price includes:
Airfare Boston/London/Boston (departures from other gateway airports may be arranged), hotel accommodations for the entire trip, all breakfasts, 17 evening meals, all airport/hotel bus transfers, and special gifts

Motorcycle provisions:
Motorcycles or automobiles are available for rent on the British Bat. Motorcycles are current BMW models and have the required liability insurance coverage. Motorcycle rental rates (with unlimited mileage) are. R80 - $950; K75 - $1,200 for the tour, which include insurance with a $500 deductible and the British Value Added Tax.

Luggage provisions:
A van accompanies each tour to carry luggage.

Running through the Scottish highlands (Photo courtesy of American Motorcyclist Assn.)

GREAT BRITAIN & IRELAND	**Four Nations Vacation**
Tour operator:	Comerford Tours
Length of tour:	16 days
Dates:	• May 25 through June 9, 1991 • June 15 through June 30, 1991 • May 27 through June 11, 1992 • June 17 through July 3, 1992
Trip begins and ends:	London

Highlights:

The Four Nations Vacation is a tour through Scotland, England, Wales and Ireland. You will use a variety of accommodations, including cottages, castles, farm houses and a Tudor coach inn, which together provide a varied taste of the United Kingdom and Ireland.

Start with a free day to rest or to explore London. But don't rush; you'll have all next day to visit this city's many attractions: Big Ben, Parliament, Buckingham Palace, the National Gallery, St. Paul's Cathedral, and Trafalgar Square. You'll even get to take in a West End show.

On the third day the tour departs London, heads north to the college town of Cambridge and then winds its way through the English countryside to Norwich before coming to rest for the evening in the Tudor town of Lincoln. After passing through the Yorkshire dales, you'll enter the beautiful English lake district.

Next, the trail leads into Scotland. Visit the famous castle in Edinburgh, Scotland's capital city, and then travel along the rugged roads that lead to Inverness, the heart of Scotland. The tour stops at Loch Ness for a chance to spot its most famous resident and then journeys south to explore the Isle of Mull, on Scotland's coast. You'll spend the night near Ben Nevis, Britain's highest mountain, before traveling to Stranraer to catch the ferry to Ireland.

Ireland, with the fewest cars per capita in Europe, is a motorcyclist's dream. Some of the roads are quite small, but an experienced rider will find them to be a unique challenge. Begin in peaceful Donegal and travel south along Ireland's west coast to county Galway. Stop at the spectacular 700 foot Cliffs of Moher in county Clare and the ancient monk's abbey Clonmacnois. You'll take a cruise of the river Shannon and enjoy a medieval banquet in Bunratty Castle. Journey across Ireland to Dublin and explore its many attractions, including Trinity College, Malahide Castle, and the Abbey Theater, or stop at one of the many pubs for a pint of Guinness with the friendly locals.

You then cross the Irish sea to Wales and travel through the Welsh mining villages to Birmingham, where you'll take a tour of the National Motorcycle Museum. Sleep in Shakespeare's home town of Stratford-Upon-Avon and then take the scenic route through the Cotswold region to London where you'll have one last night on the town before departing for home.

Price:
- All-inclusive tour, per driver $2,999
- All-inclusive tour, per passenger $2,399
- Budget tour (without air fare), per driver $1,349
- Budget tour (without air fare), per passenger $1,349

Price includes:
Round trip flight from Newark to London (other departure points in United States are available at a higher cost); accomodations for 16 nights; all breakfasts and all dinners (except for three nights); motorcycle rental and insurance; service van; $100 worth of tickets to various attractions; all ferry charges; Medieval banquet at Bunratty Castle; and a cruise of the Shannon river

Not included in price:
Fuel, road tolls, taxes, tariffs, lunches, beverages, laundry, and personal and medical insurance. The budget tour does not include service van, evening meals, air fare, show, attractions, ferry charges, or river cruise.

Motorcycle provisions:
Your choice of 1990 Kawasaki 750cc Ninja or Vulcan motorcycles is included in the price of the tour. Other motorcycles are available.

Luggage provisions:
A service van is available to carry excess luggage (limited to two suitcases per person).

Special notes:
- Participants must have an international driver's license, certified for motorcycle operation, and must comply with AAA insurance eligibility standards.
- You must be 25 years old to drive and at least 16 years old to be a passenger.
- A helmet and adequate protective clothing must be worn.
- Round trip direct flights to London are available from Boston, New York, Chicago, Los Angeles, Toronto, Atlanta, San Francisco, Tampa, Washington, D.C., Denver, Montreal, and Seattle.
- A $500 deposit is required to secure your reservation. For the 1991 tours, the deposit is nonrefundable after April 22, 1991.

ENGLAND, SCOTLAND, & IRELAND

British Isles

Tour operator:	Von Thielmann Tours
Length of tour:	21 days
Dates:	• August 10 through August 30, 1991 • Similar dates in 1992 and 1993
Trip begins and ends:	New York

Highlights:
This trip includes a visit to London, and visits to many historical sites en route. The tour takes you through England, Scotland, and the Republic of Ireland.

Price (does not include motorcycle rental):
- Single rider, double occupancy $3,220
- Two people, double occupancy $6,440
- Single passenger, double occupancy $3,220
- Supplement for single room occupancy .... $ 690

Price includes:
Round trip airfare from New York, hotel accommodations, transfers, breakfast daily, and many other meals, tour guide, and maps

Motorcycle provisions:
Rentals available

Luggage provisions:
Luggage will be carried in the support van.

ORGANIZED TOURS – WESTERN EUROPE

EUROPEAN ALPS — Beach's Alpine Adventures

Tour operator:	Beach's Motorcycle Adventures, Ltd.
Length of tour:	16-day and 22-day tours, each covering approximately 1,900 miles
Dates:	*1991* • June 8 through June 29 • July 6 through July 27 • August 3 through August 18 • September 7 through September 28 *1992* • June 6 through June 27 • July 4 through July 25 • August 1 through August 16 • September 5 through September 26 *1993* • June 5 through June 26 • July 3 through July 24 • July 31 through August 15 • September 4 through September 25

Bob Beach

Trip begins and ends:	Boston (other cities on request)

Highlights:
Do you dream of magnificent mountain riding on the finest roads in the world, breathtaking scenery, diet-shattering food, unique shopping opportunities, and enough cultural overload to last a lifetime? Then your choice has to be the Alps in Europe. It's all there — and in a small area, providing a motorcyclist's paradise.

For the past 19 years the Beach family has combined the best of Germany, Austria, northern Italy, Switzerland, a bit of France, and even tiny Liechtenstein into exciting two- and three-week motorcycling adventures.

There is a pleasant flight across the Atlantic on a major scheduled airline to the jumping-off point, Munich. This location provides a glimpse of the friendly Bavarian capital with its magnificent museums, famous beer halls, and German efficiency. The September tour permits a visit to the historical Oktoberfest. With so much to do, see, and experience, many tour members choose to arrive a few days early or stay a few days beyond the tour.

Austria offers beautiful scenery and the world famous Grossglockner mountain highway. The area around Salzburg was the setting for the well-known movie, *The Sound of Music*. The rugged Dolomite Mountains, beautiful lakes, and formidable castles are part of the scenery of northern Italy.

One can sample French cuisine on a short side trip into the French Alps, an area with a romance all its own. A spectacular view of both the Swiss and French Alps is found by riding a cable car up the mighty Mont Blanc, the highest mountain in the Alps. In Switzerland the mountains, high meadows, ringing cowbells, and superb roads create memories that never fade.

Beach's Alpine Adventures are structured to avoid the big cities and the usual gathering spots for tourists. Riding in large groups is discouraged, giving everyone the opportunity to schedule his own daily activities.

If you dream of motorcycling with mountains, glaciers, gorges, vineyards, waterfalls, picnics, gentle curves, switchbacks, tunnels, bridges, castles, palaces, lakes, mountain streams, hiking trails, and resting vistas, join the Beach family for the adventure of a lifetime!

Price (does not include motorcycle rental):
- 16-day tour, per person $2,850
- Supplement for single room occupancy ....$ 170
- 22-day tour, per person $3,700
- Supplement for single room occupancy ....$ 250

Price includes:
Airfare Boston/Munich/Boston (departure from other major gateway cities may be arranged), all hotels, all breakfasts, 17 evening meals on 22-day tours (13 evening meals included on 16-day tours), airport/hotel bus transfers, individual tour book, tour map, and special tour gifts

Motorcycle provisions:
Automobiles or motorcycles are available for rent on the Alpine Adventure. Motorcycles are all late model BMWs and have the required liability and collision insurance coverage. Rental rates, with unlimited mileage, are as follows:
- 16-day tour ....$ 785
- 22-day tour $1,100

Tour members may retain a motorcycle for additional time at the end of a tour at no additional charge.

Luggage provisions:
A luggage van accompanies each tour. A seat in the van may be available for passenger transport.

Special notes:
Riders must have a state driver's license as well as an International Driver's License, both valid for motorcycle operation. Riders must be at least 25 years of age.

THE BLACK FOREST AND SWITZERLAND — Bikes and Buddies

Tour operator:	Big Bike Tours
Length of tour:	4 days
Dates:	• June 8 through June 11, 1991 • July 27 through July 30, 1991 • August 24 through August 27, 1991
Trip begins and ends:	Geislingen, Germany

Highlights:
Though this gourmet tour of the Black Forest would be a delight for anyone to join, it has become popular as a reunion for past participants of Big Bike Tours' USA tours.

The trip begins at Lukas Duffner's house, a completely intact farmhouse in the Black Forest where hams are smoked and where serfs' and peasants' quarters can still be seen in the large living area. Enjoy a meal of smoked Black Forest ham and bread and wash it down with some schnaps and homemade cider.

Early next morning, Urs Tobler, a Swiss motorcycle driving instructor, will coach you on safe driving techniques and then assist you in developing your skills through practical road experience. The tour travels into Switzerland and concludes with a fondue dinner at the base of 2,502-meter-high Santis Mountain.

Price:
• Per person .... DM 849
• Per passenger .... DM 549

Price includes:
All accommodations, and safety training on Mt. Tobler

Motorcycle provisions:
Participants are responsible for providing their own motorcycle.

Luggage provisions:
Participants are responsible for carrying their own luggage.

Special notes:
German is the only language spoken on this tour.

ORGANIZED TOURS – WESTERN EUROPE 153

EUROPEAN ALPS	**Alpine and Dolomites Excursion**
Tour operator:	Bosenberg Motorcycle Excursions
Length of tour:	21 days, covering approximately 2,350 miles
Dates:	*1991* • June 9 through June 29 • July 7 through July 27 • September 8 through September 28 *1992* • June 14 through July 4 • July 12 through August 1 • September 6 through September 26
Trip begins and ends:	Bad Kreuznach, Germany

Highlights:

The Alpine regions offer motorcyclists more excitement per mile than any other region in Europe. Great scenery and plenty of curves, climbs and switchbacks are truly a biker's paradise on earth. Looking up in the valleys is just as exciting as looking down while on the passes and peaks.

Experience the best riding areas of four countries on this excursion. With the extended stays in one location, you have the chance to thoroughly explore each region for an extra day or two. Over 50 passes introduce themselves to you over the course of your travels in the Adula and Engadin regions of Switzerland, the Dolomites of Italy, and the eastern Alpine regions of Austria.

Besides riding little-used country roads, explore interesting towns and sights. Visit the Olympic city of Innsbruck with its Goldenes Dachl of Emperor Maximilian and Salzburg with Mozart's birthplace and the Hellbrunn castle. See Munich and its BMW museum, the Glockenspiel am Marienplatz, and the world famous Hofbrauhaus and its Biergarten. Other highlights include the Passion Play village of Oberammergau, and the King Ludwig fairy-tale castles, Neuschwanstein and the Linderhof.

Price (does not include airfare):
• Single rider, double occupancy $3,775
• Passenger, double occupancy $2,975
• Supplement for single room occupancy ....$ 325

Price Includes:
Transfers to/from Frankfurt airport, use of insured 1991 model BMW R80RT, 19 nights in select inns/hotels, 19 breakfasts, 9 lunches, 11 dinners, multilingual excursion leader on motorcycle, daily route briefings,

comprehensive sightseeing program on travel days, luggage van use, information packet and maps, motoring laws and rider safety slide show, Rhine river cruise, and excursion gift

Motorcycle provisions:
Use of insured 1991 model BMW R80RT included in excursion price or upgrade to K75RT, K100LT, or K100RS (at additional cost)

Luggage provisions:
Luggage van accompanies tour.

Special notes:
- Car or van can be rented for accompanying family members and/or friends
- Option of using airfare arrangements made by BME's representing travel agency or the option to make your own air travel arrangements through your local agency

ALSACE AND MOSEL WINE REGIONS PLUS LUXEMBOURG Castles & Grapes Excursion

Tour operator:	Bosenberg Motorcycle Excursions
Length of tour:	14 days, covering approximately 1,200 miles
Dates:	*1991* • May 12 through May 25 • August 4 through August 17 • September 29 through October 12 *1992* • May 10 through May 23 • August 9 through August 22 • September 27 through October 10
Trip begins and ends:	Bad Kreuznach, Germany

Highlights:
This tours offers you a fair share of curves, climbs, and superb scenery, but also the chance to learn a bit more about the Rhine and Mosel wine regions, Luxembourg, and France/Alsace through wine tastings and cel-

ORGANIZED TOURS – WESTERN EUROPE   155

Which way to the castles and grapes?

lar visits. Three countries and three cultures share the common thread surrounding the grape and its yearly fermenting of wine.

Cross the Rhine by ferry and visit the Lorely. Ride a loop on the Nurburgring race track. Pass through the Luxembourger Swiss Alps and the sleepy farm villages in the Ardennes highlands. Climb the Lorraine hills and sample the winding curves, French style, for the first time.

This excursion is for those who take their motorcycling as serious as the wine master in his cellar. Both know that life is a little bit better and a little more enjoyable when practicing their trade. You have a chance to experience the best of two worlds. On this tour you'll find out why wine masters toast their wines with a Zum Wohl.

Price (does not include airfare):
- Single rider, double occupancy $2,775
- Passenger, double occupancy $2,175
- Supplement for single room occupancy ....$ 225

Price includes:
Transfers to/from Frankfurt airport, use of insured 1991 model BMW R80RT, 12 nights in select inns/hotels, 12 breakfasts, 4 lunches, 6 dinners, multilingual excursion leader on motorcycle, daily route briefings, comprehensive sightseeing program on travel days, luggage van use, information packet and maps, motoring laws and rider safety slide show, Rhine river cruise, and excursion gift

Motorcycle provisions:
Use of insured 1991 model BMW R80RT included in excursion price or upgrade to K75RT, K100LT, or K100RS (at additional cost)

156 ORGANIZED TOURS – WESTERN EUROPE

Luggage provisions:
Luggage van accompanies tour.

Special notes:
- Car or van can be rented for accompanying family members and/or friends
- Option of using airfare arrangements made by BME's representing travel agency or the option to make your own air travel arrangements through your local agency

GERMANY	**United Germany Excursion**
Tour operator:	Bosenberg Motorcycle Excursions
Length of tour:	15 days, covering approximately 1,400 miles
Dates:	*1991* • May 26 through June 9 • June 23 through July 7 • August 25 through September 8 • September 22 through October 6 *1992* • May 24 through June 7 • June 28 through July 12 • August 23 through September 6 • September 20 through October 4
Trip begins and ends:	Bad Kreuznach, Germany

Highlights:
In 1989 this excursion could not have been offered, because of motorcycle use entry restrictions for visitors to the former East Germany. Germany is now united and the entire country offers new and superb motorcycling opportunities. You have a remarkable chance to meet and understand both *"Ossis"* (Germans in the East) and *"Wessis"* (Germans in the West).

The changes of the past year are highlighted by a weekend visit to Berlin. Visit the Berlin Wall, the fast disappearing monument of man's inhumanity to man; view the House at "Check-point Charlie" and tour the BMW motorcycle plant.

See where Soviet and United States ground forces met in the closing weeks of World War II in the town of Torgau on the Elbe river. Travel a

Follow me . . .

portion of the officially designated German beer road and sample the best of Bavarian beers. Stay at the medieval walled town of Rothenburg ob der Tauber.

History is around every curve and this excursion offers not only great roads and routes, but helps you to understand the Germans and their focus on reconstructing their once-divided country. A chance to meet and speak with fellow motorcyclists from both "sides" are one of the many features. This trip is a once-in-a-lifetime opportunity to see the changes firsthand sweeping through a united Germany.

Price (does not include airfare):
- Single rider, double occupancy $2,965
- Passenger, double occupancy $2,365
- Supplement for single room occupancy ....$ 285

Price includes:
Transfers to/from Frankfurt airport, use of insured 1991 model BMW R80RT, 13 nights in select inns/hotels, 13 breakfasts, 8 lunches, 10 dinners, multilingual excursion leader on motorcycle, daily route briefings, comprehensive sightseeing program on travel days, luggage van use, information packet and maps, motoring laws and rider safety slide show, Rhine river cruise, and excursion gift.

Motorcycle provisions:
Use of insured 1991 model BMW R80RT included in excursion price or upgrade to K75RT, K100LT, or K100RS (at additional cost).

Luggage provisions:
Luggage van accompanies tour.

Special notes:
- Car or van can be rented for accompanying family members and/or friends
- Option of using airfare arrangements made by BME's representing travel agency or the option to make your own air travel arrangements through your local agency

EUROPEAN ALPS — AlpenTour™ East

Tour operator:	Desmond Adventures, Inc.
Length of tour:	16 days
	Dates: *1991* • June 14 through June 30 • July 5 through July 21 • July 26 through August 11 • September 6 through September 22 [Contact Desmond Adventures for 1992 dates (probably around the same times).]
Trip begins and ends:	New York – JFK Airport

Highlights:
On this spectacular trip, you'll soar through the breathtaking European Alps and the Italian Dolomites, the most jagged, stunning mountains available for motorcycling. Explore the palaces and castles of King Ludwig of Bavaria. These opulent strongholds were the inspiration for Walt Disney's Fantasyland. Visit Mozart's birthplace in Salzburg, Austria, a city popularized in the movie *The Sound of Music.* Near Europe's highest waterfall, you'll curl through a mountain pass that is so narrow and winding that it only accommodates one-way traffic, changing direction every half-hour. You'll spend a charming night in an operating Austrian hunting lodge and then dash on to Italy to the picturesque village of Cortina D'-Ampezzo. Then you'll see the chic chalets and commanding ski slopes of St. Moritz and Interlaken. From dramatic mountain passes to dense mossy forests, you'll sample the rich flavor of the Eastern Alps and some thrilling motorcycling.

Price (includes motorcycle rental):
- Driver, double occupancy $3,995
- Passenger, double occupancy $3,395
- High season surcharge (July trip, per person) .... $ 100
- Supplement for single room occupancy .... $ 280

Price includes:
Round trip airfare New York/Zurich/New York, all required insurance, motorcycle rental (additional surcharge applies to some motorcycle models), all accommodations, airport/hotel transfers, all breakfasts, and dinner is provided every evening except when the tour spends more than

Twisties that make you want to come back for more

one night in a particular town. On the second night guests are free to make their own arrangements. When dinner is provided it is a group setting enabling riders to share their experiences and plan for the next day's travel.

Motorcycle provisions:
A wide variety of motorcycles are available, averaging less than one year old, from BMW (K75S, K75C, K100RT, K100RS); Honda (CBR 600 and 1000, TransAlp, Shadow, VFR 750, ST1100); Suzuki (Katana 600, 750 ,and 1100); and Kawasaki (Concours 1000). On specific bikes there is a surcharge; contact Desmond Adventures for complete information.

Luggage provisions:
A van accompanies each tour to carry luggage. Luggage is picked up from your hotel room as you leave a hotel, and delivered to your room at the destination. This service saves a lot of trips up and down stairs.

Special notes:
- For those wishing to ship their own motorcycle to Europe, deduct $600.
- Single room occupancy is available only on the first and last trip of each season.
- People wishing to arrange their own transatlantic transportation to Zurich can deduct $500 from the prices above.

160 ORGANIZED TOURS – WESTERN EUROPE

EUROPEAN ALPS	**AlpenTour™ West**
Tour operator:	Desmond Adventures, Inc.
Length of tour:	16 days

The AlpenTour

Dates:
1991
- May 24 through June 9
- August 16 through September 1
- September 27 through October 13

[Contact Desmond Adventures for 1992 dates (probably around the same times).]

Trip begins and ends:	New York – JFK Airport

Highlights:

You'll meet challenge on every turn in this thrilling and romantic tour. Conquer the mighty Matterhorn, charging past postcard-perfect villages improbably perched on those forbidding slopes. Near San Vittorio, Italy, you run the best road in motorcycle touring. After hours of full-throttle driving on the Autostrada, you'll sweep onto a deserted but well-paved two-lane road that cries to be ridden hard. Winding through endless curves, the tree-lined mountain road forces you to deep-leaning turns. Another day of spectacular riding ends at Monte Carlo, glamour capital of the world.

Resist the temptation to compete with Italian

The incredible Lauterbruhnen Velley, near Interlaken, Switzerland

bikers on their favorite sport, riding. Instead, delight in the landscape of vineyards and walled medieval villages. The narrow road delivers you right through the ancient gates of Ceriana, a small olive processing village dated five hundred years before Christ. When you finally tear yourself away from the topless beaches of the French Riviera, you discover the true grandeur of the Alps, following roads used by the conquerors Napoleon and Hannibal. From the massive granite cliffs of Canyon de Verdon to a route in Sestriere, Italy that includes six magnificent passes in one day, the panoramic scenery found on this trip is unequaled.

Price (includes motorcycle rental):
- Driver, double occupancy $3,995
- Passenger, double occupancy $3,395
- High season surcharge (July trip, per person) ....$ 100
- Supplement for single room occupancy ....$ 280

Price includes:
Round trip airfare New York/Zurich/New York, all required insurance, motorcycle rental (additional surcharge applies to some motorcycle models), hotel accommodations, airport/hotel transfers, all breakfasts, and dinner is provided every evening except when the tour spends more than one night in a particular town. On the second night guests are free to make their own arrangements. When dinner is provided it is a group setting enabling riders to share their experiences and plan for the next day's travel.

Motorcycle provisions:
A wide variety of motorcycles are available, averaging less than one year old, from BMW (K75S, K75C, K100RT, K100RS); Honda (CBR 600 and 1000, TransAlp, Shadow, VFR 750, ST1100); Suzuki (Katana 600, 750, and 1100); and Kawasaki (Concours 1000). On specific bikes there is a surcharge; contact Desmond Adventures for complete information.

Luggage provisions:
A van accompanies each tour to carry luggage. Luggage is picked up from your hotel room as you leave a hotel, and delivered to your room at the destination. This service saves a lot of trips up and down stairs.

Special notes:
- For those wishing to ship their own motorcycle to Europe, deduct $600.
- Single room occupancy is available only on the first and last trip of each season.
- People wishing to arrange their own transatlantic transportation to Zurich can deduct $500 from the prices above.

EUROPEAN ALPS — Affordable Alps

Tour operator:	Edelweiss Bike Travel
Length of tour:	12 days, covering approximately 1,400 miles
Dates:	• June 3 through June 14, 1991 • July 8 through July 19, 1991 • July 22 through August 2, 1991 • August 26 through September 6, 1991
Trip begins and ends:	Munich, Germany

Highlights:
Benefit from Edelweiss' decade of experience guiding motorcycle tours through the Alps. Thrill to the pinnacle of mountain motorcycling with experts. The Alps are the basis for comparing any other mountains in the world and this tour provides a singular opportunity to experience this unique area in a short time and inexpensively. It offers the essence of great motorcycling.

The tour starts in Munich and moves in a great circle through some of the most picturesque scenery on earth. You'll see historic Salzburg, Austria, then ride through Berchtesgaden and over the Grossglockner, the highest mountain in Austria. There's time for a side trip to Cortina d'Ampezzo and the grand Dolomites in northern Italy. Ride over the Gerlospass for a visit to the town of Innsbruck. Wind through vineyards and orchards on your way to romantic Lake Garda, the beautiful Italian resort area. You'll spend an extra day on Lake Garda to give you a chance to rest and explore. Next day, move on to Switzerland, over the Bernina Pass. Sample St. Moritz and tiny Liechtenstein as you return to Austria. Pass by the fairytale castles of Neuschwanstein on the way to Munich. The last day in Munich is free for you to explore, shop, and rest from your journey before returning home.

Price (includes motorcycle rental):
- Single rider, double occupancy $1,995
- Motorcycle passenger (or rider who brings his own motorcycle), double occupancy $1,395
- Single room supplement .... $ 175
- Supplement for 1000cc touring bike .... $ 275

Price includes:
Tour information package, transfers from and to Munich airport, accommodations for 11 nights in comfortable hotels, 11 breakfasts, 11 dinners, motorcycle rental (including insurance), two tour directors, safety and

ORGANIZED TOURS – WESTERN EUROPE

Mountains and valleys as far as you can see

traffic rule instruction, luggage transportation, welcome and farewell evenings, and a tour gift

Motorcycle provisions:
Three types of motorcycle are available: a 500cc for the sporty solo rider, a comfortable 750cc to 800cc touring motorcycle for two, and a 1000cc touring motorcycle is available at a premium price. All machines have a fairing or windshield.

Luggage provisions:
A luggage van accompanies this tour.

Special notes:
It can rain in the Alps, although this is unusual; it is important to bring a rain suit. At high altitudes the air can be chilly even under sunny skies, so long underwear and a windbreaker are essential.

EUROPEAN ALPS	**Best of the Alps**
Tour operator:	Edelweiss Bike Travel
Length of tour:	15 days, covering approximately 2,000 miles
Dates:	• June 16 through June 30, 1991 • August 4 through August 18, 1991 • September 8 through September 22, 1991 (Oktoberfest in Munich!)
Trip begins and ends:	Munich, Germany

Highlights:
This tour shows you the best of the Alps in Germany, Austria, Italy, France, Switzerland, and Liechtenstein. Edelweiss' decade of experience guiding motorcycle tours through the Alps has been distilled into this trip for motorcycling connoisseurs.

The adventure begins in Munich as you assemble with the others on your tour, pick up your motorcycle and get to know one another. Then it's off to historic Innsbruck, Austria, in a pleasant ride away from the city and into the mountains. Try the narrow curves of the Timmelsjoch and sail over the Jaufenpass on your way to Brixen. Next day you'll experience the eerie grandeur of the Dolomites on your way to beautiful Lake Garda. Then head westward along narrow, winding mountain roads to Lago d'Isco and onto the Autostrada to Torino. Next you'll take to the high roads and passes through the famous winter resorts to the village of Chamonix, France. There, you'll have a chance to take the cable car to the glaciers of Mont Blanc. Andermatt, Switzerland is your next stop, a charming village at the foot of three great alpine motorcycling roads. The scenery changes as you head north, out of the mountains of Switzerland and into the Black Forest of Bavaria. There you will have an extra day to explore and rest. Glide across rolling farmlands on your way past Lake Constance and on to the Bregenzer Wald. The final leg of your journey takes you by the fairytale castles of Neuschwanstein and back to Munich.

Price (includes motorcycle rental):
• Single rider, double occupancy $2,995
• Motorcycle passenger (or rider who brings his own motorcycle), double occupancy $2,395
• Single room supplement .... $ 275
• Supplement for 1000cc touring motorcycle .... $ 275

Price includes:
Tour information package, transfers from and to Munich airport, accommodations for 14 nights in comfortable hotels, 14 breakfasts, 14 dinners,

motorcycle rental (including insurance), two tour directors, safety and traffic rule instruction, luggage transportation, welcome and farewell evenings, and a tour gift

Motorcycle provisions:
Three types of motorcycle are available: a 500cc for the sporty solo rider, a comfortable 750cc to 800cc touring motorcycle for two, and a 1000cc touring motorcycle is available at a premium price. All machines have a fairing or windshield.

Luggage provisions:
A luggage van accompanies this tour.

The great Italian Dolomites: designed for motorcycling!

Special notes:
It can rain in the Alps, although this is unusual; it is important to bring a rain suit. At high altitudes the air can be chilly even under sunny skies, so long underwear and a windbreaker are essential.

EUROPEAN ALPS	**Austrian Tyrol**
Tour operator:	European Adventures
Length of tour:	14 days
Dates:	July 20 through August 3, 1991
Trip begins and ends:	London

Highlights:
This tour begins in London on Saturday night and arrives at St. Johann in Tyrol on Monday, after a one night stay in Schotten. Tuesday you will be free to explore St. Johann's many offerings, such as a walk through its quaint streets, a ride on the cable cars or a bus trip into Kitzbuhl. Scenic rides are planned to the Gross Glockner Pass, the Thurn Pass, the Konig See, Krimml waterfalls and the Kaprun Power station where there is usually snow.

During the journey home you will stop for two nights in Gundelsheim on the Neckar, a beautiful old town. Your accommodations, which are located in the Pedestrian Zone, has received Gold and Silver Awards for the cuisine and the owner has his own private motorcycle museum. From here you may visit Heidelberg, wander around the town or join in on the planned trip to Rothenburg on the Tauber. After two days the trip continues on to Hachenburg in Westerwald where you will stay for two days to explore the many interesting places that region offers.

Price:
- Rider and machine £517
- Pillion passenger £500

Price includes:
Two overnight sailings with cabin accommodations, 12 evening meals, and bed and breakfast in Germany. All accommodations are in pensions or hotels, where the atmosphere is both homey and comfortable. The minimum standard is that rooms have hot and cold water, with access to shower and bath, but the majority have in-room facilities.

Motorcycle provisions:
Each rider is responsible for providing his own motorcycle.

Luggage provisions:
Riders are responsible for transporting their own luggage.

Special notes:
Motorcycles should be at least 450 cc for this trip. A green card should be obtained by rider's insurance agent in order to verify that driver has adequate insurance.

GERMANY	**Bayerischer Wald**
Tour operator:	European Adventures
Length of tour:	14 days
Dates:	June 29 through July 13, 1991
Trip begins and ends:	London

Highlights:
This tour begins in London. Travel for one day across the Netherlands and Germany and spend the night in Vogelsburg. On Monday afternoon you will arrive at your destination of Bayerischer Wald, right next to the Czechoslovakian border. Your hotel, which is located 1,500 feet above sea

level, is right in the heart of the Weisser Regen Valley. Day tours include a trip into Czechoslovakia, a tour of the silver mine at Bodenmais and, as the area is renowned for its colored glass, a visit to some of its glass craftsmen.

On the return journey you will spend two nights in Gundelsheim on the Neckar river and visit the Transportation Museum at Sinsheim, which has a large display of motorcycles, cars, airplanes, and even a U-boat. From there the journey moves up to the Eifel mountains and where you will stay in a guest house for the last two nights. This area is close to the Nurburgring racetrack, which is a must for many motorcyclists. After a quick stop in the old town of Moschau, you will return by overnight ferry to London, where the trip ends on Saturday morning.

Price:
- Rider and machine £517
- Pillion passenger £500

Price includes:
Two overnight sailings with cabin accommodations, 12 evening meals, and bed and breakfast in Germany. All accommodations are in pensions or hotels, where the atmosphere is both homey and comfortable. The minimum standard is that rooms have hot and cold water, with access to shower and bath, but the majority have in-room facilities.

Motorcycle provisions:
Each rider is responsible for providing his own motorcycle.

Luggage provisions:
Riders are responsible for transporting their own luggage.

Special notes:
Motorcycles should be at least 450 cc for this trip. A green card should be obtained by rider's insurance agent in order to verify that driver has adequate insurance.

Alone, somewhere in the Alps
(photo courtesy of Beach's MCA)

GERMANY — Eifel Mountains

Tour operator:	European Adventures
Length of tour:	Seven days
Dates:	June 8 through June 15, 1991
Trip begins and ends:	London

Highlights:
This trip departs London on Saturday night and arrives in the Netherlands on Sunday morning. You will drive through Belgium, passing the famous Grand Prix circuit at Spa and arrive at the hotel just south of Daun (your home base for the trip) by early afternoon. Day tours include trips to the Nurburgring racetrack and the museum there, the old towns of Mayen and Monreal, and excursions into Luxembourg and the Mosel valley.

Price:
- Rider and machine £277
- pillion passenger £265

Price includes:
Two overnight sailings with cabin accommodations, five evening meals, and bed and breakfast in Germany. All accommodations are in pensions or hotels, where the atmosphere is both homey and comfortable. The minimum standard is that rooms have hot and cold water, with access to shower and bath, but the majority have in-room facilities.

Motorcycle provisions:
Each rider is responsible for providing his own motorcycle.

Luggage provisions:
Riders are responsible for transporting their own luggage.

Special notes:
Motorcycles should be at least 450 cc for this trip. A green card should be obtained by rider's insurance agent in order to verify that driver has adequate insurance.

GERMANY — Eifel Mountains, Black Forest, Mosel

Tour operator:	European Adventures
Length of tour:	14 days
Dates:	September 21 through October 5, 1991
Trip begins and ends:	London

Highlights:
Take the overnight ferry from London, arriving in the Netherlands on Sunday morning. Ride through the Ardennes to your first stop near Daun in the Eifel mountains, where you'll stay for four days. Visit the Nurburgring racetrack, the beautiful old towns of Monreal and Mayen, and see Maars, lakes in volcanic craters particular to this part of Germany. Next, travel the Autobahn to spend five nights in the Black Forest. There, you'll test your skills on the hairpin turns and winding roads. Stop at the top of Kandel and look out over the Rhine into France and into the Swiss Alps.

On then to Mosel, where you spend four nights in a hotel along the river Mosel. Here you can enjoy the local wines, visit Burg Elz and Hunstruck, with its aircraft museum or watch gems being cut in an old water-powered Scheiferei. Your last day on the continent is spent in the old walled town of Herrstein, before returning to London on Saturday.

Price:
- Rider and machine £517
- Pillion passenger £500

Price includes:
Two overnight sailings with cabin accommodations, 12 evening meals, and bed and breakfast in Germany. All accommodations are in pensions or hotels, where the atmosphere is both homey and comfortable. The minimum standard is that rooms have hot and cold water, with access to shower and bath, but the majority have in room facilities.

Motorcycle provisions:
Each rider is responsible for providing his own motorcycle.

Luggage provisions:
Riders are responsible for transporting their own luggage.

Special notes:
Motorcycles should be at least 450 cc for this trip. A green card should be obtained by rider's insurance agent in order to verify that driver has adequate insurance.

GERMANY — Southern Bavaria

Tour operator:	European Adventures
Length of tour:	14 days
Dates:	August 10 through August 24, 1991
Trip begins and ends:	London

Highlights:
This tour incorporates the best of Southern Bavaria and the Allgau. The tour leaves from London on Saturday night and travels for two days to reach Fussen, stopping overnight in Schotten. The hotel, which is 7,200 feet above sea level, lies in the foothills of the Alps. From there you will take day trips to visit Oberammergau, the famous castles of King Ludwig at Neuschwanstein and Linderhof and cross Lake Konstanz into Switzerland. You will use the area's many winding roads and climb over scenic mountains into Austria. Also, you will spend the day on Zugspitz, Germany's highest mountain.

The return trip will stop at the Mosel river for two evenings where you will visit the Nurburgring racetrack and Bad Munstereifel, an old walled town. The tour ends in London on Saturday morning.

Price:
- Rider and machine £517
- Pillion passenger £500

Price includes:
Two overnight sailings with cabin accommodations, 12 evening meals, and bed and breakfast in Germany. All accommodations are in pensions or hotels, where the atmosphere is both homey and comfortable. The minimum standard is that rooms have hot and cold water, with access to shower and bath, but the majority have in-room facilities.

Motorcycle provisions:
Each rider is responsible for providing his own motorcycle.

Luggage provisions:
Riders are responsible for transporting their own luggage.

Special notes:
Motorcycles should be at least 450 cc for this trip. A green card should be obtained by rider's insurance agent in order to verify that driver has adequate insurance.

GERMANY — Vogelsberg, Sauerland, Harz Mtns

Tour operator:	European Adventures
Length of tour:	14 days
Dates:	September 1 through September 15, 1991
Trip begins and ends:	London

Highlights:
Depart from London on Sunday night and arrive at Vlissingen, the Netherlands, Monday morning. Travel to Schotten in Vogelsberg, where you will spend three days exploring the castles at Muzenberg and Budingen, and the scenic roads that connect them. From Schotten travel to Petersbourn, stopping at Mohne Dam for a lake cruise. The tour stops in Petersbourn for four days, where you will visit Winterberg, the winter sports center, and the Sauerland, known as the area of 100 lakes and 1,000 peaks. On Sunday visit Hamlin to see the re-enactment of the Pied Piper story and return through Teotuburger Wald. Continue up to the Harz mountains where you will stay for four nights. There you will have a chance to ride the cable cars at Boxberg and Braunlage, and spend the day in the old town of Goslar, which has a good selection of shops and beautiful buildings. Spend your last night in Hachenberg, Westerwald, giving you a short ride to the ferry on Friday.

Price:
- Rider and machine £532
- Pillion passenger £515

Price includes:
Two overnight sailings with cabin accommodations, 12 evening meals, and bed and breakfast in Germany. All accommodations are in pensions or hotels, where the atmosphere is both homey and comfortable. The minimum standard is that rooms have hot and cold water, with access to shower and bath, but the majority have in-room facilities.

Motorcycle provisions:
Each rider is responsible for providing his own motorcycle.

Luggage provisions:
Riders are responsible for transporting their own luggage.

Special notes:
Motorcycles should be at least 150 cc for this trip. A green card should be obtained by rider's insurance agent to verify adequate insurance.

ORGANIZED TOURS – WESTERN EUROPE

GERMANY	**Westerwald**
Tour operator:	European Adventures
Length of tour:	Seven days
Dates:	April 27 through May 4, 1991
Trip begins and ends:	London

Highlights:
This trip departs from London on Saturday night and arrives, via ferry, in Vlissingen, the Netherlands on Sunday morning. From there you will drive across scenic Holland and arrive in Hachenburg, Germany, your home base for this trip, in time for a late lunch. The rest of the day is yours. Daily trips include one to the Rhine and another to Kannenbackerland, where Westerwald pottery is produced. Other trips take you along Westerwald's winding roads and through its many villages. The hotel is noted for its excellent food. Evening activities include a concert. Also, this trip enables you to take part in the Fest, which is a long weekend celebration for the coming May.

Price:
- Rider and machine £315
- Pillion passenger £265

Price includes:
Two overnight sailings with cabin accommodations, five evening meals, and bed and breakfast in Germany. All accommodations are in pensions or hotels, where the atmosphere is both homey and comfortable. The minimum standard is that rooms have hot and cold water, with access to shower and bath, but the majority have in-room facilities.

Motorcycle provisions:
Each rider is responsible for providing his own motorcycle.

Luggage provisions:
Riders are responsible for transporting their own luggage.

Special notes:
Motorcycles should be at least 450 cc for this trip. A green card should be obtained by rider's insurance agent in order to verify that driver has adequate insurance.

GERMANY — Westerwald and Mosel

Tour operator:	European Adventures
Length of tour:	Seven days
Dates:	May 25 through June 2, 1991
Trip begins and ends:	London

Highlights:
This new tour for 1991 works from two areas: Hachenburg and Mosel. Leave London on Saturday night and arrive in Hachenburg early Sunday afternoon. For three days explore this beautiful area of Westerwald and visit its castles and the Bigge See. The second half of the trip is spent in the wine-producing area along the Mosel river. Here accommodations are in a riverside hotel. Day trips follow the Mosel valley and lead to Burg Eltz and Hunstruck.

Price:
- Rider and machine £317
- Pillion passenger £305

Price includes:
Two overnight sailings with cabin accommodations, six evening meals, and bed and breakfast in Germany. All accommodations are in pensions or hotels, where the atmosphere is both homey and comfortable. The minimum standard is that rooms have hot and cold water, with access to shower and bath, but the majority have in-room facilities.

Motorcycle provisions:
Each rider is responsible for providing his own motorcycle.

Luggage provisions:
Riders are responsible for transporting their own luggage.

Special notes:
Motorcycles should be at least 450 cc for this trip. A green card should be obtained by rider's insurance agent in order to verify that driver has adequate insurance.

SWITZERLAND	**S.A.P. Tour**
Tour operator:	S.A.P. Tour
Length of tour:	Seven days
Dates:	• July 6 through July 12, 1991 • Dates for 1992 not yet available; check with Jed Halpern
Trip begins and ends:	Not announced until start of tour

Highlights:
This nonprofit trip was designed six years ago as a means for Honda Gold Wing owners to get together and tour the Swiss Alps and passes (hence, "S.A.P"). For this reason the tour has been scheduled to coincide with the Swiss Gold Wing Treffen (rally) in Buron (near Lucerne, July 11–14, 1991).

S.A.P. Tour will arrange daily trips from a base camp where you will be pitching a tent for the week. These trips, which cover some of the most scenic areas you will ever see, are designed by you and your group, with the tour guides providing their input on routes, speeds, and places to eat along the way.

The goals of this tour are to bring you in contact with the trials and pleasures of high altitude touring, to enhance and broaden your knowledge of handling your motorcycle in the Swiss Alpine environment, and to form friendships with other Gold Wing riders.

Price:
15 Swiss francs registration fee, per person; 13.10 Swiss francs per night camping fee for two people

Price includes:
Campground, complete with all modern facilities, and postage and packaging of all information

Not included in price:
Meals, tents, or camping equipment

Motorcycle provisions:
Each participant is responsible for providing his own motorcycle.

Luggage provisions:
Each participant is responsible for carrying his own luggage.

ORGANIZED TOURS – WESTERN EUROPE 175

Special notes:
- This tour covers terrain at very high altitudes and uses roads that sometimes have very sharp turns and quick drops and rises. Those who have any aversion to heights may not wish to participate.
- You will be sleeping in a tent at the base campsite. If you don't enjoy camping this tour would not be right for you. Participants must provide their own camping equipment, including a tent.
- To ensure that this tour remains an event for Gold Wing owners only, Jed Halpern, tour organizer and director, has required that participants be members of one of the following groups: Gold Wing European Federation, Gold Wing Road Riders Association, or GWTA. Only fifteen Gold Wing motorcycles are allowed to participate each year.

EUROPEAN ALPS — Enduro High Alps Tour

Tour operator:	mhs Motorradtouren GmbH
Length of tour:	Seven days, approximately 1,400 km; and 14 days, approximately 2,800 km

Dates:
Seven-day tour
- July 7 through July 13, 1991 and 1992
- August 12 through August 18, 1991 and 1992

14-day tour
- June 17 through June 30, 1991 and 1992
- September 1 through September 14, 1991 and 1992

Trip begins and ends:
Wolfratshausen, West Germany

Highlights:
After their great success with off-road tours last year, two new trips have been organized for mountain-loving enduro riders. As the popularity of the mountains in Piemonte along the French-Italian border grew among German and Swiss bikers, many of the roads were closed to the public.

The new 14-day enduro trip offers everything for those who have always wanted a real enduro adventure: off-roading, swimming, relaxing, and good eating. The tour encompasses southern Tyrol, the Lake Garda

Reaching the peak of Monte Genevris, on a trail for experts

region, Cinque Terre, the Riviera, and the Côte d'Azur of the Mediterranean, the mountains of Liguria and Piemonte, the Rhone Alps, the Aosta Valley, and Switzerland.

Even beginning off-roaders will find the trip to be great fun, while the more experienced riders will find plenty to test their skills. For those who desire a less expensive or shorter expedition a seven-day trip to southern Tyrol is also available.

FRANCE	**Southern France**
Tour operator:	mhs Motorradtouren GmbH
Length of tour:	14 days, approximately 3,200 km
Dates:	• June 17 through June 30, 1991 • September 1 through September 14, 1991 • Similar dates in 1992
Trip begins and ends:	Munich, Germany

Highlights:
This trip explores the less-traveled western Alps, which boast the highest passes in the middle European mountains, as well as the largest canyon, the Grand Cañon du Verdon. You'll pass through a small dukedom on your way to Switzerland.

The mountains are higher here, with the roads often set adventurously into the steep slopes. You will cross such well-known passes as the Furka, the Iseran, the Izoard, the Vars, and the Restefond-La Bonette, the highest paved pass at an altitude of 2,802 meters. Shortly afterward you'll come to the breathtaking sights of the canyon dug 800 meters into the mountains by the Verdon River.

Your journey takes you furthur to the Côte d'Azur and Provence, with opportunities to relax at the beach or visit such world famous cities as Nice, Monte Carlo, or Menton. You will ride a short distance on the route of the Rallye Monte Carlo, when passing into the Camargue. This region has inspired photographers and artists — like nowhere else — to the most famous paintings and pictures. You will see flamingos, wild horses, and buffaloes, and the most important cities, many of them founded by the Romans or in the Middle Ages. After five days in Southern France you will continue your trip through the high Alps of Italy and Switzerland back to Germany.

Price (does not include motorcycle rental):

	1991	1992
• Single rider, double occupancy	DM 2,695	DM 2,795
• Motorcycle passenger, double occupancy	DM 2,095	DM 2,195
• Supplement for single room occupancy	DM 600	DM 600

Price includes:
Accommodation in middle-class hotels, or better (always with private bath); half board (often à la carte) with fine French or Italian food; and entry fees

Motorcycle provisions:
Suzuki and other rental bikes available, starting at DM 1,350

Luggage provisions:
Rental bikes are equipped with panniers.

Special notes:
Languages spoken: German, Italian, French, and English.

GERMANY	**Sport-Bike Tour**
Tour operator:	mhs Motorradtouren GmbH
Length of tour:	Seven days, approximately 2,700 km, average 350 to 500 km per day
Dates:	• May 27 through June 2, 1991 (to Hungary) • August 15 through August 21, 1991 (to Southern France)
Trip begins and ends:	Munich, Germany

Highlights:
With Herbert Schellhorn as the group leader, this tour is especially for experienced drivers who place a high value on accommodations and service.

 Each day's riding is a bit longer than other mhs Motorradtouren trips and you'll get lots of curves — curves, curves, curves. The basic program is similar to mhs's other tours to Hungary and Southern France but this trip has its extra share of excitement.

Price (does not include motorcycle rental):

	Hungary tour	Southern France tour
• Single rider, single occupancy	DM 1,950	DM 2,250
• Passenger, double occupancy	DM 1,690	DM 1,895

You must register early for this trip, as the number of participants is limited.

Price includes:
Accommodations in hotels of higher class, full service with typical good cuisine, drinks at the table, fuel, tolls, and entry fees

Motorcycle provisions:
• Suzuki GSX 750F or DR 800 BIG, rental price: DM 1,000
• Others on request

Luggage provisions:
Rental bikes are equipped with luggage carriers and panniers.

Special notes:
The primary languages are German, English, Hungarian, or French.

Fabulous views from Passo Gian, Italian Dolomites

ORGANIZED TOURS – WESTERN EUROPE 179

ITALY	**The Dolomites**
Tour operator:	mhs Motorradtouren GmbH
Length of tour:	Five days, approximately 1,200 km
Dates:	• July 2 through July 6, 1991 • August 6 through August 10, 1991 • September 3 through September 7, 1991 • Same dates in 1992
Trip begins and ends:	Munich, Germany

Highlights:
Southern Tyrolia is a beloved destination for a vacation, and with good reason. In the summer months the streets are filled with autos, buses, and trucks, but this trip has been planned for paths which are as unknown and untraveled as possible and which lead to the most beautiful points. You'll visit the lakes at Molveno, Tenno, and Valvestino, unknown Alpine crossings and passages like Manghen, Tremalzo or Giau, as well as some of the famous passes such as Sella, Pordol, and Falzarego. At times you'll spend the night on the tip of a mountain, sometimes in a sport hotel, and at other times in a small, homey pension. You'll have plenty of opportunity to try regional cuisine specialties, as well as the good wine.

Price (does not include motorcycle rental):

	1991	1992
• Single rider, double occupancy	DM 895	DM 945
• Motorcycle passenger, double occupancy	DM 695	DM 745
• Supplement for single room occupancy	DM 160	DM 160

Price includes:
Accommodation in middle-class hotels (one night on top of a mountain in a simple house); breakfast and evening meals with good, typical Southern Tyrolian food; entry fees; and cable car ride to top of a mountain

Motorcycle provisions:
The following rental bikes are available: Suzuki mid-size bikes, like DR 800 BIG and VX 800. Minimum rental price starts at DM 540 for five days.

Luggage provisions:
No minibus available. Rental bikes have panniers.

Special notes:
The primary languages for this tour are German, English, and Italian.

AUSTRIA	**Upper Austria**
Tour operator:	mhs Motorradtouren GmbH
Length of tour:	Five days
Dates:	• July 11 through July 15, 1991 • July 23 through July 27, 1991 • August 26 through August 30, 1991 • September 9 through September 13, 1991 • Similar dates in 1992
Trip begins and ends:	Munich, Germany

Highlights:
Do you have only a little time? Then try this five-day trip. You'll see the tallest brick building in the world, the longest castle in Europe (about one kilometer long), and the world's biggest church organ. Visit the marvelous city of Mühldorf (translation: Mill-village) with its typical houses, a never-finished Second World War underground airport, and come to the border of Czechoslovakia. You will see the forest of Böhmen, where the famous poet Adalbert Stifter was born, and have a view of Lake Moldau in Czechoslovakia.

Continue the tour farther to the East. Pass the medieval city of Freistadt and Kefermarkt with its beautiful carved altar from the Gothic era. You'll see the grapevines of the Wachau and taste the good wine produced there. On the way back to Munich you'll pass the towns of Linz and Passau before you reach Landshut and the world's tallest brick building.

Price (does not include motorcycle rental):
• Single rider, double occupancy .... DM 895
• Motorcycle passenger, double occupancy .... DM 645
• Supplement for single room occupancy .... DM 140

Price includes:
Accommodation in middle-class hotels (double-occupancy room) with shower and bath, breakfast and evening meals, entry fees, and tour guidance

Motorcycle provisions:
Several Suzuki and BMW models are available. Prices start at DM 600.

Luggage provisions:
There is no luggage van on this trip, as all rental bikes are equipped with luggage holders and saddlebags.

Special notes:
The primary languages for this tour are German and English.

Price (does not include motorcycle rental):

	Seven-day tour	14-day tour
• Single rider, double occupancy	DM 1,345	DM 2,695
• Motorcycle or vehicle passenger, double occ.	DM 1,095	DM 2,095
• Supplement for single room occupancy	DM 200	DM 600

Price includes:
Accommodation in middle class hotels in double bed rooms, breakfast and evening meals (meals are typical southern Tyrolian food on seven-day trips or a variety of the best Italian and French food on 14-day tours), club bus for luggage transportation, passenger service, return service for any broken down bikes back to Germany, and entrance fees

Motorcycle provisions:
Suzuki TS 250, DR 600, or KTM 600 bikes are available. Prices range from DM 540 to DM 1,800, depending on length of trip and the bike desired. Rental price: starts at DM 600 for seven days and DM 1,350 for 14 days.

Luggage provisions:
Club bus accompanies trip to transport luggage.

Special notes:
The minimum number of participants is five. When there are more than ten participants, there will be two tour guides.

A club bus will accompany the party to carry luggage and passengers and to provide transportation back to Germany for riders and bikes in the case of a breakdown. Languages spoken: German, Italian, English; or German, Italian, French, and English.

Reward for the morning's climb: beautiful panorama of the Dachstein, Austria

EUROPEAN ALPS	**Alps and Southern France**
Tour operator:	Motorrad-Reisen
Length of tour:	12 days, approximately 2,150 miles
Dates:	• May 9 through May 20, 1991 • June 2 through June 13, 1991 • August 21 through September 1, 1991
Trip begins and ends:	Munich, Germany

Highlights:
If you're a mountain enthusiast with *joie de vivre* and enjoy cultural pursuits, this is the perfect tour. Run the high Alps, then delight in the Mediterranean Sea and the sensual pleasures of food, sun, and scenery in an area that has attracted Roman nobles and artistic giants. Cross the Alps through high Swiss and French passes to reach the Massif Central, steam toward Nice and Monte Carlo, and finally Provence and the fabulous city of Arles. Van Gogh's home was also the farthest summer seat of Roman emperors. You'll see well-preserved arenas, amphitheaters, forums, and temples from Roman times. Marvel at the prehistoric caves. Visit historic Avignon, formerly the residence of Popes in exile. The fabulous Château-Noeuf-du-Pape is also located in Avignon. Live like a king in France. Return to Munich through mountains along the Rhone Valley.

Price (does not include motorcycle rental):
- Rider and passenger, double occupancy $4,380
- Single rider, double occupancy $2,330
- Motorcycle rental $1,250

Price includes:
All land arrangements, bilingual (German and English) tour guide on motorcycle, board and lodging in twin bed rooms at comfortable inns, free transportation for you and/or your motorcycle to Munich in case of illness or accident, and technical assistance from tour guide

Motorcycle provisions:
Purchase a BMW through Motorrad-Reisen, rent their motorcycles, or ship your own to Munich. You can rent accessories and gear or purchase additional insurance from the agency. You must have an international driver's license valid for motorcycle operation. If you ship your motorcycle, bring the registration card and an international insurance card.

Luggage provisions:
Contact agent.

Special note:
U.S. agent can make arrangements for air travel to Munich and additional land and air arrangements including shipping your own motorcycle.

EUROPEAN ALPS	**High Alpine Circular Trip**
Tour operator:	Motorrad-Reisen
Length of tour:	• Five days, covering approximately 620 miles • Seven days, covering approximately 930 miles • Ten days, covering approximately 1,490 miles
Dates:	*Five-day tour* • May 22 through May 26, 1991 • June 12 through June 16, 1991 • July 13 – 17 and 24 – 28, 1991 • September 4 – 8, and 18 – 22, 1991 *Seven-day tour:* • June 23 through June 29, 1991 • July 21 through July 27, 1991 • August 25 through August 31, 1991 *Ten-day tour* • June 21 through June 30, 1991 • August 1 through August 10, 1991
Trip begins and ends:	Munich, Germany

Highlights:
Accept the challenge of mile upon mile of hairpin turns and the ecstasy of Alpine motorcycling. You'll find rolling hills, sapphire lakes, and romantic sunsets along with the thrill of endless serpentine curves. Steam through the Lower Alps to the more impenetrable highlands, a panorama of rugged rock walls and sheer cliffs. Run backroads through the most beautiful and impressive Alpine regions. Climb the bare rock face of the Dolomites, the pinnacle of Alpine touring. Claim the splendor of the great Dolomite passes such as Sella, Pordoi Joch, and Falzarego. Relax with a day on the banks of romantic Lake Garda, enjoying fabulous Chianti and Italian food. Crisscross countries as you travel twisty Alpine roads. You'll know the journey is ending when the roads become wider and the curves more gentle.

184 ORGANIZED TOURS – WESTERN EUROPE

Passing through snow-capped peaks, a little touch of winter

Price (does not include motorcycle rental):

	Five-day tour	Seven-day tour	Ten-day tour
• Rider and passenger, double occupancy	$1,315	$2,275	$3,370
• Single rider, double occupancy	$ 790	$1,295	$1,875
• Motorcycle rental	$ 650	$ 650	$1,250
• Supplement for single room occupancy	$ 180	$ 270	$ 450

Price includes:
All land arrangements, bilingual (German and English) tour guide on motorcycle, board and lodging in twin bed rooms at comfortable inns, free transportation for you and/or your motorcycle to Munich in case of illness or accident, technical assistance from tour guide

Motorcycle provisions:
Purchase a BMW through Motorrad-Reisen, rent their motorcycles, or ship your own motorcycle to Munich. You can rent complete accessories and gear or purchase additional insurance from the agency. You must have an international driver's license valid for motorcycle operation. If you ship your motorcycle, bring the registration card and an international insurance card.

Luggage provisions:
Contact agent.

Special notes:
U.S. agent can make arrangement for air travel to Munich and additional land and air arrangements including shipping your own motorcycle.

ORGANIZED TOURS – WESTERN EUROPE

AUSTRIA	**Magic Austria**
Tour operator:	Motorrad-Reisen
Length of tour:	• Two days, covering approximately 600 miles • Four days, covering approximately 589 miles • Five days, covering approximately 775 miles • Seven days, covering approximately 1,055 miles
Dates:	*Two-day tour* • Every weekend starting with April 13 to 14, 1991 and finishing October 26 to 27, 1991 *Four day tour* • May 9 through May 12, 1991 • May 30 through June 2, 1991 • June 13 through June 16, 1991 • July 13 through July 16, 1991 • August 15 through August 18, 1991 • August 30 through September 2, 1991 • October 3 through October 6, 1991 *Five-day tour* • May 29 through June 2, 1991 • July 3 through July 7, 1991 • August 7 through August 11, 1991 *Seven-day tour* • July 21 through July 27, 1991 • August 5 through August 11, 1991 • September 16 through September 22, 1991
Trip begins and ends:	Munich, Germany

Highlights:
From the Bavarian Mountains, venture to the remarkable massifs of Tennengebirge. Climb a hidden pass and push through the picturesque Dachstein range. Spend the night in a hidden mountain inn. Fish for trout. Laze around the campfire or warm your backside by the tiled stove in the parlor. At Admont, gateway to the Gesäuse, you'll visit the Stiftsbibliothek, one of the world's most famous libraries. Storm the high mountains and the deep clefts and chasms of the Gesause. Run the forgotten pathways of this famous as well as notorious region. Follow the current of the river Enns on roads that become narrower and narrower as they twist around the mountain. Stay at a quaint mountain inn perched at 4,920 ft. Taste homemade goat and sheep cheese. Wash it down with local

186 ORGANIZED TOURS – WESTERN EUROPE

Gathering in town square, preparing to start the Dikes Tour (photo courtesy of MSV Ophemert)

beer. Descend through the mountains along the river Enns. You'll cross the border to Germany at a place so small you must ring a bell to call the border guard to the gate. Finish your tour with a farewell party at a local Bavarian restaurant. Extend your stay in charming Austria with the five-day tour that includes Maria Zell, Jogland, Graz Basin, and Pongau. Add another two days for a seven-day trip that adds Murtal, Carinthia, Gurktal Alps, Tyrol, and Grossglockner to the itinerary.

Price (except as noted, motorcycle rental not included):

	Two-day tour	Four-day tour	Five-day tour	Seven-day tour
• Rider & passenger, double occ.	$520	$990	$1,325	$2,155
• Single rider, double occupancy	$350	$580	$ 745	$1,195
• Motorcycle rental	included	$650	$ 650	$ 650
• Supplement, single room occ.	$45	$135	$ 180	$ 270

Price includes:
All land arrangements, bilingual (German and English) tour guide on motorcycle, board and lodging in twin bed rooms at comfortable inns, free transportation for you and/or your motorcycle to Munich in case of illness or accident, and technical assistance from tour guide

Motorcycle provisions:
Purchase a BMW through Motorrad-Reisen, rent their motorcycles, or ship your own motorcycle to Munich. You can rent complete accessories and gear or purchase additional insurance from agency. You must have

driver's license valid for motorcycle operation and international driver's license. If you bring your own motorcycle, you'll need the motorcycle registration and an international insurance card.

Luggage provisions:
Check with agent.

Special notes:
Motorrad-Reisen's U.S. agent will arrange air travel to Munich and additional land and air arrangements including shipping your own motorcycle.

GERMANY	**The Black Forest**
Tour operator:	Motorrad-Reisen
Length of tour:	Six days
Dates:	• June 11 through June 16, 1991 • September 10 through September 15, 1991 • October 1 through October 6, 1991
Trip begins:	Freiburg, Germany
Trip ends:	Baden-Baden, Germany

Highlights:
On both sides of the Rhine River, you'll find extraordinary landscape for motorcycling. Glide through the romantic scenery of the Black Forest and the Vosges Mountains; any road offers fine riding and beautiful scenery. Wind through the narrow roads of the Alsace. Taste the wine and enjoy French cuisine. You'll delight to the combination of nature, culture, and *joie de vivre*.

Price (does not include motorcycle rental):
• Rider and passenger, double occupancy $2,155
• Single rider, double occupancy $1,195
• Supplement for single room occupancy ....$ 225

Price includes:
Contact agent.

Motorcycle provisions:
A motorcycle can be rented for $650 for the tour.

HOLLAND	**Dikes Tour**
Tour operator:	Motorsportvereniging Ophemert (MSV Ophemert)
Length of tour:	Choice of 93-mile and 124-mile tour
Dates:	Easter Sunday, March 31, 1991
Trip begins and ends:	Ophemert, The Netherlands

Highlights:
The Dikes Tour is a one-day event that takes place annually on Easter Sunday. The tour, which is listed on the FIM tour calender, begins at the Kapelhof canteen in Ophemert. Here you'll stop to have a cup of coffee before receiving your tour directions. The tour then travels along the dikes of the rivers Waal, Linge, Lek, Hollandse Ijssel, and Merwedekanaal. As you make your way across the wide and narrow dikes, you'll encounter beautiful surroundings and winding roads. Everyone begins the tour together, but half way through the tour you have to choose between the long and short route home. Also, a break is taken during the day for you to eat and have a rest.

Price:
12.50 Dutch florin (f.) per person entrance fee with momento; f. 10 per person entrance fee without momento.

Price includes:
Tour course directions, free coffee before the tour, and prizes

Not included in price:
Accommodations, meals, motorcycle rentals, insurance, air fare, and fuel

Motorcycle provisions:
Each participant is responsible for providing his own motorcycle.

Luggage provisions:
Each participant is responsible for carrying his own luggage.

Special notes:
Several campsites are available in the Ophemert area.

GERMANY	**The Wandervogel Rider**
Tour operator:	TransCyclist International
Length of tour:	Seven days, covering approximately 1,300 km
Dates:	Monthly during May, July, September (subject to booking requests; minimum six people)
Trip begins and ends:	Munich, Germany

Highlights:
This exhilarating tour of European Alps includes visits to the famous Hofbräuhaus in Munich and Hofburg in Innsbruck. Small mountain roads turn into wide sweeping turns as you navigate breathtaking Alpine valleys with awesome mountain peaks above. Hundreds upon hundreds of kilometers of fantastic mountain scenery seen from a birds-eye view. Enjoy those rustic, homey feelings created by Alpine farms, churches, and colorful village pubs. Warm, friendly people invite you to rest in preparation for mountain peaks and passes, creeks and rivers, and Alpine meadows and glaciers. The spicy-red Alpine wine and Tyrolean dumplings you will enjoy at night in the cozy Gasthaus after a full day's ride add to your memories of a spectacular ride you'll never forget.

Price (includes motorcycle rental):
- Single rider, double occupancy $1,400
- Passenger (pillion), double occupancy ....$ 900

Note: A U.S. $500 refundable insurance bond is required when renting a motorcycle.

Price includes:
Six nights in comfortable hotels, six breakfasts, six dinners, safety and traffic rule instruction, warm-up loop, welcome and farewell evenings, daily route briefing, various sightseeing tours (Hofbräuhaus, Hofburg, and others), tour gift, motorcycle rental, tour information packet, and tour guide on motorcycle

Not included in price:
Fuel, lunch, snacks, riding wear, and insurance

Motorcycle provisions:
BMW K75, BMW K100, or Japanese makes of equal capacity

Luggage provisions:
A van accompanies the tour to carry luggage, provided a 15-member group is booked.

Special notes:
International driver's license valid for motorcycle operation is required. You are advised to book at least three months ahead. In addition to this tour, a colorful choice of one week Wandervogel Rider Tours originating in various European and neighboring countries is offered from June 1 through September 30 each year. Prices range from $1,400 to $1,800, usually all-inclusive except for fuel, lunch snacks, and insurance. Also self-guided touring is possible. Send a self-addressed envelope and one international reply coupon (available from the post office) when inquiring about the tours.

EUROPEAN ALPS — Destination High Alps

Tour operator:	Von Thielmann Tours
Length of tour:	21 days
Dates:	• September 6 through September 26, 1991 • Similar dates in 1992 and 1993
Trip begins and ends:	New York (or other airports)

Highlights:
Travel through the most scenic Alpine countries, including Germany, Austria, Switzerland, Italy, and France. Return via the Riviera and the High Alps, to the original Oktoberfest in Munich.

Price (does not include motorcycle rental):
- Single rider, double occupancy $3,385
- Two people, double occupancy $6,770
- Single passenger, double occupancy $3,385
- Supplement for single room occupancy .... $ 680

Price includes:
Round trip airfare from New York, hotels, most meals, transfers, Oktoberfest reservation with fried chicken and beer, and a tour guide

Motorcycle provisions:
Bring your own, purchase a BMW tax-free, or rent a motorcycle.

Luggage provisions:
Luggage van with motorcycle trailer is provided.

EUROPEAN ALPS	**Grand Alpine Tour**
Tour operator:	Von Thielmann Tours
Length of tour:	15 days
Dates:	• May 30 through June 13, 1991 • Similar dates in 1992 and 1993
Trip begins and ends:	New York (or other airports)

Highlights:
Enjoy spring in the Alps! Austria, Bavaria, Switzerland, Italy, Yugoslavia, and Liechtenstein. Very comfortable mileage through this mostly scenic area. A good tour at a budget price.

Price (does not include motorcycle rental):
• Single rider, double occupancy $2,300
• Two people, double occupancy $3,900
• Single passenger, double occupancy $1,950
• Supplement for single room occupancy ....$ 580

Price includes:
Round trip airfare from New York, hotel accommodations, breakfast daily, welcome and farewell dinners, transfers, and a tour guide

Motorcycle provisions:
Bring your own motorcycle, purchase a BMW tax-free, or rent a motorcycle.

Luggage provisions:
Support van with motorcycle trailer is provided.

A bit of old Europe on this tour

EUROPEAN ALPS	**Alpine Countries**
Tour operator:	World Motorcycle Tours
Length of tour:	21 days
Dates:	• May 11, 1991 through June 1, 1991 • September 14, 1991 through October 5, 1991
Trip begins and ends:	New York, Chicago, or Los Angeles

Highlights:
Begin your Alpine adventure in the luxurious resort area of northern Yugoslavia by enjoying the delightful meals and service offered by one of the finest "old-world-style" hotels in Europe. From there climb over the interesting Loibel Pass into Austria for more exciting terrain and equally comfortable hotels. The selection of tour routes will take you over and around some of the most desirable motorcycle touring roads in Europe. You'll start each day with a buffet style breakfast and average about five hours of riding between hotels, leaving time to appreciate each destination and relax before dinner.

Price (does not include motorcycle rental or shipping):
• Per person, double occupancy, from New York City $3,495
• Per person, double occupancy, from Chicago $3,595
• Per person, double occupancy, from Los Angeles $3,750
• Supplement for single room .... $ 250

Price includes:
Round trip airfare, and luxury hotels with two meals daily

Motorcycle provisions:
Mr. Goodman specializes in shipping the client's motorcycle uncrated. The cost is about $.90 per pound from New York City, $1.05 from Chicago, and $1.20 from Los Angeles. Liability insurance in Europe will cost $101.

Luggage provisions:
Luggage van will accompany tour.

ORGANIZED TOURS – EASTERN EUROPE

CZECHOSLOVAKIA AND GERMANY — Bavaria and Bohemia Excursion

Tour operator:	Bosenberg Motorcycle Excursions
Length of tour:	15 days, covering approximately 1,600 miles
Dates:	*1991* • July 14 through July 28 • August 18 through September 1 *1992* • July 19 through August 2 • August 30 through September 13
Trip begins and ends:	Bad Kreuznach, Germany

Highlights:
Experience the best of Bavaria and the rich heritage of Bohemia, the western portion of Czechoslovakia. Highlighted by stopovers in Prague and Munich, explore centuries-old traditions from two kingdoms sharing a common heritage.

Ride the German Beer Road and sample some of the best beer available anywhere. Enter Czechoslovakia through the Kaiserwald and take country roads to its capital of Prague, the city of seven hills and 100 towers. Visit the famous Wenceslav square where democracy was rekindled in the fall of 1989.

Discover the city of Ceske Budejovice, more easily said by its German pronunciation of Budweiser. You will be able to sample the original beer with your evening meal. Ride hidden meadows and streams in southern Bohemia, and enjoy its forests and lakes, the traditional folk customs, and the simple, contrasting beauty of the new and old, as this country strives to rebuild itself.

Visit Munich and see the BMW museum, Hofbrauhaus, Marienplatz and its Glockenspiel; relax at one of the sidewalk cafes or a Biergarten, enjoying a *Hefe Weissen mit Brezeln*. Travel along the Neckar river, visit the NSU motorcycle museum at Neckarsulm, and see Heidelberg and its castle overlooking the Neckar river.

Price (does not include airfare):
- Single rider, double occupancy $3,375
- Passenger, double occupancy $2,775
- Supplement for single room occupancy .... $ 375

Price includes:
Transfers to/from Frankfurt airport, use of insured BMW R80RT motorcycle, 13 nights in select inns/hotels, 13 breakfasts, 7 lunches, 9 dinners, multilingual excursion leader on motorcycle, daily route briefings, comprehensive sightseeing program on travel days, luggage van use, information packet and maps, motoring laws and rider safety slide show, Rhine river cruise, and excursion gift

Motorcycle provisions:
Use of insured BMW R80RT motorcycle included in excursion price or upgrade to K75RT, K100LT, or K100RS (at additional cost)

Luggage provisions:
Luggage van accompanies tour.

Special notes:
- Car or van can be rented for accompanying family members and/or friends
- Option of using airfare arrangements made by BME's representing travel agency or the option to make your own air travel arrangements through your local agency

SOVIET UNION	Soviet Union '91
Tour operator:	Edelweiss Bike Travel
Length of tour:	21 days, covering approximately 3,400 miles
Dates:	• June 15 through July 5, 1991 • July 6 through July 26, 1991 • July 27 through August 16, 1991 • August 17 through September 7, 1991
Trip begins and ends:	Munich, Germany

Highlights:
After your arrival in Munich, you collect your rental motorcycle and get acquainted with some of your travelling companions. Start your trip by riding from Germany, stopping in Vienna and Budapest, and traveling through the Hungarian lowlands to the Russian border. Then you'll follow twisting roads over the Carpathian Mountains to Lvov, where you'll have a free day to explore the city and meet the local citizens.

196 ORGANIZED TOURS – EASTERN EUROPE

Throughout this tour, you'll make close contact and spontaneous friendships with Soviet citizens. It's 500 km through the Ukraine to Brest, site of a great military fortress. You'll be travelling through spacious woods of white Russia to Smolensk and on to Moscow where you have two days to visit the splendid metropolitan capital of this superpower nation. In Moscow, don't miss the fabulous Russian circus, the Cosmonaut museum and, of course, the Kremlin. Then move on along the Volga to Novgorod, one of the oldest towns in Russia. It's only a half-day trip to Leningrad, one of the most beautiful cities in Russia. You'll learn about the history of czarist Russia in Leningrad. See the splendor of the Hermitage, formerly the winter palace of Czar Peter the Great, now one of the world's great art museums. You leave the Soviet Union and travel to Helsinki, Finland, where you and your motorcycle board a ferry to return to Germany via Travemunde. The last two days take you through Hanover and back to Munich where the trip comes to an end.

Ah, the ecstasy of the warm sun after a long journey

Price (includes motorcycle rental):
- Single rider, double occupancy $4,395
- Motorcycle passenger, double occupancy $3,395
- Single room supplement .... $ 695
- Supplement for 1000cc touring motorcycle .... $ 550

Price includes:
Tour information package, accommodations for 19 nights in comfortable hotels plus one on the ferry, 19 breakfasts and evening meals, motorcycle rental (including insurance), three tour directors, sightseeing and entry fees, cultural programs, luggage transportation, introductory and farewell get-togethers, and a tour gift

Motorcycle provisions:
Three types of motorcycle are available: a 500cc for the sporty solo rider; a comfortable 750cc to 800cc touring motorcycle for two; a 1000cc touring motorcycle, available at a premium price. All machines have a fairing or windshield.

Luggage provisions:
A luggage van accompanies this tour.

Special notes:
Amenities in the Soviet Union are not equivalent to American standards. Riders expecting the same services and conveniences as they would find in America will be disappointed. The daily distances are sometimes long and therefore endurance is required. Consumer goods can be limited. Think of this trip as an adventure rather than a holiday.

YUGOSLAVIA	Istra — a gourmet tour
Tour operator:	mhs Motorradtouren GmbH
Length of tour:	Eight days, approximately 2,200 km (average 250 to 300 km per day)
Dates:	• April 14 through April 21, 1991 • September 29 through October 6, 1991 • Similar dates in 1992
Trip begins and ends:	Munich, Germany

Highlights:
It's only a short hop from Germany to northern Yugoslavia, but the climactic difference is great. This tour, the first and last trips in Europe for mhs Motorradtouren each year, leads you to the highlights of Austria and Istra. You will see the beautiful mountains of Salzburg and the Steiermark, a region with little industry but with beautiful farmhouses in original Austrian country style.

Crossing the border to Yugoslavia, the landscape changes. Winding roads lead over the hills to the Mediterranean, where you will stop at the coastline and stay in a fine hotel. You will make excursions to the famous grottoes of Postoijna and to the undiscovered interior of the peninsula of Istra. You will see castles and medieval villages and will meet local people that are friendly and interested in your high tech bike. You will be astonished at the fine food, served in excellent restaurants.

Continue on to the lakes of Plitvice, where several movies were filmed, before you start back to Austria. The final leg is a marvelous ride through mountains and untouched nature, an experience that has become rare in Europe. This trip is a holiday with the utmost of fine food and the best hotels offered in Austria and Yugoslavia.

198 ORGANIZED TOURS – EASTERN EUROPE

Loading the bike trailer in Istra, Yugoslavia; skyline of Rovinj is beyond

Price (does not include motorcycle rental):

	1991	1992
• Single rider, double occupancy	DM 1,995	DM 2,095
• Motorcycle passenger, double occupancy	DM 1,645	DM 1,795
• Supplement for single room occupancy	DM 200	DM 240

Price includes:
Seven nights in a first-class hotel, double occupancy room with private bath; gourmet full board, often à la carte; table drinks; tolls; entry fees; and tour guide

Motorcycle provisions:
• The following models are available (rentals from DM 750):Suzuki GS 500 E, DR 750 BIG, VX 800, GSX 750 F, GSX 1100 F or G

Luggage provisions:
Rental bikes are equipped with luggage holders and panniers.

Special notes:
The primary languages for this tour are German and English.

CZECHOSLOVAKIA	Czechoslovakia
Tour operator:	Motorrad-Reisen
Length of tour:	Five days
Dates:	• June 5 through June 9, 1991 • July 3 through July 7, 1991 • August 13 through August 17, 1991 • September 4 through September 8, 1991
Trip begins and ends:	Munich, Germany

Highlights:
See the splendid countryside as you step behind the former "iron curtain." Look over from the Czechoslovakian side past the watch-towers and across the death-strip. You'll also see the churches and villages and meet the friendly people and witness this dramatic change in history. Enjoy world famous beer where it is brewed. Have fun with a night in a castle and ferry boat crossing of lake Moldau. Make a "step back to the future."

Price (does not include motorcycle rental):
- Rider and passenger, double occupancy .... U.S. $1,070
- Single rider, double occupancy .... U.S. $ 635
- Motorcycle rental .... U.S. $ 650

Price includes:
All land arrangements, bilingual (German and English) tour guide on motorcycle, board and lodging in twin bed rooms at comfortable inns, room reservation in Munich for arrival day, free transportation for you and/or your motorcycle to Munich in case of illness or accident, and technical assistance from tour guide

Motorcycle provisions:
Purchase a BMW through Motorrad-Reisen, rent their motorcycles, or ship your own motorcycle to Munich. You can rent complete accessories and gear or purchase additional insurance from the agency. You must have an international driver's license valid for motorcycle operation. If you ship your motorcycle, bring the registration card and an international insurance card.

Luggage provisions:	Contact agent.

Special notes:
U.S. agent can make arrangements for air travel to Munich and additional land and air arrangements including shipping your own motorcycle.

SOVIET UNION	**Destination Moscow**
Tour operator:	Von Thielmann Tours
Length of tour:	21 days
Dates:	• July 15 through August 4, 1991 • July 13 through August 2, 1992 • Similar dates in 1993
Trip begins and ends:	New York (or other airport) and Munich

Highlights:

Starting in Munich you'll travel through Austria, Czechoslovakia, Poland, through Belorussia to Moscow, and back through the Ukraine, into Hungary, Austria, and Bavaria. Scenery will vary widely, and include visits to Munich, Prague, Krakau, Warsaw, Minsk, Moscow, Kiev, Budapest, and Vienna. As in the past, riders on this trip shall be allowed to travel independently at their own pace, if they wish to do so. Special receptions, parties and sightseeing are included.

Price (does not include motorcycle rental):
- Single rider, double occupancy $3,625
- Two people, double occupancy $7,250
- Single passenger, double occupancy $3,625
- Supplement for single room occupancy .... $ 685

Price includes:

Round trip air fare New York/Munich (or from other airports), hotel accommodations, breakfast daily and several other meals, transfers, and a multilingual tour guide(s).

Motorcycle provisions:

Rental motorcycles are available. You may bring your own motorcycle or purchase a motorcycle tax-free.

Luggage provisions:

A luggage van with motorcycle trailer accompanies this tour.

ORGANIZED TOURS – MEDITERRANEAN AREA

CORSICA & SARDINIA	**Corsica and Sardinia**
Tour operator:	mhs Motorradtouren GmbH
Length of tour:	14 days, approximately 3,500 km
Dates:	• April 28 through May 11, 1991 • September 29 through October 13, 1991 • Similar dates in 1992
Trip begins:	Lugano, Switzerland
Trip ends:	Munich, Germany

Highlights:
As a motorcyclist, you'll be welcomed to Sardinia and Corsica. You will see lots of strange buildings on both islands called nurages, built like towers more than two thousand years ago. The narrow, winding roads are sometimes gravelled but always in good condition. There is hardly any traffic, and the landscape is overwhelming. You will see the grotto of Neptune, the well-fortified city Su nuraxi, built in the nurage-style, and medieval fortresses dating from Genoan invaders.

After visiting Cagliari, the capitol of Sardinia, you proceed into the quiet wilderness of the Gennargentu Mountains. Here, you'll find lots of ancient political graffiti painted on the walls in beautiful colors, showing the protest against the government of Rome. The next day you will reach the Costa Smeralda, where the Aga Khan had beautiful houses built in the sixties. These houses are well integrated into nature.

You will have one day off for relaxing and swimming before you start to Corsica. Corsica is much wilder than Sardinia. The highest mountain is 8,400 feet. Napoleon, the French emperor of the early 19th century, was born here. You will visit his home, see artifacts from the stone age and have time for swimming in one of the lonely bays.

After six days riding on the island, you will leave Corsica for La Spezia, which is the major harbor for marines in Italy. A last night at the Italian coast in a nice medieval city gives you the real feeling for *la dolce vita,* the sweet life, before you start your last day, bringing you back to Munich.

Prices for 1991 and 1992 (does not include motorcycle rental):
• Single rider, double occupancy . . . . DM 3,995
• Motorcycle passenger, double occupancy . . . . DM 3,345
• Supplement for single room occupancy . . . . DM 600

Price includes:
Overnight stays in middle-class hotels (double occupancy), full board with typical fine food (French and Italian cuisine), passage in first-class cabins from Genoa to Sardinia, passage from Sardinia to Corsica, passage from Corsica to La Spezia, table drinks, and all entry fees and tolls

Motorcycle provisions:
Motorcycle rental only to and from Munich are provided. Rental prices start at DM 1,500.

Luggage provisions:
Rental bikes are equipped with luggage holders and panniers.

Special notes:
Primary languages: German, Italian, French, and English, if American travelers are on the tour.

ITALY — Sicily and Southern Italy (a gourmet tour)

Tour operator:	mhs Motorradtouren GmbH
Length of tour:	13 days, approximately 3,800 km, average 350 km per day
Dates:	• April 28 through May 10, 1991 • September 29 through October 12, 1991 • Similar dates in 1992
Trip begins:	Lugano, Switzerland
Trip ends:	Munich, Germany

Highlights:
This is a special trip for connoisseurs of Italy, whether you're interested in history, bathing, or the best Italian seafood.

Ride up to the Monte Pellegrino, which the great German poet Schiller called one of the most beautiful spots in the world. Visit the catacombs of Palermo and the cathedrals of the harbor city and Monreale. In Trápani, on the west coast of the island, you can even see the coast of northern Africa on a clear day.

On the trip through the island you'll see Selinunte, formerly a Greek city; Licata with its marvelous lonely bay; Enna, the geographical and once political center of Sicily; the romantic fishing village of Cefalu; Mount Etna, Europe's largest active volcano; and Taormina or Siracusa. Frequently you'll encounter traces of the ancient Greek and Roman cultures.

After this, you'll leave the island for the lovely coast of Southern Italy. Journey to the National Park of Calábria, a place of astonishing vistas reminiscent of the Canadian Rockies. In Puglia you will encounter the strange round houses called "trulli," built in natural stone without mortar. You'll stay one night in a very comfortable hotel with an absolutely beautiful park — a night you may never forget. Near Alberobello, the center of the trulli region, you'll visit the grottoes of Castellana before starting north. See the forest umbra, a wild and romantic wood, the Adriatic coastline, Lake Trasimeno, and a great many other sights on the way to Tuscany, and then to the trip's ending point at Munich.

Each tour offers its own special flair: the blooms of springtime in Italy, where the sea is often warm enough for swimming even though it is still quite cool in Germany, the fresh fruit of autumn, and the chance to spend hours basking in the warm sun or in the sea.

Prices (does not include motorcycle rental):
1991
- Single rider, double occupancy .... DM 3,895
- Motorcycle passenger, double occupancy .... DM 3,195
- Supplement for single room occupancy .... DM   600

1992
- Single rider, double occupancy .... DM 3,995
- Motorcycle passenger, double occupancy .... DM 3,295
- Supplement for single room occupancy .... DM   600

Price includes:
Accommodation in very good hotels (double occupancy), full board with best Italian food (often seafood), table drinks, ferry from Genoa to Palermo in first-class cabins (no single rooms possible), and entry fees and tolls

Motorcycle provisions:
Rental bikes are available from DM 1,400 upwards. Bike rentals are available only from and to Wolfratshausen.

Luggage provisions:
Rental bikes are equipped with panniers.

Special notes:
The primary languages for this tour are German, English, and Italian. Also important, don't forget your swimming suit since some of the hotels lie directly on the sea.

ITALY	**Tuscany (a gourmet tour)**
Tour operator:	mhs Motorradtouren GmbH
Length of tour:	10 days, approximately 2,400 km, average 300 km per day
Dates:	• May 15 through May 24, 1991 • June 6 through June 15, 1991 • September 19 through September 28, 1991 • Similar dates in 1992
Trip begins and ends:	Munich, Germany

Highlights:
On your way to Tuscany you'll pass beautiful landscapes: the lakes of Molveno and Garda, the Cinque Terre, a small region on the Mediterranean, the five villages of which have been accessible by road for only a few decades. You'll pass along the beaches of the Riviera and reach Pisa, with its famous leaning tower. After climbing the tower you leave this center of tourism for the quietness of nature.

Volterra, the city of alabaster, and San Gimignano, with its popular skyline of palace and church towers from the Middle Ages are the next destinations. Close to the house where Arnbolfo di Cambio, the most important architect of the 13th century, was born, you'll take rooms in a cozy hotel. The chef de cuisine will present the delights of middle Italian fare.

The next stations are Montepulciano, the pearl of the Renaissance, Perugia, one of the centers of the Etruscan culture, and Assisi, the home town of St. Francis. There will be some time to relax, swim, or ride while you stay in an old but very good guest house, once a farmhouse. You will stay in a 16th century villa, from which you will journey to Florence by bus — a real adventure on these narrow, twisting roads.

On your way back to Germany you'll want to stop at the new Ferrari Museum, and the small town of Cutigliano in the heights of the Apennines. A night in a castle in southern Tyrol will conclude your stay in Italy.

Prices for 1991 and 1992 (does not include motorcycle rental):
• Single rider, double occupancy .... DM 2,795
• Motorcycle passenger, double occupancy .... DM 2,345
• Supplement for single room occupancy .... DM 500

Price includes:
Accommodation in very good hotels (often in castles or other medieval houses), full board with finest Italian food, table drinks, and tolls and entry fees

Motorcycle provisions:
Rental bikes are available from DM 1,200 upwards

Luggage provisions:
Rental bikes have panniers.

Special notes:
The primary languages for this tour are German, English, and Italian.

ITALY	**Tuscany: The Magic Spell of Italy**
Tour operator:	Motorrad-Reisen
Length of tour:	Ten days
Dates:	• June 14 through June 23, 1991 • August 23 through September 1, 1991 • September 13 through September 22, 1991
Trip begins and ends:	Munich, Germany

Highlights:
Journey to Tuscany through the Italian Dolomites, skirting beautiful Lake Garda, and arriving in Florence, art capital of the world. Roll through the gentle hills of Tuscany, a region that nurtured many famous creative spirits including Michelangelo, Dante, Galileo, Filippo Brunelleschi, Leonardo da Vinci, Puccini, and Boccaccio. See Etruscan design in Sienna, the gem of medieval architecture. Sweep through an ochre landscape dotted with cyprus and olive trees to visit Arezzo, Sorano, Savona, and other charming but less well-known villages. Luxuriate in the richness and variety of Italian cuisine. Don't forget, the Italians taught the French how to enjoy food. Drink a glass of robust Chianti wine at sunset, listen to the delicate evening bells, and feel the enchantment that has nourished the Italian spirit for ages.

Price (does not include motorcycle rental):
• Rider and passenger, double occupancy $3,730
• Single rider, double occupancy $2,080
• Motorcycle rental $1,250

Price includes:

All land arrangements, bilingual (German and English) tour guide on motorcycle, board and lodging in twin bed rooms at comfortable inns, free transportation for you and/or your motorcycle to Munich in case of illness or accident, and technical assistance from tour guide

Motorcycle provisions:

Purchase a BMW through Motorrad-Reisen, rent their motorcycles, or ship your own motorcycle to Munich. You can rent complete accessories and gear or purchase additional insurance from agency. You must have an international driver's license valid for motorcycle operation. If you ship your motorcycle, bring the registration card and an international insurance card.

Luggage provisions:

Check with agent.

Tasting the sea breeze at a stop along the Mediterranean

Special notes:

U.S. agent can make arrangements for air travel to Munich and additional land and air arrangements including shipping your own motorcycle.

TURKEY	Lykien on Motorcycle
Tour operator:	Motorrad Spaett, KG
Length of tour:	14 days
Dates:	• April 13 through April 27, 1991 • June 1 through June 15, 1991 • July 6 through July 20, 1991 • September 21 through October 5, 1991

Trip begins and ends:

Munich, West Germany. For overseas customers, Motorrad Spaett can arrange a combination one-week tour through the Alps and two weeks in Turkey. They can book flights from any location to Munich.

Highlights:
Intended principally for sightseeing, this guided tour leaves from Antalya, a city on the south coast with its harbor castle and bazaar. The tour visits the most important archeological sites including the chalk terraces at Pamukkale, the ancient city of Ephesos and Bodrum, the "St. Tropez" of Turkey's Aegean coast where there will be enough time to relax, swim, and sail.

In this area of Turkey, 90 percent of the roads are paved and the climate is excellent with little likelihood of rain. The hotels are of international standard since they cater to a visitors from all countries who come to see the famous Grecian, Persian, and Roman historical sites.

Price (includes motorcycle rental):
- Rider, double occupancy .... DM 3,950
- Passenger, double occupancy .... DM 3,250
- Supplement for single room occupancy .... DM   350

Price includes:
Round trip airfare from Munich to Antalya, all transfers, hotels, half-board (hotel includes Turkish breakfast and dinner), English-speaking guide, and sightseeing expenses

Motorcycle provisions:
Yamaha XT600Z (Ténéré), XJ650, XJ550, and Honda CM400T

Luggage provisions:
Luggage is transported by a van and is limited to two pieces per person and a maximum of 30 kilograms (66 lbs. limit on the flight to Turkey).

Special notes:
The principal language of this tour is German; the tour guide also speaks English. Temperatures in south Turkey are high, but cool in the mountain highlands; pack accordingly. Riding gear is not available in Turkey.

TURKEY & CYPRUS	**South Turkey and Cyprus**
Tour operator:	Motorrad Spaett, KG
Length of tour:	14 days
Dates:	• April 27 through May 11, 1991

- June 15 through June 29, 1991
- July 20 through August 3, 1991
- September 7 through September 21, 1991

Trip begins and ends:
Munich, West Germany. For overseas customers, Motorrad Spaett can arrange a combination one-week tour through the Alps and two weeks in Turkey. They can book flights from any location to Munich.

Highlights:
Intended principally for sightseeing, this guided tour leaves from Antalya, a city on the south coast with its harbor castle and bazaar and travels about 100 to 150 miles per day.

First the tour travels northeast to central Turkey, to Kappadokia, to Konya with its dancing dervishes, to Navsehir and Goreme to a city built into a mountain of lava. Then the tour goes south to the coast and from Silifke to Cyprus by ferry where you'll spend three days. Finally, after returning from Cyprus on the ferry, you'll follow the coast back to Antalya.

In this area of Turkey, 90 percent of the roads are paved and the climate is
excellent with little likelihood of rain. The hotels are of international standard since they cater to a visitors from all countries who come to see the famous Grecian, Persian, and Roman historical sites.

Price (includes motorcycle rental):
- Rider, double occupancy .... DM 3,950
- Passenger, double occupancy .... DM 3,250
- Supplement for single room occupancy .... DM   350

Price includes:
Round trip airfare from Munich to Antalya, all transfers, hotels, half-board (hotel includes Turkish breakfast and dinner), English-speaking guide, and sightseeing expenses

Motorcycle provisions:
Yamaha XT600Z (Ténéré), XJ650, XJ550, and Honda CM400T

Luggage provisions:
Luggage is transported by a van and is limited to two pieces per person and a maximum of 30 kilograms (66 lbs. limit on the flight to Turkey).

Special notes:
The principal language of this tour is German; the tour guide also speaks English. Temperatures in south Turkey are high, but cool in the mountain highlands; pack accordingly. Riding gear is not available in Turkey.

CYPRUS — Cyprus

Tour operator:	Prima Klima Reisen GmbH
Length of tour:	14 days (extensions possible)
Dates:	Twice a month from March through December. Contact Prima Klima Reisen (PKR) for specific dates.

Trip begins and ends:
Larnaca Airport, Cyprus. Home base on Cyprus is the romantic village of Polis, 200 miles from the airport. PKR provides the transfers between the airport and Polis.

Highlights:
Cyprus is a beautiful mountainous island with scenic areas to explore and beaches to sample. Legend says that Aphrodite, greek goddess of love, was born of the sea foam on these shores. The island has been inhabited since the Stone Age. Artifacts from Cyprus date back 8,000 years.

The island's winding mountain trails are perfect for enduro riders of any level experience. Mount Olympus, home of the gods of Greek mythology, is 1,995 meters high. You can zigzag up the mountain through olive groves and return to the beach on another road that descends past citrus groves. When you tire of the heights, there are always beautiful coastal towns and old fishing villages to explore.

Price (includes motorcycle rental):
- Driver, riding double, double occupancy .... DM 1,690
- Passenger, riding double, double occupancy .... DM 1,090
- Single rider, single occupancy .... DM 2,690

Price includes:
Round trip charter flight from Hamburg, Berlin, Frankfurt, and Dusseldorf (other cites cost more or less); accommodations for 14 days; and breakfasts. You should plan on at least DM 400 for other food for two weeks.

Motorcycle provisions:
A wide variety of motorcycles are available. The enduro bikes include: Yamaha XT 350, Yamaha DT 175, and Honda XL 600R. Others available are: Honda 650 and 750 (four-cylinder) soft-chopper style, Cagiva 350 two-stroke super sport, and other smaller machines.

Exploring the far reaches in Cyprus

Luggage provisions:
During this trip, you will stay in Polis every night except for two nights in the mountains of Troodos. Each person is responsible for carrying his own luggage.

Special notes:
Cyprus was a British Colony until 1960, so nearly everyone speaks and understands English. Most of the tourists who go to Cyprus annually are West Europeans. PKR's German tour guides speak English fluently.

GREECE	**Athens and The Cyclades**
Tour operator:	Von Thielmann Tours
Length of tour:	15 days
Dates:	• April 20 through May 4, 1991 • October 12 through October 26, 1991 • Similar dates in 1992 and 1993

Trip begins and ends: Athens, Greece

Highlights:
This tour starts with sightseeing of Athens, followed by island hopping in the Aegean, including those picturesque islands of Mykonos, Paros, Santorini, and Crete. Even though a motorcycle tour, this trip includes many visits to historical places. Following the tour, extension of your stay may be arranged.

Price (does not include motorcycle rental):
- Single rider, double occupancy $2,570
- Two people, double occupancy $5,140
- Single passenger, double occupancy $2,570
- Supplement for single room occupancy .... $ 685

Price includes:
Round trip air fare New York/Athens (or from other airports), hotel accommodations, breakfast daily (continental or buffet), domestic air fare from Crete to Athens, ferry boat transfers, half-day sightseeing tour of Athens including Acropolis, an original Taverna party (including dinner and music), airport/hotel/pier transfers, road maps, and a tour guide

Motorcycle provisions:
Rental motorcycles are available starting at $350, or you may bring your own.

Luggage provisions:
Luggage transportation is included in the tour price.

Lots of natural beauty to discover in Cyprus
(photo courtesy of Prima Klima Reisen)

TURKEY	**East Turkey**
Tour operator:	Von Thielmann Tours
Length of tour:	14 days
Dates:	April through October; biweekly departures
Trip begins and ends:	Munich, Germany

Highlights:
This tour features 14 days in the important border region of Turkey. This small group (ten or under) travels with their tour guide to the coast of the Black Sea, along the border of Russian Georgia to Mt. Ararat, which is 17,000 feet above sea level. They continue through the mountainous border region with Iraq and Iran and return to the city of Erzurum.

Price (includes motorcycle rental):
- Single rider, double occupancy .... DM 3,850
- Passenger, double occupancy .... DM 3,150

Price includes:
Airfare from Munich to Erzurum, hotels, half-board (daily breakfast plus either lunch or dinner), gasoline, guide, and sightseeing expenses

Motorcycle provisions:
Enduro type motorcycles with dual seat

Luggage provisions:
A support vehicle carries luggage. Bring your own riding gear and helmet.

TURKEY	**West Turkey**
Tour operator:	Von Thielmann Tours
Length of tour:	14 days
Dates:	April through October; biweekly departures
Trip begins and ends:	Munich, West Germany

Highlights:
Guided sightseeing tour leaves from the Aegean city of Bodrum. The 14-day trip visits the ancient cities of Ephesus and Pamukkal, the south of Turkey and the Aegean coast.

Price (includes motorcycle rental):
- Single rider, double occupancy .... DM 3,850
- Passenger, double occupancy .... DM 3,150

Price includes:
Airfare from Munich to Bodrum, hotels, half-board (daily breakfast and either lunch or dinner), gasoline, guide, and sightseeing expenses

Motorcycle provisions:
Enduro type motorcycles with dual seat

Luggage provisions:
A support vehicle carries luggage. Bring your own riding gear and helmet.

Time out for a picnic
(photo courtesy of Prima Klima Reisen)

ORGANIZED TOURS – AFRICA & MIDDLE EAST

216 ORGANIZED TOURS – AFRICA & MIDDLE EAST

ALGERIA

Algeria and Niger (Explo-Tours #TEN)

White dessert!

Tour operator:	Explo-Tours
Length of tour:	Four and one half weeks, covering approximately 7,000 km; 4,000 km off-road
Dates:	March 7 through April 7, 1992
Trip begins:	Genoa, Italy
Trip ends:	Marseille, France

Highlights:
Explo-Tours calls this tour "Arbre du Tenere" (Tree of the Desert). Thousands of years ago there was no desert in this huge area; instead, there existed vegetation and animals that allowed men to live in comfort. In Niger still today you can find many tools of this stone age when the land flourished. As time went on the land grew barren and eventually there was left only one single tree, the "Arbre du Tenere", a meeting point of many caravans. On this trip you will follow the tracks of the last camel convoys with your motorcycle through a sea of hard dunes. You will see people who still live in medieval style.

Price (does not include motorcycle rental):
- Single rider, double occupancy .... DM 4,480
- Pillion passenger, double occupancy .... DM 4,380

- Surcharge for single tent . . . . DM   100

Price includes:
Ship from Genoa to Tunis and back from Tunis to Marseille for cycle and driver, tour guide, transportation, luggage, fuel, all meals in Africa, camping fees, and two hotels in Tunis

Not included in price:
Gasoline, drinks, and additional hotel accommodations

Motorcycle provisions:
A good enduro motorcycle is suggested for this trip. You may bring your own or you may rent one from Explo-Tours. Rental available (new Suzuki DR 350, 27 hp) for DM 490 per week. Price includes mileage, insurance, fuel, and gas.

Luggage provisions:
A van will accompany this tour to carry luggage.

Special notes:
The common language of this tour is German. The language in the countries in which you travel is French. The guide is also fluent in English and French. Clients come from throughout Europe. Physical and mental endurance, with endurocycle experience is required for this trip.

NORTH AFRICA	**Dakar to Tunis (Explo-Tours #M7)**
Tour operator:	Explo-Tours
Length of tour:	Three weeks
Dates:	March 12 through April 6, 1991
Trip begins:	Munich
Trip ends:	Genoa, Italy

Highlights:
This tour starts in Dakar, Africa's most westerly point and the capital of Senegal. It proceeds through Mali and Algeria and ends in Tunis, Tunisia. The climate will be hot and dry in the west and excellent summer-like weather in Tunisia.

Price (does not include motorcycle rental):
- Single rider, double occupancy .... DM 4,950
- Passenger in van, double occupancy .... DM 4,450

Price includes:
Flight from Munich to Dakar, ferry from Tunis to Genoa, transport for your motorcycle from Munich to Dakar and from Tunis to Genoa, hotel for one night in Dakar and Tunis, welcome banquet in Senegal, two-person tent accomodations, full meals throughout the tour, and transport for your luggage

Not included in price:
Gasoline, drinks, food on ferry, or hotel accommodations

Motorcycle provisions:
Your motorcycle will be containerized and shipped from Munich to Tunis, and from Tunis to Genoa by sea. When Explo-Tours receives your DM 400 deposit for space, they will tell you whether your reservation has been accepted.

Rental available (new Suzuki DR 350, 27 hp) for DM 490 per week. Price includes mileage, insurance, fuel, and gas.

Luggage provisions:
A van will accompany this tour to carry luggage.

Special notes:
The common language of this tour is German. Guide also fluent in English and French. Clients come from throughout Europe. Physical and mental endurance, along with endurocycle experience is strongly suggested for this trip.

CENTRAL AFRICA	**Douala to Mombasa (Explo-Tours #MOM)**
Tour operator:	Explo-Tours
Length of tour:	Four weeks, covering approximately 6,000 km along the equator; 4,000 km off-road
Dates:	November 25 through December 23, 1991
Trip begins and ends:	Munich, West Germany

Highlights:
You'll need steady nerves for this trip. Follow ever-changing trails from the white sands of Limbet to the black sands of Mombasa. Roll through Cameroon on red dusty paths that become impassable mud trenches in a sudden tropical downpour. Push through the rain forest in Zaire. Cross one of Africa's largest rivers on a primitive raft. Perhaps you'll see members of the Bambuti tribe; these pygmies are the world's smallest people. From the slogging mud of the rain forest, you'll steam up mountains and zoom down the valleys of Uganda on your way to Africa's highest peak at Mt. Kilamanjaro. Unwind on the last run of tar road into Mombasa on the shores of the Indian Ocean.

"How come the bike gets to ride and I get to walk?"

Price (does not include motorcycle rental):
- Single rider, double occupancy .... DM 5,900
- Pillion passenger, double occupancy .... DM 4,950
- Supplement for single tent .... DM 100

Price includes:
Flights from Munich to Douala and Nairobi to Munich, tour guide, food in Africa, tents, and camping fees

Not included in price:
Gasoline, food on ferry, drinks, or hotel accommodations

Motorcycle provisions:
Your motorcycle will be containerized and shipped from Munich to Douala and from Nairobi to Munich by sea as part of the tour cost. Rental available (new Suzuki DR 350, 27 hp) for DM 490 per week. Price includes mileage, insurance, fuel, and gas.

Luggage provisions:
A van will accompany this tour to carry luggage.

Special notes:
The common language of this tour is German. Guide also fluent in English and French. Clients come from throughout Europe. Physical and mental endurance, with endurocycle experience required for this trip.

ALGERIA

High Dunes and Deep Valleys: Algeria (Explo-Tours #M2)

Tour operator:
Explo-Tours

Length of tour:
Three weeks, covering approximately 4,000 km (1,800 rough km)

Dates:
April 4 through April 27, 1992

Trip begins and ends:
Genoa, Italy

Highlights:
Only 500 kilometers of asphalt before you thrust into the desert sand track of Algeria. Leave El Oued Oasis, pass Arab market villages, and bear south across the dunes of the Great Western Plateau. Conquer the 600 meter sand dune. Storm off of the barely visible track for even more challenging trails across the dunes. Brave the northern boundaries of Plateau of the Dead. Climb the high plateau for a stunning view of the Tassili Mountains, part of the Hoggar Range. Navigate the wadis that crease the high plateau. You'll visit an important center for oil pumping in In Amenas. Master the descent from the plateau; migrate across the Great Eastern Desert toward the oasis of El Oued and the beautiful shining Mediterranean.

Making camp, Hoggar Mountains

Price (does not include motorcycle rental):
- Single rider, double occupancy .... DM 3,290
- Motorcycle passenger, double occupancy .... DM 3,190
- Surcharge for single tent .... DM   100

Price includes:
Round trip ferry Genoa to Tunis, tour guide, all meals in Africa, tents and camping fees, and two hotels in Tunis

Not included in price:
Gasoline, food on ferry, drinks, and additional hotel accommodations

Motorcycle provisions:
Your own motorcycle accompanies you round trip from Genoa to Tunis. Rental available (new Suzuki DR 350, 27 hp) for DM 490 per week. Price includes mileage, insurance, fuel, and gas.

Luggage provisions:
A van will accompany this tour to carry luggage.

Special notes:
The common language of this tour is German. Guide also fluent in English and French. Clients come from throughout Europe. Physical and mental endurance, along with endurocycle experience is strongly suggested for this trip.

SOUTH AFRICA — Mombasa to Capetown (Explo-Tours #CAP)

Tour operator:	Explo-Tours
Length of tour:	Four weeks
Dates:	December 28, 1991 through January 26, 1992
Trip begins and ends:	Munich, West Germany

Highlights:
Within a few miles after leaving Mombasa, you'll cross into Tanzania, one of the wildest countries in Africa. Visit the Mikumi National Park where zebras, elephants, hyenas, gazelles, even lions and other animals will frequently cross your path. You'll see great rivers, great Ruaha, Sambesi, Victoria Falls, and many other well-known natural sites.

You finish your journey in Capetown, South Africa and fly back to Munich from there.

Price (does not include motorcycle rental):
- Single rider, double occupancy .... DM 5,950
- Pillion passenger, double occupancy .... DM 5,150
- Supplement for single tent .... DM 100

Price includes:
Flights Munich to Mombasa and Capetown to Munich, tour guide, food in Africa, tents, camping fees, and hotel in Mombasa and Capetown

Not included in price:
Gasoline, food on ship, drinks, or hotel accommodations

Motorcycle provisions:
Your motorcycle will be containerized and shipped from Munich to Mombasa and Capetown to Munich by sea as part of the tour cost. Rental available (new Suzuki DR 350, 27 hp) for DM 490 per week. Price includes mileage, insurance, fuel, and gas.

Luggage provisions:
A van will accompany this tour to carry luggage.

Special notes:
The common language of this tour is German. The language in the countries from Kenya to South Africa is English. Guide also fluent in English and French. Clients come from throughout Europe. Physical and mental endurance, with endurocycle experience required for this trip.

WEST AFRICA — Tunis to Douala (Explo-Tours #DLA)

Tour operator:	Explo-Tours
Length of tour:	28 days, approx. 6,000 km; 2,000 km off-road
Dates:	October 26 through November 22, 1991
Trip begins:	Genoa, Italy
Trip ends:	Munich, West Germany

Highlights:
Drive through desert, brush, and tropical forest from the Mediterranean to the Gulf of Guinea. In the Great Sahara, you'll feel as if your motorcycle stands still and the earth rotates under you. You'll lose your sense of perspective in the endless yellow sand of the dunes and feel as if you move in a third dimension. Navigate the perils of sand with conditions ranging from soft powder to hard pack. Plunge into the Nigerian brush. Ride through Yankari Game Reserve in the company of jungle apes. With luck, you'll spot elephants or lions. Cross smooth roads to the Cameroon border. Then a short but difficult ride on the muddy Malfe Road brings you to beautiful Cameroon highlands. Except for lush banana, mango, and

ORGANIZED TOURS – AFRICA & MIDDLE EAST

Full power!

avocado trees along the road, you'll believe you're in the Swiss Alps. You'll need endurance for this tour, but it is accessible to every good rider.

Price (does not include motorcycle rental):
- Single rider, double occupancy .... DM 5,350
- Pillion passenger, double occupancy .... DM 4,850
- Surcharge for single tent .... DM   100

Price includes:
Ship from Genoa to Tunis for cycle and driver, tour guide, transportation by air from Douala to Munich, all meals in Africa, tents, and camping fees

Not included in price:
Gasoline, food on ferry, drinks, or hotel accommodations

Motorcycle provisions:
Containerized shipping of your motorcycle from Douala to Munich by ship. A good enduro motorcycle is suggested for this trip. You may bring your own or you may rent one from Explo-Tours. Rental available (new Suzuki DR 350, 27 hp) for DM 490 per week. Price includes mileage, insurance, fuel, and gas.

Luggage provisions:
A van will accompany this tour to carry luggage.

Special notes:
The common language of this tour is German. Guide also fluent in English and French. Clients come from throughout Europe. Physical and mental endurance, along with endurocycle experience is strongly suggested for this trip.

SOUTH AFRICA	**South Africa**
Tour operator:	mhs Motorradtouren GmbH
Length of tour:	17 days, or 22 days
Dates:	*17-day tours* • February 24 through March 12, 1991 • December 21, 1991 through January 6, 1992 • Similar dates in 1992 *22-day tours* • November 29 through December 20, 1991 • January 12 through February 3, 1992 • Similar dates in 1992
Trip begins and ends:	Frankfurt, Germany

Highlights:

You have probably heard about the overwhelming beauty of South Africa. Because of the Apartheid policy of the white minority government the country has been held in poor regard for several years, and was under an international embargo. Since Nelson Mandela was set free, many of the inhuman laws have been abolished, and South Africa has become more than ever worth a holiday trip.

Now you have the opportunity to see the country from the saddle of a motorcycle. Sunshine, warm temperatures, and excellent roads make this trip very pleasant. South Africa's hotels and food are among the best in the world, and the game reserves are famous for their variety and number of wild animals. You will learn that riots, of which much is heard in our news, have little influence on everyday life. On a day-to-day basis there is little tension between people of different colors.

Your trip begins in Johannesburg, where you pick up your rental bike from BMW and head toward Eastern Transvaal. Set among beautiful landscapes similar to the Scottish Highlands you'll find your first hotel, a beautiful countryside house with individually designed lodges. The tour continues to Blyde River Canyon, "God's Window" and Kruger National Park. One of your destinations is a two-night stay at a private game park with fully equipped bungalows and a friendly staff to take care of you. Enjoy wandering with a ranger or join the night game drive with a spotlight.

Continue southward, passing the citrus plantations of Nelspruit before reaching the Kingdom of Swaziland, one of the rare places where gambling is allowed. Return the next day to South Africa and spend an afternoon in Hluhluwe National Park, where the world's largest population of the rare "white" rhino lives. After a fabulous ride along the coastline of the Indian Ocean, you'll visit a real Zulu village. Travel on to Transkei, where Nelson Mandela was born, and visit a very original part of South Africa. East London, Port Elizabeth, and the Garden Route are your next stops along the coastline of the Indian Ocean before turning into the Little Karoo, a semidesert. Nearly 90 percent of all ostriches in the world are living there.

Continue to Cape Town, one of the most beautiful cities in the world. Climb up to the lighthouse on the Cape of Good Hope and visit the vineyards on the Cape Peninsula. The 17-day trip ends with a comfortable ride in the Trans Karoo Express train back to Johannesburg. The 22-day trip continues by motorcycle to Johannesburg.

While this trip is not a cheap holiday, mhs Motorradtouren believes it is worth more than the price. They want you to sample the finest food, excellent hotels, and the best of nature and game this country has to offer.

Price (includes motorcycle rental):

	17-day tour	22-day tour
• Single rider, double occupancy	DM 7,995	DM 9,350
• Motorcycle or van passenger, dbl. occupancy	DM 6,995	DM 7,950
• Supplement for single room occupancy	DM 900	DM 1,200
• Supplement for trip during Christmas	DM 300	

Note: For both trips a deposit of Rand (R) 1,000 is required when taking a rental bike. The deposit is fully refundable when the bike is returned undamaged.

Price includes:
Round trip flight between Frankfurt and Johannesburg, accommodation in first-class and deluxe hotels, best food (full board, often à la carte), entry fees to National Parks, game drives, and a tour guide. The 17-day trip
includes a sleeping compartment on the Trans Karoo Express train, but without food during the train trip.

Motorcycle provisions:
BMW rental bikes are included in the tour price. Available bikes include R80 RT, R80G/S Paris-Dakar, or K75 C with windscreen. (All bikes are fully insured with a deductible of ZAR 250 min. or 5 percent of damage costs.)

Luggage provisions:
A minibus accompanies this trip to carry luggage and passengers. This car also is used for sightseeing trips and for some of the game drives.

Special notes:
The primary languages for this tour are English and German.

EGYPT	**Motorrad Expedition Sahara**
Tour operator:	Motorrad Expedition Sahara
Length of tour:	Seven days and 14 days
Dates:	*Seven-day tour* • March 27 through April 3, 1991 *14-day tour* • March 10 through March 24, 1991 • April 7 through April 21, 1991 Other dates available; contact tour operator.
Trip begins and ends:	Cairo, Egypt

Highlights:
The Sahara tour takes you through the harsh and vast Egyptian desert. You will fly past the pyramids of Giza and under the eyes of the Sphinx. Using old caravan trails you will travel deep into the Sahara Desert past ancient Roman forts, over huge sand dunes and through oases that are a thousand years old. The tour descends into the Nile river valley and crosses the river into Luxor, the ancient capital of Eygpt, to see Karnak, the Mortuary Temples, and the Valley of the Kings. Spend a day at the Red Sea sailing, snorkeling, and scuba diving.

At night you'll cook on an open fire and camp under a clear sky filled with a billion stars. Test your endurance in some of the toughest conditions on earth.

Price:
• Seven days, per person .... U.S. $1,800
• 14 days, per person .... U.S. $2,500

Price includes:
Motorcycle rental, fuel, accommodations (camping gear and hotels), meals (participants are expected to help prepare food), entry fees to attractions, service vehicles, medical, and mechanical assistance if needed

Not included in price:
Air fare to Cairo, damage to motorcycles

Motorcycle provisions:
Rental of an XT600 Ténéré, XR600R, or XTZ750 is included in the price of the tour.

Luggage provisions:
A service vehicle carries excess luggage, but each person is expected to carry his own sleeping bag and a small backpack for personal items.

Special notes:
- This tour requires you to travel and camp in harsh desert conditions.
- The principal language of this tour is German, but English can be spoken if necessary.
- This tour is for experienced motorcyclists in good physical condition.
- The tour organizers reserve the right to refuse and select customers.
- Group size is restricted to five to ten people per tour.
- Participants are responsible for providing their own gear, including helmets, jackets, boots, sleeping bag, water bottle, etc.
- At least five participants are required for a tour to take place.

EGYPT	Egypt Short Tour
Tour operator:	Sahara Cross
Length of tour:	One week
Dates:	• September 14 through September 20, 1991 • September 21 through September 27, 1991 • Similar dates in 1992
Trip begins and ends:	Munich, Germany

Highlights:
This short tour is designed to give you a good taste of Cairo, Alexandria, and the surrounding places of interest.

The trip starts with a sightseeing tour of Cairo and one night in a campsite bungalow. Travel to Alexandria over asphalt roads and return to Cairo via the Nile Valley. Visit the Fayum oasis, leaving a free day that you'll plan while on your journey.

Price (includes motorcycle rental):
- Single rider, double occupancy .... DM 1,960
- Passenger, double occupancy .... DM 1,760

228 ORGANIZED TOURS – AFRICA & MIDDLE EAST

Price includes:
Round trip airfare Munich/Cairo/Munich, transfers, hotel accommodations with breakfast, tools and spare parts, experienced tour guide and gasoline.

Not included in price:
Insurance, meals, and entrance fees

Motorcycle provisions:
Yamaha XT 500 is included in the price of tour.

Luggage provisions:
A van accompanies each tour to carry luggage.

EGYPT — Egypt Tour

Tour operator:	Sahara Cross
Length of tour:	Three weeks, covering approximately 3,000 km (Cairo to Aswan and back)
Dates:	• October 5 through October 25, 1991 • October 3 through October 23, 1992
Trip begins and ends:	Munich, Germany

Highlights:
Revel in an enduro paradise from Cairo to the head of the Nile River and back to Cairo. Battle sand and biting sandstorms from the limestone formations in the white desert to grandiose landscapes where yellow sand stretches from horizon to horizon. Camp in the oasis of Farafra. Bathe in its hot springs in the midst of the desert. Superior

"What do you mean, 'there's sand on the bike'?"

drivers press on to the mountain desert. Trek through 150 kilometers of sand, stone, and gravel to Luxor. Journey over mountains and valleys to Aswan, head of the Nile River Valley. Leave the road for 30 kilometers of rough gravel riding to an ancient Roman fortress. Run through deep red granite gorges and over wadis, dry beds that become rushing streams in the rainy season. You'll persevere through rock, sand, and desert heat for a motorcycling adventurer's thrills in the land of ancient pyramids.

Price (includes motorcycle rental):
- Single rider, double occupancy .... DM 4,090
- Passenger, double occupancy .... DM 3,330
- Passenger, riding in the luggage van .... DM 2,500

Price includes:
Round trip airfare Munich/Cairo/Munich, transfers, hotel accommodations with breakfast, tools and spare parts, lunch and dinner in desert camps, farewell banquet, experienced tour guide, medical treatment, damage insurance — covered up to DM 50 and over DM 1,000 (guest pays up to 1,000 DM for serious damage), baggage loss insurance

Price does not include:
Gasoline (about DM 220); lunch and dinner in Cairo, Karga, Luxor, and Safaga (total cost, about DM 100); or malaria pills

Motorcycle provisions:
Yamaha XT 500 is included in the price of tour.

Luggage provisions:
A van accompanies each tour to carry luggage.

Special notes:
This tour is for experienced enduro riders only. It requires considerable physical stamina and will place exceptional demands on riders. The tour guide speaks fluent English as well as German. The last half day will be spent cleaning the motorcycles before turning them in.

NORTH AFRICA	**Sinai Tour**
Tour operator:	Sahara Cross
Length of tour:	14 days, approximately 1,500 km
Dates:	• November 2 through November 15, 1991 • November 7 through November 20, 1991
Trip begins and ends:	Munich, Germany

Highlights:
Watch the sun rise on the commanding peak of majestic Mt. Sinai. You'll always remember the wildness of this overpowering mountain world and the colorful array of rocks in the sunlight. Visit the Katherina monastery. Camp at spectacular beaches along the bays of the Sinai. In the Gulf of Aqaba, you'll snorkel in the world's most beautiful coral reefs. Alternate days of water sport with one- and two-day forays into the desert.

Price (includes motorcycle rental):
- Single rider, double occupancy .... DM 3,090
- Passenger, double occupancy .... DM 2,290
- Passengers riding in the luggage van .... DM 1,590

Price includes:
Round trip airfare; transfers; hotel accommodations with breakfast; tools and spare parts; lunch and dinner; farewell banquet; experienced tour guide; medical treatment; damage insurance — covered up to DM 50 and over DM 1,000 (guest pays up to DM 1,000 for serious damage); and baggage loss insurance.

Not included in price:
Gasoline

Motorcycle provisions:
Yamaha XT 500 is included in price of tour.

Luggage provisions:
Luggage van accompanies tour.

Special notes:
This tour is for experienced enduro riders only. It requires considerable physical stamina and will place exceptional demands on riders. The tour guide speaks fluent English as well as German.

SOUTH AFRICA	**The Safari Rider**
Tour operator:	TransCyclist International
Length of tour:	One week to ten days (subject to request), covering approximately 2,000 to 3,000 km

Dates:
Monthly year round (dates subject to booking requests and minimum six participants)

Trip begins and ends:	Johannesburg, South Africa

Highlights:
Experience the true African *Born Free* on TransCyclist's (TC) ultimate bike adventure: The Safari Rider Tour. Enjoy clean spacious roadways with generous turnouts next to breathtaking views of a steamy wilderness. Bring your camera, there are plenty of photo opportunities. Big game graze along the side of the trail. Sounds, smells, and tastes from Africa will be deeply engraved in your memory. Have a chat with the friendly natives, children of the sun. Explore the remote areas in Southern Africa where you can still find the genuine Africa away from commercialization. The Safari Rider Tour is a challenge for the long-distance tourer and off-road enthusiast.

Price (includes motorcycle rental):
- Single rider, double occupancy $1,600
- Passenger (van), double occupancy ....$ 990

Price includes:
All hotels and bush camps, breakfasts and dinners, information packet, guiding, luggage transport, four-wheel drive van, airport transfers, game reserve visits, and motorcycle rental

Not included in price:
Fuel, oil, lunch, snacks, travel accident insurance, and a $500 U.S. refundable insurance bond

Motorcycle provisions:
Mostly Japanese makes — 500cc and up

Luggage provisions:
Four-wheel drive van will carry luggage for groups of ten or more participants.

Special notes:
International driver's license valid for motorcycle operation required by participants. You are advised to book at least three months in advance. Departure dates and prices are subject to change. Tour departure requires six minimum bookings. Send a self-addressed envelope and one international reply coupon (available from the post office) when inquiring about the tour.

"How far back did you see that gas station?"

ORGANIZED TOURS – ASIA & INDONESIA

CHINA China Motorcycle Expedition 1991

A crowd gathers to greet a very unusual visitor.

Tour operator:	Aushina Tours
Length of tour:	22 days including international air time
Dates:	April 13 through May 4, 1991, from Australia
Trip begins:	Hong Kong
Trip ends:	Beijing

Highlights:
The tour begins in Hong Kong where you will have two and a half days for sightseeing and shopping before departing for Hangzhou, China. There you will start your thirteen-day journey over mountains and rivers along China's eastern coast, through remote villages and small towns. You will cross the water to an off-coast Buddhist pilgrim island, and encounter an occasional rural bazaar in addition to farmers with their buffaloes working in the paddy fields.

Turning inland you will see different ethnic peoples and mountain tribes. Then travel by cable car up the Huangshan mountains, which for hundreds of years, have been the subject of Chinese scroll paintings. There you will stay overnight in a summit guest house before descending the mountain past West Lake and into the city of Hangzhou. You will travel by air to Beijing to explore China's ancient capital. This three-day stop allows you to visit Beijing's many attractions, such as the Forbidden City and the Great Wall. The tour ends in Beijing.

Price (includes motorcycle rental):
- Per rider, double occupancy .... AUS $3,581
- Passenger, double occupancy .... AUS $3,281

Note: Prices are subject to change in accordance with Chinese and Hong Kong tariffs.

Price includes:
Hotel accommodations for 20 nights, all meals in China, breakfasts only in Hong Kong, 13 days of motorcycle rental in China, fuel, service vehicle, guides, and three days of bus tours in China

Not included in price:
Participants originating elsewhere than Australia must make their own flight arrangements to Hong Kong and home from Beijing. No travel insurance is included in the tour price. Each traveler is responsible for his or her own insurance, including coverage for injury.

Motorcycle provisions:
A Chinese Xihu-250c motorcycle (brand new for 1991) is provided to each rider.

Luggage provisions:
A service vehicle is available to carry your luggage.

Special notes:
Tour is limited to fifteen motorcycles and their passengers. Passengers (paying AUS $300 less than riders) may travel in the service van if they wish. Participants must make sure that their insurance provides full coverage for trip.

Cyclists gather at water's edge for ferry ride in China
(photo courtesy of Von Thielmann Tours)

BALI	Motorcycle Vacation in Bali
Tour operator:	Bike Tours Australia
Length of tour:	19 days
Dates:	Whenever you want to go
Trip begins and ends:	Frankfurt, Germany

Highlights:
Combine your hot, dusty Australia trip with a stopover in beautiful Bali. Here you can relax on the beach, or participate in one of the many festivals and processions throughout the island. This is a paradise of friendly, gentle people, with deep religious beliefs. Unlike the guided tours in this directory, this is actually a trip to Bali where you can sightsee and travel on your own around the island on a motorcycle.

Price (includes motorcycle rental):
- Single rider .... DM 3,450

Price includes:
Hotel accommodations for 19 nights at Rita's House, a beautiful inn near Kuta Beach (single rooms, private bath, tea, and bananas); round trip airfare from Frankfurt; touring information; maps; and motorcycle rental

Motorcycle provisions:
125cc to 250cc bikes provided

Luggage provisions:
Luggage provisions are not needed. The traveler is based in one inn, free to visit other parts of the island as the urge arises.

Special notes:
This tour is for European guests only, since the flight arrangements are from Frankfurt. However, for all travelers who want to enjoy a stopover on Bali and who will make their own flight arrangements, Bike Tours Australia will organize your Bali stop in the same beautiful inn near Kuta Beach. A single room is DM 25, a double room is DM 30, motorcycle rental is DM 30 per day, and transfers between airport and hotel are DM 30.

SOUTHEAST ASIA

Thailand Tour

Tour operator:
Bivak International

Length of tour:
17 days, with an option for a seven-day extension into western Thailand

Dates:
- July 13 through July 29, 1991
- July 27 thorugh August 12, 1991
- December 21, 1991 through January 5, 1992
- January 6 through January 20, 1992

"Where's the nearest laundramat?"

Trip begins and ends:	Amsterdam

Highlights:
Upon arrival in Bangkok the group travels by air to Chaing Mai where the motorcycling trip begins. The first half of the trip covers the North of Thailand, including the "Golden Triangle" and the area of the "hill tribes." The second half takes you through the western part of Thailand, an area covered by jungles and largely unexplored.

A seven-day off-road extension is also offered for this tour, covering western Thailand. During this extension, you'll travel from one extreme to another. From steep slopes paved with mud to knee-deep channels. Explore beautiful waterfalls and a desert island. Highlights include a visit to the bridge on the River Kwai and to a secret cave where in the evening thousands of bats make room for swallows.

Price (in Dutch florin):
- Basic tour, per person .... f. 4,309
- Seven-day off-road extension to western Thailand, per person .. f. 1,153

Price includes:
The price includes air fare from Amsterdam to Bangkok and return, air fare from Bangkok to Chiang Mai, bus fare from Chiang Mai to Bangkok, service van to carry luggage, rental of Honda 125 cc motorcycle, Thai cook, and Dutch tour guide. Seven-day extension includes: meals, motorcycle rental, fuel, lodging, transfer to western Thailand, luggage transportation, and a guide.

Not included in price:
Meals (approximately f. 165), fuel (approx. f. 45), airport taxes (approx. $8), camping equipment (approx. f. 140), and camping site fees

Motorcycle provisions:
Motorcycles are included in the tour price (Honda 125 cc).

Luggage provisions:
A service van is provided to carry luggage.

Special notes:
This tour travels through some fairly remote areas of Thailand. Riders are required to ride and camp in jungle terrain.
Camping equipment is available for rent from Bivak, but participants should bring a sleeping bag.

THAILAND	Chiang Mai Tour
Tour operator:	Chiang Mai Motorcycle Touring Club
Length of tour:	Anywhere from one to four weeks, depending on how long you want to stay
Dates:	Tours are available any time during the year. However, the wettest months of the rainy season are July through September and are not recommended for touring.
Trip begins and ends:	Chiang Mai, North Thailand

Highlights:
Chiang Mai Motorcycle Touring Club offers tours of northern Thailand that are tailored to your schedule and riding ability. They prefer working this way because it allows you to set the pace of the tour, giving you the most personal enjoyment.

All tours start with a two-day stay in Chiang Mai. This allows you some time to get accustomed to your motorcycle and the terrain that you will be riding on. It also allows you to explore Chiang Mai, Thailand's second-largest city.

On the third day you begin the tour that you and your guide have planned. Ride on roller coaster asphalt roads that crest mountains and meander through scenic valleys to remote locations or get serious and tackle the dirt trails, forging streams and crossing crude bridges that lead up steep mountains to isolated villages. Many diverse and colorful hill tribes reside here, each with its own history and customs.

Venture into the back woods of northern Thailand and visit the Golden Triangle, where Thailand's, Laos', and Burma's borders meet. Visit tranquil Buddhist temples, ride an elephant or tour the ruins of ancient civilizations. Experience the drama of precipitous waterfalls, hot springs, and geysers. Sample the world renown Thai cuisine or try some of the local liquor.

David Unkovich and a fellow rider pose with several budding Thai beauties

Price:
Chiang Mai Motorcycle Touring Club offers several price rates:
- Guide only; minimum of three motorcycles;
  per person per day .... Thai Baht (฿)   600
- All-inclusive package; minimum of four motorcycles;
  per person per day .... ฿ 1,500
- All-inclusive custom package; set tours of four to fourteen days;
  per person .... ฿8,300 to ฿ 25,000
- *Tour 1 - Golden Triangle:* seven nights, eight days .... ฿ 10,350
- *Tour 2 - Golden Triangle & Short Laos Border Run:*
  eight nights, nine days .... ฿ 11,600
- *Tour 3 - Laos Border Run:* 12 nights, 13 days .... ฿ 16,950
- *Tour 4 - Burma Border Run:* seven nights, eight days .... ฿ 10,150
- *Burma Border & Salween River Run:* 10 nights, 11 days .... ฿ 16,200

Price includes:
The second and third ("all-inclusive") price rates cover all breakfast and evening meals, fuel, motorcycle rental, and shared accommodations in anything from thatched huts to good hotels. The first price rate pays for the guide only. Riders must pay for everything else (food, fuel, motorcycle rental, and accommodations), except the guide's expenses.

Not included in price:
Insurance is not included in any of the tour prices and participants are urged to have proper insurance before leaving home; transportation from Bangkok to Chiang Mai is not included.

Motorcycle provisions:
Motorcycles (Honda 125 cc) are provide by Chiang Mai Motorcycle Touring to those who are in the tour.

Luggage provisions:
Participants are required to carry their own luggage and are advised to travel light: a small kit bag is adequate.

Special notes:
- Tour is limited to a minimum of three motorcycles and a maximum of eight motorcycles.
- Helmets are available for rent from Chiang Mai Motorcycle Touring.
- This tour travels through some fairly remote areas of Thailand. Riders are required to ride in jungle terrain and, depending on your choice of itinerary, you might stay in a thatched hut other local accommodations.
- David is a particularly keen photographer and welcomes photographers to join him. He carries a sturdy tripod on all tours.

SINGAPORE & MALAYSIA

Singapore–Malaysia Motorcycle Tour

Tour operator:	Cycle-East Adventures
Length of tour:	10 days, covering about 2,250 km
Dates:	• February 23 through March 4, 1991 • April 20 through April 29, 1991 • May 11 through May 20, 1991 • June 8 through June 17, 1991 • July 13 through July 22, 1991 • August 17 through August 26, 1991 • September 14 through September 23, 1991 • October 12 through October 21, 1991
Trip begins and ends:	Singapore

Highlights:
The Singapore–Malaysia Tour begins in the island nation of Singapore and heads north along the east coast of the Malaysian Peninsula to the city of Kota Bahru. You'll move along the Thailand border to Penang Island, on the west coast of Malaysia, to try some of the local cuisine and stay for the evening. Ride high up into the cool climate of Cameron High-

lands to visit a tea plantation. Ride south to the ancient city of Malacca for an evening's stay and end your trip in Singapore after a day of sightseeing.

Price (does not include motorcycle rental):
• Per person .... U.S. $1,000

Price includes:
A Continental/American breakfast each morning, at least five dinners, accommodations in comfortable rooms with air conditioning and full amenities, and 24-hour breakdown service

Not included in price:
Lunches, fuel, and handling charges for those shipping their motorcycle

Motorcycle provisions:
Harley-Davidson motorcycles are available for rent, to tour participants only, for a price of approximately U.S. $1,000, including insurance. Cycle-East will arrange for your motorcycle to be transported to Singapore, if desired.

Luggage provisions:
A luggage van is available to carry excess luggage.

INDIA	**Desert Tour**
Tour operator:	Indsun Adventure Tours
Length of tour:	22 days, covering approximately 3,000 km (Alternate tour is 15 days, covering approximately 2,200 km and omitting some of the places described below.)
Dates:	*1991* • January 5 through January 26 • February 2 through February 23 • March 2 through March 23 • March 30 through April 20 • April 27 through May 18 • October 5 through October 26 • November 2 through November 23 • November 30 through December 21 • December 21, 1991 through January 11, 1992

1992
- January 18 through February 8
- February 15 through March 7
- March 14 through April 4
- April 11 through May 2
- October 3 through October 24
- October 31 through November 21
- November 28 through December 19
- December 19, 1992 through January 9, 1993

Trip begins and ends:	Delhi

Highlights:

Begin your tour with an afternoon of sightseeing around Delhi. The next day you will tarvel by bus to Alwar, where the motorcycle tour begins. You'll then proceed to Mandawa, which is famous for its wall paintings, and stay in the Maharaja's palace. The next stop is Bikaner, famous for its camel-breeding farm. You'll then move into the Great Indian Desert via the city of Jaisalmer.

Next, climb the mountain roads until you reach the hilltop station Mount Abu. From here it is only a short distance to Udaipur, the city of lakes. Before reaching Bundi, home of the erstwhile Maharaja of Bundi, you will visit the world's largest fort, in Chittaurgarh.

Next is the ancient city of Pushkar, with its holy lake. This city dates back to the fourth century when it was cited by Chinese traveller Fa Hien as a great pilgrim center. The next stop is Jaipur, the capital of Rajasthan.

You will travel through Bharatpur and Fatehpur Sikri, the abandoned city, until you reach Agra and the Taj Mahal, one of the architectural wonders of the world. On the way to the Sariska Tiger Sanctuary, you'll visit Lord Krishna's birthplace, Vrindavan. Continue through the quiet serenity of Sariska to Delhi, where the tour ends.

The alternate tour follows the same route as the desert tour except that it makes a detour at Jaisalmer and journeys through Jodhpur instead of going south through Mount Abu and Bundi. It reconnects with the desert tour route at Pushkar and heads north to Jaipur, Alwar and Delhi, where it ends.

Price (includes motorcycle rental):
- Per person $2,625
- Shorter tour, per person $2,430

Price includes:

Twin bed accommodations in modest to five star hotels, accompanying service team and van, fuel, helmet, airport transfers for group flight passengers only, entrance fees to all major sites, all meals, and motorcycle rental, insurance, and maintenance

Price does not include:
Drinks, laundry, phone, tips, visa, international and internal Indian flights, or airport departure taxes

Motorcycle provisions:
Enfield motorcycles are provided by Indsun Adventure Tours and are included in the tour price.

Luggage provisions:
A service vehicle is provided for excess luggage.

INDIA — Garwhal Mountain Tour

Tour operator:	Indsun Adventure Tours
Length of tour:	15 days, covering approximately 1,800 km
Dates:	*1991* • March 2 through March 16 • March 30 through April 13 • April 27 through May 11 • October 5 through October 19 • November 2 through November 16 • November 30 through December 14 • December 21, 1991 through January 4, 1992 *1992* • January 18 through February 1 • February 15 through February 29 • March 14 through March 28 • April 11 through April 25 • October 3 through October 17 • October 31 through November 14 • November 28 through December 12 • December 19, 1992 through January 2, 1993
Trip begins and ends:	New Delhi

Tour guides Himmat Gingh and Hans-Joachim Klein inspect their vehicles

Highlights:
Once you get the feeling for the Indian traffic in Delhi, you'll start for Nainital. Those who love the mountains are in for a treat because from here on you travel northwest over 1100 kilometers of mountain roads

through Almora, Kausani, Ranikhet, Corbett National Park, and Lansdowne to Rishikesh. Near Rishikesh you board a boat for a rafting expedition on the Ganga river. For three days you'll have to fight the rapids of the mighty Ganga and at night you'll stay in jungle camps. After leaving the mountains and riding down the Indian plains, you return to Delhi where the tour ends.

Price (includes motorcycle rental):
Per person $2,430

Price includes:
Twin bed accommodations in a modest to five star hotel, an accompanying service team, fuel, helmet, airport transfers for group passengers only, boat fare, entrance fees to all major sites, all meals, and motorcycle rental, insurance, and maintenance

Price does not include:
Drinks, laundry, phone, tips, visa, international and internal Indian flights, and airport departure taxes

Motorcycle provisions:
Enfield motorcycles are provided by Indsun Adventure Tours and are included in the price of the tour.

Luggage provisions:
A service vehicle is available to carry your excess luggage.

Special notes:
You must carry a sleeping bag on this tour.

INDIA	**Grand India Tour**
Tour operator:	Indsun Adventure Tours
Length of tour:	22 days, covering approximately 4,200 km
Dates:	*1991* • August 3 through August 24 • September 7 through September 28 • October 5 through October 26 • November 9 through November 30 • December 14, 1991 through January 4, 1992

1992
- January 18 through February 8
- August 8 through August 29
- September 12 through October 3
- October 17 through November 7
- November 21 through December 12
- December 19, 1992 through January 9, 1993

Trip begins and ends:
Begins in Delhi, ends in Bombay or vice versa

Highlights:
This tour begins with an afternoon of sightseeing in Delhi. The next day you will take a bus ride to Alwar, where the motorcycle tour begins. Ride to Jaipur, which is rich in Indian culuture, via Amber and Nahargarh Fort. The next day you will reach Pushkar, known for its holy lake, and then procede to Udaipur, which is nestled in the fold of the Arravali hills.

Take the Delhi-Bombay highway until you reach Ahmedabad, home of Mahatama Gandhi. It is from there that Gandhi began his famous march to Dandi beach. You'll stop in Daman, a small town on the Arabian Sea and then proceed into Matheran and the Western Ghats, where the mountain range begins.

The tour then travels down the coast through Mahabaleshwar and Ratanagiri to Goa, where it stops for a few days for you to enjoy the beaches there. Continue further south to Jog falls, India's highest water fall, and then on to Calicut, on the Spice Coast. Here, Vasco da Gama landed in 1498, resulting in Europe's direct access to Indian spices.

Still following the coast south, you will visit Kanyakumari and India's finest wooden building, Padmanabhapuram Palace. At the southernmost tip of India you will visit Vivekananda Rock Memorial. You'll travel north to Kottayam and then by boat to Cochin. For a day of sightseeing you stay in Bombay before the tour ends.

"May I bring a quart of oil for your motorcycle, sir?"

Price (includes motorcycle rental):
Per person $2,625

Price includes:
Twin bed accommodations in modest to five star hotels, accompanying service team and van, fuel, helmet, airport transfers for group passengers only, entrance fees to all major sites, all meals, and motorcycle rental, insurance and maintenance

Price does not include:
Drinks, laundry, phone, tips, visa, international and internal Indian flights, and airport departure taxes

Motorcycle provisions:
Enfield motorcycles are provided by Indsun Adventure Tours and are included in the price of the tour.

Luggage provisions:
A service van is available to carry excess luggage.

Special notes:
This tour covers 150-180 miles per day and reqiures a lot of stamina.

INDIA AND NEPAL	**Himalaya Tour**
Tour operator:	Indsun Adventure Tours
Length of tour:	22 days, covering approximately 3,800 km
Dates:	*1991* • June 15 through July 6 • July 20 through August 10 • August 24 through September 14 • September 28 through October 19 • November 2 through November 23 *1992* • June 13 through July 4 • July 18 through August 8 • August 22 through September 12 • September 26 through October 17 • October 31 through November 21
Trip begins and ends:	New Delhi

Highlights:
From the capital city of Delhi ride north climbing steadily to the popular hill resort of Mussoorie. Along the mountains, you'll go westward to Nahan, famous for the discovery of prehistoric animals. Through the lower Himalaya ranges you'll climb up to Mandi leaving behind the hot Indian plains. At Dharmsala you might be able to see His Holiness, the Dalai-Lama; this part of the Kangra Valley has a strong Tibetan influence. The next stop, Dalhousie, transports you back to the times of the British Raj. You'll then pass through Jammu until you reach Kud. After crossing the pass there is a fine view of the Kashmir Valley. In Srinagar you'll enjoy

the luxury of a houseboat. Here you'll rest because the road to Ladakh is a demanding ride.

Sonamarg is your last stop before you enter Ladakh. Here you might wonder if you are still on the earth or swallowed by the mighty Himalayas. From Leh to Rothang Pass you have to cross the highest mountain passes in the world. Coming down to Manali you enter the Kulu Valley. This beautifully placed hill resort is known for its hot sulphur springs. Take a bath in the springs and soak away your travel tiredness. After visiting Chandigarh, you'll return to Delhi where the tour ends.

Price (includes motorcycle rental):
Per person $2,625

Price includes:
Twin bed accommodations in modest to five star hotels, entrance fees to all major sites, airport transfers for group flight passengers only, all meals, fuel, helmet, accompanying service team, houseboat ride in Srinagar, and motorcycle rental, insurance, and maintenance

Price does not include:
Drinks, laundry, phone, tips, visa, International and internal Indian flights, and sleeping bag (needed for trip)

Motorcycle provisions:
Enfield motorcycles are provided by Indsun Adventure Tours and are included in the tour price.

Luggage provisions:
Limited excess luggage will be carried by the service vehicle.

INDIA — **Nilgiri Tour**

Tour operator:	Indsun Adventure Tours
Length of tour:	22 days
Dates:	*1991* • August 31 through September 9 • November 2 through November 23 • December 14, 1991 through January 4, 1992 *1992* • January 11 through February 1

- February 8 through February 29
- August 29 through September 19
- October 3 through October 24
- November 7 through November 28
- December 12, 1992 through January 2, 1993

Trip begins and ends:	Bombay

Highlights:
This tour travels within the southern section of India. It begins in Kottayam and then moves on through the paddy fields to Quilon. The next destination is Kovalam beach, where you can take a swim in the warm Arabian sea or enjoy a walk along the beach that is referred to as the "Venus of the East."

The next stop is Kanyakumari, where a boat trip is planned to visit the Vivekananda Rock Memorial. After that you then move on through Madurai, where you will visit the Shree Meenakshi Temple, to Tanjore and Pondicherry. It is only a short ride to Mahabalipuram, where you can relax or visit the romantic Shore temples before the long ride to Bangalore.

Gradually you will notice the climate becoming less hot as you climb up the Deccan plateau and into the Bangalore. You'll stop for the evening in Mysore, famous for its sandalwood and silk weaving, and the next day you'll visit the Mudumalai Wildlife Sanctuary. The tour then moves through Anamalai, Kodaikanal, and Periyar, slowly descending through the tea gardens and rubber plantations to Kottayam. From Kottayam you will travel by boat along the backwaters and lovely tree-lined lagoons to Cochin, where Mattancherry and Fort Cochin await your exploration. After enjoying a night of entertainment by traditional Kerala dancers, you will fly back to Bombay where your tour ends.

Price (includes motorcycle rental):
Per person $2,625

Price includes:
Twin bed accommodations in a modest to five star hotel, an accompanying service team, fuel, helmet, airport transfers for group passengers only, boat fare, entrance fees to all major sites, all meals, and motorcycle rental, insurance, and maintenance

Price does not include:
Drinks, laundry, phone, tips, visa, international and internal Indian flights, and airport departure taxes

Motorcycle provisions:
Enfield motorcycles are provided by Indsun Adventure Tours and are included in the price of the tour.

Luggage provisions:
A service vehicle is available to carry your excess luggage.

Special notes:
No sleeping bag is required on this tour.

INDIA	**Temple Tour**
Tour operator:	Indsun Adventure Tours
Length of tour:	22 days, covering approximately 3,500 km
Dates:	*1991* • January 5 through January 26 • February 2 through February 23 • March 2 through March 23 • March 30 through April 20 • April 27 through May 18 • October 5 through October 26 • November 2 through November 23 • November 30 through December 21 • December 21, 1991 through January 11, 1992 *1992* • January 18 through February 8 • February 15 through March 7 • March 14 through April 4 • April 11 through May 2 • October 3 through October 24 • October 31 through November 21 • November 28 through December 19 • December 19, 1992 through January 9, 1993
Trip begins and ends:	Delhi

Highlights:
Your journey will begin in Delhi and cover mainly the state of Uttar Pradesh. Before entering Uttar Pradesh, however, you will travel through Rajasthan, Alwar and Jaipur, which is famous for its forts, palaces, and observatory. You'll then head east to Agra and visit Dayal Bagh, Red Fort, and the most famous landmark in India, the Taj Mahal.

A long ride is ahead of you before you reach the dusty Khajuraho, where you'll find the most uniquely carved sand stone temples, which display the Kama Sutra. The tour then crosses the Uttar Pradesh border and rides down the plains of the holy Ganga to Allahabad, where the sacred rivers Ganga and Jumna meet.

Next, you'll travel three hours to Varanasi, which is the symbol of Hindu renaissance and learning, and then you procede to Faizabad, which is a predominately Muslim area.

Leaving behind the dusty plains, you'll head north into the legendary Kumaon Mountains and stop at Nainital for lunch. On winding roads, you'll travel through the pilgrimage centers of Bageshwar and Baijnath and then continue on to Kausani, where you can see the spectacular Nanda Devi Trishul and other lofty peaks of the Himalayas.

Your tour then continues to Corbett National Park, where you will explore the jungle on elephant back. One might even spot a tiger in this lush wildlife sanctuary. From rural India you head into cosmopolitan Delhi where the tour ends after a day of sightseeing.

Price (includes motorcycle rental):
Per person $2,625

Price includes:
Twin bed accommodations in modest to five star hotels, an accompanying service team, fuel, helmet, airport transfers for group passengers only, entrance fees to all major attractions, all meals, and motorcycle rental, insurance, and maintenance

Price does not include:
Drinks, laundry, phone, tips, visa, international and internal Indian flights, airport departure taxes, or sleeping bag

Motorcycle provisions:
Enfield motorcycles are provided by Indsun Adventure Tours and are included in the price of the tour.

Luggage provisions:
A service van is available to carry your excess luggage.

Special notes:
You must carry a sleeping bag on this tour.

INDIA	**Goa, South Indian Coasts and Jungle by Royal Enfield**
Tour operator:	Prima Klima Reisen GmbH
Length of tour:	3 weeks, covering approximately 2,000 km, or 4 weeks, covering approximately 3,500 km
Dates:	Call Prima Klima Reisen for schedules.
Trip begins and ends:	Goa, South India

Highlights:
Ride 1950s style British Royal Enfield Silver Bullet 350cc bikes built in India. Travel 2,000 kilometers through the Indian paradise: dreamlands, jungles, and the old Portuguese colony of Goa. Travel with two guides (German and Indian), and a mechanic; stay in a variety of Indian-style hotels. Lots of adventure is guaranteed on this trip.

Three-week trips include ten days of round-trip touring and ten days in Goa. Four week trips include 21 days of round-trip touring and seven days in Goa.

Price (includes motorcycle rental):
- Per person .... DM 3,050

Price includes:
Round trip flight Frankfurt/Goa/Frankfurt, (other cities cost more or less), all accommodations, transfers, insured motorcycle, and guides

Motorcycle provisions:
350cc Royal Enfields are included in the tour price.

Luggage provisions:
All luggage is carried in a seven-seat Jeep.

Special notes:
The weather on this trip will be quite warm (28 to 40 degrees C; 82 to 104 degrees F); bring appropriate clothing. You will not need a large variety of clothing or equipment. Travelers should bear in mind that India is a Third World country, with its own culture and mentality. You should not expect western standards of service or reliability. As this trip is still in the planning stage, contact PKR after March 1991 for further details.

ORGANIZED TOURS – ASIA & INDONESIA

JAPAN	M'am Butterfly Tour Riders
Tour operator:	TransCyclist International
Length of tour:	Six to ten days, covering 500 to 1,000 km, depending upon rider's wishes
Dates:	September or October (dates subject to booking requests and minimum six participants)
Trip begins and ends:	Tokyo, Japan

Highlights:
See Madame Butterfly country by joining TransCyclist's (TC) exotic bike adventure through Japan. This tour takes you out of Tokyo's maze of concrete and steel into the hazy green mountains behind. Ride past majestic Mt. Fuji to Matsumoto and its old Samurai Castle. Scale up steep mountain passes to the Shogun town of Takayama in central Japan. Lake Biwa and beautiful Kyoto are next, with glimpses of historical temples and modern geishas called "maiko." You'll take picturesque Route 9 through Tottori's countryside, aiming for the famous sand dunes near Tottori Town. Then, across Honshu to the old town of Kurashiki on the lovely Setonaikai Inland Sea. There'll be time to relax on your return to Tokyo via a comfortable Pacific Coastal ferry boat. During each day, you can define your own itinerary; the pace is highly informal. Ride solo or with others in your party, as you wish. Each day starts with a route orientation by your experienced guide. At night share your stories of the day with others on the tour over rice wine or soaking in a Japanese bath. Or both, if you can take it!

Price (Six-day tour; includes motorcycle rental):
- Rider or passenger, two-up, double occupancy, per person $1,650

Price includes:
Japanese accommodations (including one Tokyo hotel stay prior to tour departure and after tour ends), all breakfasts and dinners, motorcycle rental, and insurance

Not included in price:
Ferry fees, lunch, fuel, oil, tolls, and additional hotel stays

Motorcycle provisions:
All Japanese makes — from 250cc up

Luggage provisions:
Travelers are expected to carry their own luggage on this tour.

Special notes:
International driver's license valid for motorcycle operation required by participants. This tour requires a minimum of six participants. You are advised to book at least three months in advance. Send a self-addressed envelope and one international reply coupon (available from the post office) when inquiring about the tour. You are advised to travel lightly (bulky luggage must be stored in Tokyo). Riding wear (helmet, boots, gloves, rain suits, etc.) must be provided by the participants themselves. The use of a motorcycle by one rider alone as well as the use of a motorcycle larger than 250cc will result in increased price. Larger displacement motorcycles can be obtained at increased cost provided the international driver's license of holder is accepted in Japan. (International driver's licenses of some nationals are not accepted, however they may still ride 250cc motorcycles.)

CHINA	**The Silk Road Rider**
Tour operator:	TransCyclist International
Length of tour:	Ten days, approximately 1,400 km by motorcycle (plus some by plane)

Dates:
Monthly during May and September (dates subject to booking requests and minimum six participants). East to west tour is followed by west to east tour.

Trip begins and ends:	Beijing Airport

Highlights:
In ancient times the Silk Road was the main trade route between Europe and China, on which the main and most desirable commodity exported from China was silk. What was and still is the throat of the Silk Road is the Hexi Corridor. On this tour you will explore the Hexi Corridor between Lanzhou on the east and Dunhuang on the west. See the precipitous Wu Qiao Ling (Black Scabbard Mountain) winding 1,200 km westward to Xing Xing Xia (the Star Gorge), the ice-capped Qilian Mountain Range to the south, and enormous Tengri and Badanjilin Deserts to the north. The Corridor passes through prairies, deserts, mountains, and oases. While part of this area is desolate, as a whole it is rich both in agricultural products and natural resources and is famous for its majestic scenery. A rustic, rugged experience by motorcycle!

Price (includes motorcycle rental):
- Group of ten people or more, per person, double occupancy $2,500
- Group of six to nine people, per person, double occupancy $3,000

(The small motorcycles used on this trip preclude riding double; there is room in the luggage van for up to four people.)

Price includes:
Beijing airport reception/farewell, welcome party, first day route and traffic orientation, all hotels (double occupancy), all meals in China, all public transportation in China (includes three domestic flights), Chinese driver's license, motorcycle rental, tour guide, camel or horse riding, all gasoline and oil, and tourist admission fees

Motorcycle provisions:
Honda, Suzuki, Kawasaki 85cc/125cc/250cc, including some motocross machines

Luggage provisions:
A van accompanies the tour to carry luggage.

Special notes:
International driver's license valid for motorcycle operation required by participants. If a minimum of ten participants are not confirmed by the booking deadline for a particular trip (one month before departure), you may change your booking to another suitable departure date or join as a member of a smaller group. Minimum of six participants. You are advised to book at least three months in advance. Some of the tour machines are motocross models and all participants need to be fit and experienced riders. Riding wear (helmet, boots, gloves, rain suit, etc.) must be provided by participants themselves. Send a self-addressed envelope and one international reply coupon (available from the post office) when inquiring about the tour.

Royal Enfields preparing for duty in India (photo courtesy of Prima Klima Reisen)

ORGANIZED TOURS – ASIA & INDONESIA

CHINA	**China**
Tour operator:	Von Thielmann Tours
Length of tour:	18 days
Dates:	• March 15 through April 1, 1991 • May 15 through June 1, 1991 • November 1 through November 18, 1991 • Similar dates in 1992 and 1993
Trip begins and ends:	Los Angeles

Highlights:
Watch the panorama of China unfold from the seat of your motorcycle. Ride through the rural villages, peaceful and everlasting, toward the misty hills, through dense forests, and green rice fields. Gaze upon mile after mile of wall receding in each direction. Know the China of flooded rice fields and of mulberry groves where silks are produced. Enjoy your status of visiting dignitary as a member of this motorcycle tour. Request special tours from the government official who escorts this American "sports team." Perhaps you'll visit an elementary school, a farm, or a factory — and see modern China along with the ancient jewels of this civilization.

Price (includes motorcycle rental):
- Single rider, double occupancy $3,235
- Two people, double occupancy $5,970
- Single passenger, double occupancy $2,985
- Supplement for single room occupancy, Hong Kong only . . . .$ 210

Price includes:
Chinese driver's license, visa application processing, airfare, motorcycle, hotel, sightseeing, transfers, and almost all meals

Motorcycle provisions:
Touring motorcycles (two or four cylinders, dual seat, U.S. models) are provided. A mechanic accompanies the tour, with spare parts.

Luggage provisions:
A support vehicle carries all luggage and offers pillion passengers a ride.

Special notes:
Special departures are being offered to groups of at least ten persons. Many itineraries available for tours of one to three weeks duration. Most itineraries start in southern China and may include Hainan Island, Guilin, and Shanghai. Tours include option to visit Beijing and the Great Wall.

THAILAND — Thailand

Tour operator:	Von Thielmann Tours
Length of tour:	15 days
Dates:	• April 10 through April 24, 1991 • October 2 through October 16, 1991 • Similar dates in 1992 and 1993
Trip begins and ends:	Los Angeles (or other airports) and Bangkok

Highlights:
Thailand, the land of smiles. Ask anyone who's spent more than a few days there if that doesn't perfectly describe how friendly the Thai people are and how stunning the country's natural beauty. Unsurpassed for its magnetic mix of ancient history, pageantry, Buddhist temples, bounties of rice, luscious seafood, and tropical fruits. You'll see rural children napping on the backs of grazing water buffalos, magnificent tropical beaches, marvelous history, and wild and exotic hill country. You may extend your stay or arrange a stopover in Honolulu, Taipei, Seoul, or Tokyo.

Price (does not include motorcycle rental):
- Single rider, double occupancy $2,758
- Two people, double occupancy $5,290
- Single passenger, double occupancy $2,645
- Supplement for single room occupancy .... $ 145

Price includes:
Round trip air fare from U.S. West Coast (Los Angeles, San Francisco, San Diego, or Phoenix) to Bangkok; hotel accommodations; all transfers; more than 30 meals including daily American breakfast; train ride from Chiang Mai to Bangkok; full-day Coral Island excursion by boat; visit to elephant camp; and Thai- and English-speaking guide

Motorcycle provisions:
Rental motorcycles from 400cc to 1100cc are available. Rental fees start at $350.

Luggage provisions:
A luggage van with driver/mechanic accompanies this tour.

ORGANIZED TOURS – AUSTRALIA

GOLD COAST

Gold Coast to Cairns: Amazing Queensland

Tour operator:	Australian-American Mototours
Length of tour:	21 days, covering approximately 2,000 miles (average rider drives over 3,000 miles)
Dates:	*1991* • August 23 through Sept. 1 (Ski Kiwiland) • September 7 through September 28 • October 5 through 26 (this trip runs in the reverse direction: Cairns to Gold Coast) *1992* • August 21 through August 30 (Ski Kiwiland) • September 5 through September 26 • October 3 through 24 (Cairns to Gold Coast)

"Please, Mr. Keown, I know I could learn to ride if you'll just let me try."

Trip begins and ends:
Brisbane (Toowoomba) to Cairns or Cairns to Brisbane, Australia

Highlights:
Enjoy open Aussie hospitality on this three-week tour of Queensland's 2,500 miles of sunny coastline. From the glittering casinos of the Gold Coast to the Great Barrier Reef, you'll love the green mountains, white beaches, and blue water of Australian paradise. Relax and pamper yourself. Work on your tan on Fraser Island with 100 miles of isolated beach. Visit Jupiters on the Gold Coast, the southern hemisphere's largest casino. Shop for opals. Cruise tropical rain forest and spectacular scenery where mountains and reef meet the shoreline. On the Gillies Highway, whirl through hundreds of hairpin turns in 17 kilometers. Spend a day on the America's cup contender Gretel in Whitsunday Islands. Take days to snorkel, scuba, and dive off the Great Barrier Reef. A spectacular float plane flight to the reef is included.

Price (does not include motorcycle rental):
• Single rider, double occupancy .... U.S. $3,620
• Supplement for single room occupancy .... U.S. $ 400

Price includes:
Round trip airfare from U.S. West Coast, accomodations for 21 nights, airport transportation, luggage transportation, personalized guide service,

daily briefing, maps, all breakfasts, dinners upon arrival in a new location, Whitsunday Island cruise on Gretel, and float plane flight to reef

Not included in price:
Motorcycle rental, gas, oil, insurance, some meals, and spending money

Motorcycle provisions:
Rent various BMW models, ranging from AUS $750 for an R65LS to AUS $1,200 for a K100. A AUS $500 damage deposit is required with rentals; it is refunded when the motorcycle is returned without damage. A few other types of motorcycles are available with special arrangements.

Luggage provisions:
A van accompanies this tour to carry luggage.

NEW SOUTH WALES The Wonders of New South Wales

Tour operator:	Australian-American Mototours
Length of tour:	21 days, covering approximately 2,300 miles (the average rider drives over 3,500 miles)
Dates:	• November 2 through November 23, 1991 • October 31 through November 21, 1992

Note: As an option you can choose to substitute the third week of the New South Wales trip with one week spent on the south island of New Zealand.

Trip begins and ends:	Brisbane (Toowoomba), Australia

On the road; Captain Cook Highway, north of Cairns, Queensland

Highlights:
Take in the friendly Aussie welcome of New South Wales on this three-week loop through the home of Australia's first settlement. Begin in Toowoomba, Australia's largest inland city and then travel south for memorable mountain riding and a sampling of the world's finest beaches — including Byron Bay, Australia's most easterly point. Visit Coff's Harbor and the original convict settlement of Port Macquarie. Wander over the scenic roads of Tuncurry/Forster and then head for the heart of the wine making district, the famous Hunter Valley. You'll sample the vintages of over 20 renowned wineries. (You'll travel by bus for this part of the tour.) Then it's on to the mysterious Blue Mountains and Katoomba for breathtaking vistas before boarding a train into Sydney, Australia's largest city. See the sights of this great city before returning to Katoomba and departure for the Snowy Mountains of Banjo Paterson fame. Retrace your steps inland to the upper Hunter region. You'll have a chance for more wine tasting before you return to Toowoomba through the fascinating New England district. Follow the original paths of the early explorers over winding mountain passes and gaze with awe on the 1,000-foot waterfalls that bear their names.

Price (does not include motorcycle rental):
- Single rider, double occupancy . . . . U.S. $3,620
- Supplement for single room occupancy . . . . U.S. $ 400

Price includes:
Round trip airfare from U.S. West Coast, accomodations for 21 nights, airport transportation, luggage transportation, personalized guide service, daily briefing, maps, all breakfasts, dinners upon arrival in a new location, and stay in downtown Sydney

Not included in price:
Motorcycle rental, gas, oil, insurance, some meals, and spending money

Motorcycle provisions:
Rent various BMW models, ranging from AUS $750 for an R65LS to AUS $1,200 for a K100. A AUS $500 damage deposit is required with rentals; it is refunded when the motorcycle is returned without damage. A few other types of motorcycles are available with special arrangements.

Luggage provisions:
A van accompanies this tour to carry luggage.

EASTERN AUSTRALIA

East Coast Australia

Tour operator:	Australian Motorcycle Adventures
Length of tour:	13 days (not including flight time)
Dates:	This tour is operated twice each month from May through December.

Trip begins and ends:
Begins at Sydney and ends in Cairns or begins in Cairns and ends in Sydney, depending on your booking date.

Highlights:
The first day of this tour you'll become better acquainted with fellow riders by taking a guided bus tour of beautiful Sydney harbour and its many offerings. At night there is an orientation to cover traffic rules and the following morning you head north into the "bush."

"Hi cutie. If you give me that bread I'll take you for a ride on my shiny new Harley."

The tour starts inland through typical Australian countryside heading for Tamworth, Australia's country music capital. Then it's onward farther north through cattle and sheep country until you reach the Gold Coast.

Surfer's Paradise is the first stop on the Gold Coast, Australia's Las Vegas. Try your luck at Jupiter's Casino or visit the Currumbin Wildlife Sanctuary, where you can pet tame kangaroos or feed flocks of the multi-colored parrots that surround you. There is also an enormous variety of restaurants, nightclubs, and discos throughout the coast for those who enjoy the nightlife. You then move on to Noosa Heads to soak up the sun on one of Australia's prettiest beaches, or visit Fraser Island, the world's largest sand island.

Bundaberg, your next stop, is a sleepy little town lying in the heart of sugar country. Have a chat with the friendly locals or visit the world famous "Bundy" Rum Distillery. You then move on to Rockhampton, which is the beef capital of Australia and where you are likely to see Australian cowboys, called "rough riders" or "jackaroos".

At Airlie beach you get your first glimpse of the Great Barrier Reef with its spectacular vivid blue waters and seductive coral islands. See coral teeming with vividly colored fish of all shapes and sizes. Go snorkeling or scuba diving and take a ride in a glass bottom boat or submarine. Your next destination is Townsville: crocodile country. It's also a great place to buy sapphires, emeralds, opals, and Thunder Eggs, a gem unique to this part of the country.

Your last stop is Cairns, where you'll remain for the balance of the trip. There you have the option of visiting Kuranda, a tropical rain forest that exhibits indigenous wild flora and Aboriginal rituals, or Wildworld, a park where animals such as koalas, emus, wombats, and kookaburras roam free, and where a spectacular Crocodile "Attack" Show is given. You have one last day at your own disposal before your departure.

Price:
- Per rider . . . . U.S. $2490
- Per passenger . . . . U.S. $1490

Price includes:
Motorcycle hire, accomodation for 14 nights in high quality motels, service vehicle, and shuttle bus to and from airport

Price does not include:
Airfare to and from Australia

Motorcycle provisions:
The tour price includes rental of 1991 Harley Davidsons (FRX Superglides).

Luggage provisions:
A 20-seat bus is available to carry any excess baggage or carry your passenger if you want to ride solo.

Special notes:
This tour is limited to ten riders and their passengers, per tour.

VICTORIA & NEW SOUTH WALES — Boomerang Tour

Tour operator:	Australian Motorcycle Touring
Length of tour:	Eight days, covering 1,414 miles
Dates:	*1991* • January 21 through January 28 • February 18 through February 25 • March 18 through March 25

ORGANIZED TOURS – AUSTRALIA

- April 22 through April 29
- October 21 through October 28
- November 18 through November 25
- December 16 through December 23

1992
- January 20 through January 27
- February 17 through February 24
- February 26 through March 5
- March 16 through March 23
- April 20 through April 27
- October 19 through October 26
- November 23 through November 30

Trip begins and ends: Melbourne, Australia

Highlights:
From the heights of the Snowy Mountains to the sweeping beaches of the Pacific Ocean, delight in Australia's best motorcycle roads. Average about 200 miles per day with plenty of time to sightsee, photograph, and enjoy Australia's unique wildlife. In Healesville, you'll pet kangaroos and befriend koalas and wombats at one of the world's great wildlife parks. Whip through switchbacks and hairpin curves that rival the

"Picnic? I thought YOU brought the picnic."

European Alps on the scenic climb up Mt. Buffalo. Ride to the top of the Snowies, dipping down from time to time to several dams and lakes in the giant hydroelectric project. Visit Canberra, the country's capital, constructed in the virgin bush by American architect Walter Burley Griffin. Speed over the grassy hills of South Gippsland to see the penguin parade on Phillip Island when these tuxedo-clad birds return from their fishing grounds to their burrows. Return to stately Melbourne, your departure point for the Boomerang Tour.

Price (includes motorcycle rental):
- Single rider, double occupancy . . . . .U.S. $1,860
- Passenger, double occupancy . . . . .U.S. $1,350

- Security deposit of AUS $500 for riders over the age of 25 (credit card accepted), refunded upon return of undamaged motorcycle

Price includes:
Accommodations for seven nights, seven breakfasts, seven dinners, and a get-acquainted dinner the night before the tour starts

Not included in price:
Personal accident insurance (available through travel agent), lunch, snacks, nor personal items

Motorcycle provisions:
Nearly new BMW Model R80 sport touring bikes are provided as part of the price; they are fitted with a windshield and lockable luggage cases.

Luggage provisions:
Travelers are expected to carry their own luggage on their bikes.

Special notes:
Deposit of AUS $200 needed to secure tour reservation; balance due 30 days prior to tour commencement. If reservation is cancelled within 30 days prior to tour, 50 percent refund; seven days prior to tour, no refund.

SOUTHERN AUSTRALIA

Mulga Tour

Tour operator:	Australian Motorcycle Touring
Length of tour:	11 days
Dates:	*1991* • January 7 through January 17 • February 4 through February 14 • March 4 through March 14 • April 8 through April 18 • May 6 through May 16 • August 5 through August 15 • September 2 through September 12 • October 7 through October 17 • November 4 through November 14 • December 2 through December 12

1992
- January 6 through January 16
- February 3 through February 13
- March 2 through March 12
- April 6 through April 16
- May 4 through May 14
- August 3 through August 13
- September 7 through September 17
- October 5 through October 15
- November 2 through November 12
- December 7 through December 17

Trip begins and ends:
Melbourne, Australia

It's never lonely in the outback

Highlights:
Penetrate the desiccated heart of the driest continent on the planet. Discover the real Australia. From desert outback to a motorcyclist's dream on the Great Ocean Road, you'll get an unequalled picture of the past and present of the Land Down Under. Visit Sovereign Hill, a recreation of an 1850's gold mining town. See the center of present-day mining country at Broken Hill. Visit the remote Flinders Range at the end of civilization. Roll down the vine-covered hills in Barossa Valley, world famous wine country. Ride through wheat fields and pine forest to Mount Gambier and its renowned Blue Lake. Twist along Great Ocean Road past the Cliffs of the Twelve Apostles and the Bay of Islands.

Price (includes motorcycle rental):
- Single rider, double occupancy ........................U.S. $2,550
- Passenger, double occupancy ..........................U.S. $1,850
- Security deposit of AUS $500 for riders over the age of 25 (credit card accepted), refunded upon return of undamaged motorcycle.

Price includes:
Accommodations for nine nights, nine breakfasts, nine dinners, and a get-acquainted Australian barbecue the night before the tour starts

Not included in price:
Personal accident insurance (available through travel agent), lunch, snacks, nor personal items

Motorcycle provisions:
Nearly new BMW Model R80 sport touring bikes are provided as part of the price; they are fitted with a windshield and lockable luggage cases.

Luggage provisions:
Travelers are expected to carry their own luggage on their bikes.

Special notes:
Deposit of AUS $200 needed to secure reservation on tour; balance due 30 days prior to tour commencement. If reservation is cancelled within 30 days prior to tour, 50 percent refund; if reservation is cancelled within seven days prior to tour, no refund.

VICTORIA & NORTHERN TERRITORY — Bike Tours Special '91

Tour operator:	Bike Tours Australia
Length of tour:	Five weeks, covering approximately 8,000 km; 300 km per day (6,000 km rough roads, trails)
Dates:	• June 16 through July 20, 1991 • Contact Bike Tours Australia for dates in future years
Trip begins:	Perth, Australia
Trip ends:	Cairns, Australia

Highlights:
Enduro adventurers, pack your gear and head across 8,000 kilometers of Aussie road with 6,000 kilometers of extreme challenge. You'll need strength and experience to master the most difficult terrain in Australia. For five weeks, you'll travel the most beautiful and the loneliest paths of this continent. Course through the plains of the eastern states past herds of sheep and cattle. Stop at Alice Springs, the most northern outpost of civilization in the outback. Push on to legendary Ayers Rock. Toward the end of the expedition you will be riding in tropical jungles, enjoying lots of waterfalls, rivers, and the sandy beaches of the great Pacific Ocean.

Price (includes motorcycle rental):
- Single rider . . . . DM 6,500
- Vehicle passenger . . . . DM 2,850

Price includes:
Camping equipment (except sleeping bag), food, fuel, transfer from airport to camp, campground fees, tents, and motorcycle rental, maintenance, and repairs

Not included in price:
All-risk insurance (voluntary), available for AUS $35 (or AUS $60 with no deductible) per week per motorcycle

Motorcycle provisions:
Yamaha XT 600 (electric starter)

Luggage provisions:
A van accompanies tour to carry all luggage, food, and fuel.

Special notes:
The principal language of this tour is German. English can be spoken if necessary.

EASTERN AUSTRALIA

East Coast Tour

Tour operator:	Bike Tours Australia
Length of tour:	Three weeks, covering approximately 6,000 km; 300 km per day
Dates:	• March 10 through March 30, 1991 (for reference only) • December 15, 1991 through January 4, 1992 • January 12 through February 1, 1992 • February 9 through February 29, 1992 • March 8 through March 28, 1992
Trip begins and ends:	Melbourne, Australia

On top of the bottom of the world

Highlights:
Escape winter. Head for the beach and summer weather in Australia. Sprint over 6,000 kilometers of Aussie road from the spectacular mountain world to the edge of the

primitive outback and along the endless Pacific coast. Take a diving expedition to the marvels of the Great Barrier Reef. Enjoy Australia's exceptional surfing. From Melbourne you'll wander through the mountainous world of Victoria, New South Wales, and Queensland to splendid Paradise Falls. Speed through the planes of Bogong National Park to Mt. Kosciusko, Australia's highest peak. Visit Croajingalong National Park with the 100-meter-high sand dune. Drive to the southernmost tip of Australia for spectacular ocean views. Wind through countless bays on the southern tip of Australia.

Price (includes motorcycle rental):
- Single rider .... DM 3,250
- Motorcycle passenger .... DM   950
- Vehicle passenger .... DM 1,850

Price includes:
Camping equipment (except sleeping bag), transfer from airport to camp, campground fees, tents, motorcycle rental, maintenance, and repairs

Not included in price:
Food (cost approximately AUS $180 per tour per person), fuel (cost approximately AUS $120 per tour per motorcycle), and all-risk insurance (voluntary), available for $35 (or $60 with no deductible) per week per motorcycle

Motorcycle provisions:
Yamaha XT 600 (electric starter)

Luggage provisions:
A luggage van accompanies this tour.

Special notes:
The principal language of this tour is German. English can be spoken if necessary.

"First one to Darwin gets a Fosters on me."

SOUTH & WEST AUSTRALIA	Explorer Darwin to Perth
Tour operator:	Bike Tours Australia
Length of tour:	Three weeks, covering approximately 5,000 km; 300 km per day (2,000 km of rough roads and trails)
Dates:	May 12 through June 1, 1991
Trip begins:	Darwin, Australia
Trip ends:	Perth, Australia

Highlights:
Only enduro enthusiasts in good shape should take this tour. It is a combination of sightseeing and lots of off-road fun (2,000 km). You will see Crocodile Dundee's country, enjoy the hot springs of Mataranka, climb Ayers Rock and course down the Gunbarrel 'Highway' through the Gibson and Great Victoria deserts. Spend one week camping under the starry skies of the outback, to escape from the constraints of civilization. The tour ends in beautiful Perth.

Price (includes motorcycle rental):
- Single rider .... DM 3,250
- Vehicle passenger .... DM 1,850

Price includes:
Camping equipment (except sleeping bag), transfer from airport to camp, campground fees, tents, and motorcycle rental, maintenance, and repairs

Not included in price:
Food (cost approximately AUS $180 per tour per person), fuel (cost approximately AUS $120 per tour per motorcycle), and all-risk insurance (voluntary), available for $35 (or $60 with no deductible) per week per motorcycle

Motorcycle provisions:
Yamaha XT 600 (electric starter)

Luggage provisions:
A van accompanies tour to carry all luggage.

270 ORGANIZED TOURS – AUSTRALIA

Special notes:
The principal language of this tour is German. English can be spoken if necessary.

OUTBACK	**Outbacker** **Melbourne to Darwin or Darwin to Melbourne**
Tour operator:	Bike Tours Australia
Length of tour:	Three weeks, covering approximately 5,000 km; 300 km per day
Dates:	*Melbourne to Darwin* • April 7 through April 27, 1991 • October 13 through November 2, 1991 • April 5 through April 25, 1992 • October 4 through October 24, 1992 *Darwin to Melbourne* • September 15 through October 5, 1991 • November 10 through November 30, 1991 • May 3 through May 23, 1992 • November 1 through November 21, 1992
Trip begins and ends:	Melbourne to Darwin or Darwin to Melbourne, Australia

Highlights:
Bisect the Australian continent with this run from Melbourne to Darwin. Start in Melbourne where the climate is as temperate as Ireland. Follow the Great Ocean Road along sandy bays and fantastical rock formations. Breathtaking views open at every turn of the road. Roar onto the legendary Stuart Highway that runs 3,000

"It's a good thing this Aussie beer is so great!"

miles hell-bent for Darwin. Travel the deserted roads of the outback past herds of sheep and cattle with eucalyptus trees marking the landscape. See koalas and kangaroos in the wild. Go through Coober Pedy, a desert town where people live in dugouts — comfortable apartments carved into soft boulders. Discover the variety of the Land Down Under with climates that range from mild in the south to tropical in the north.

Price (includes motorcycle rental):
- Single rider .... DM 3,250
- Motorcycle passenger .... DM 950
- Vehicle passenger .... DM 1,850

Price includes:
Camping equipment (except sleeping bag), transfer from airport to camp, campground fees, tents, and motorcycle rental, maintenance, and repairs

Not included in price:
Food (cost approximately AUS $180 per tour per person), fuel (cost approximately AUS $120 per tour per motorcycle), and all-risk insurance (voluntary), available for $35 (or $60 with no deductible) per week per motorcycle

Motorcycle provisions:
Yamaha XT 600 (electric starter)

Luggage provisions:
A van accompanies tour to carry all luggage.

Special notes:
The principal language of this tour is German. English can be spoken if necessary.

NORTHERN AUSTRALIA Tropicana

Tour operator:	Bike Tours Australia
Length of tour:	Three weeks, covering approximately 4,000 km (3,000 km off road and dirt roads)
Dates:	August 4 through August 24, 1991

"Did you hear them say I'd have to get wet?"

Trip begins:	Cairns, Australia
Trip ends:	Darwin, Australia

Highlights:
This is a very hot tour, since the trip goes through the tropical north of Australia. Though it is the shortest (4,000 km) tour offered by Bike Tours Australia, this tour is certainly not the easiest. The main part of the trip takes unpaved dirt roads or jungle tracks. You will have to cross several rivers; be prepared to get wet. You'll drive along the Pacific Ocean and visit Cooktown, Captain Cook's historical anchorage. The highlight for enduro enthusiasts is certainly Cape Tribulation (see for yourself). You will enjoy the popular Litchfield National Park and finally relax in Darwin at the Timor Sea, a town with a typical 'easy-going' atmosphere.

Price (includes motorcycle rental):
- Single rider .... DM 3,250
- Vehicle passenger .... DM 1,850

Price includes:
Camping equipment (except sleeping bag), transfer from airport to camp, campground fees, tents, and motorcycle rental, maintenance, and repairs

Not included in price:
Food (cost approximately AUS $180 per tour per person), fuel (cost approximately AUS $120 per tour per motorcycle), and all-risk insurance (voluntary), available for $35 (or $60 with no deductible) per week per motorcycle

Motorcycle provisions:
Yamaha XT 600 (electric starter)

Luggage provisions:
A van accompanies tour to carry all luggage.

Special notes:
The principal language of this tour is German. English can be spoken if necessary.

VICTORIA & NEW SOUTH WALES — **Aussie Tour**

Tour operator:	Edelweiss Bike Travel
Length of tour:	15 days, covering 1,800 miles
Dates:	• January 4 through January 18, 1991 • February 1 through February 15, 1991 • March 1 through March 15, 1991 • April 5 through April 19, 1991 • October 4 through October 18, 1991 • November 1 through November 15, 1991 • November 29 through December 13, 1991
Trip begins and ends:	Melbourne, Australia

Highlights:
In just two weeks this tour provides a good insight into the contrasting Australian landscape: desert, mountains, and coastline. The daily stretches are not excessively long and the hotels are comfortable. Comfort is also a major factor in the choice of bikes. Tour guide Geoff Coat (Australian Motorcycle Touring) takes his time to make your journey informative and enjoyable.

Start your trip by heading north to find the old gold mines near Ballarat. Ride across the Great Divide to Echuca on the mighty Murray River. Visit Hattah Kulkyne National Park at the edge of the desert. Ride along the Darling River through the Australian outback to Broken Hill, where you will have a free day to relax or take an airplane excursion to the surrounding deserts and lakes. Drive west from the desert almost to the sea and reach the Flinders Ranges and Wilpena Pound, a natural amphitheater, and perhaps the most spectacular part of the Ranges. Turning south you travel into the vine-covered hills of the Clare and Barossa Valleys. Visit Adelaide, the capital of South Australia, and its National Motor

Museum at Birdwood. Sample the Adelaide Hills and the best of the back mountain roads on your way to Robe, South Australia. Wind your way through pine forests on your way to Port Fairy, Victoria, where you'll once again discover the breathtaking beauty of the coast. Finally, ride the most fantastic motorcycling road in Australia, the coastal road to Melbourne, with its marvelous view of the Southern Ocean. Your final day in Australia allows time to relax and see the sights of Melbourne.

Price (includes motorcycle rental):
- Single rider, double occupancy $2,550
- Motorcycle passenger, double occupancy $1,850
- Single room supplement .... $ 275

Price includes:
Tour information package, transfer from and to airport in Melbourne, accommodations for 12 nights in comfortable hotels plus one on the ferry, two meals per day (normally breakfast and evening meal), motorcycle rental (including insurance), tour director, introductory get-togethers, and a tour gift

Motorcycle provisions:
BMW R80 touring bike with two large BMW cases

Luggage provisions:
Travelers are expected to carry their luggage on their own bike.

Special notes:
Temperature differences can be extreme on this tour. From November to April it is really hot in the outback. It is possible to extend your stay (at a supplement), but without bike rental.

SOUTHERN AUSTRALIA	**Outback Tour One** **Outback Tour Two** **Outback Tour Three** **Ayers Rock - Alice Springs**
Tour operator:	Motorcycle Adventures Australia
Length of tour:	• Outback Tour One: 13 days, 12 nights • Outback Tour Two: Seven days, six nights • Outback Tour Three: Seven days, six nights • Ayers Rock - Alice Springs: 13 days, 12 nights

Dates:

Outback Tour One
- May 13, 1991
- October 21, 1991
- May 11, 1992
- October 19, 1992

Outback Two and Three
- November 11, 1991
- November 9, 1992

Ayers Rock - Alice Springs
- August 19, 1991
- September 23, 1991
- August 17, 1992
- September 21, 1992

"Faster, I think that kangaroo really likes you."

Trips begins and ends:
Outback Tours: Adelaide Airport, South Australia;
Ayers Rock – Alice Springs Tours: Alice Springs Airport, Northern Territory

Highlights, Outback Tours One, Two, and Three:
The outback rides take you into the diverse and interesting heart of Australia, well off the beaten track. They are designed to give visitors the maximum amount of enjoyment by providing a varied mix of riding terrain, with scenic and historic features, combined with a look at some of Australia's unique and plentiful wildlife.

The general areas covered in the outback rides are in Northern and Northeastern parts of South Australia and in Western New South Wales.

Highlights, Ayers Rock - Alice Springs:
This ride, beginning and ending in Alice Springs, combines most of the features mentioned in the outback rides, but participants also visit such unique landmarks as Ayers Rock, The Olgas, Mount Conner, Palm Valley, and many other beautiful places of interest. This ride is a photographer's dream and participants are urged to bring plenty of film.

Highlights, all tours:
All the above tours include hotel/motel accommodation with some camping, often with only kangaroos and emus around for miles and miles, and under the brightest stars you can imagine. If you are lucky, after rain in the outback, the desert will become a sea of flowers for just a few days. Sit around the campfire drinking "billy tea" and swapping stories. This is what motorcycle touring is all about. A light aircraft or helicopter flight is provided on each ride at the most scenic locations.

276 ORGANIZED TOURS – AUSTRALIA

"Did you see it move? I swear I saw it move."

Price (includes motorcycle rental):
Single rider, double occupancy:
- Outback Tour One: .... U.S. $1,575
- Outback Tour Two and Three: .... U.S. $1,260
- Ayers Rock - Alice Springs: .... U.S. $1,575

Price includes:
All fuel, accommodations, meals, and entry fees, light aircraft flight, a Dri-Rider wet weather suit, a complimentary pictorial book about Australia, and a Motorcycle Adventures Australia tee shirt

Not included in price:
Personal accident and illness insurance (available through your travel agent), all drinks, and personal items

Motorcycle provisions:
An insured Honda NX 650 is included with the price.

Luggage provisions:
Toyota 4WD accompanies each tour to carry luggage.

Special notes:
Desert areas can be cold at night, so warm clothing is advisable. Participants must bring all their own riding gear. Participants may be asked to bring a warm sleeping bag, depending on the time of the year and the particular trip. Helmets are mandatory in Australia.

Motorcycle Adventures Australia reserves the right to cancel or reschedule a trip if there is insufficient booking.

VICTORIA & TASMANIA	Victoria One Victoria Two Tasmania
Tour operator:	Motorcycle Adventures Australia
Length of tour:	• Victoria One: 13 days, 12 nights • Victoria Two: Seven days, six nights • Tasmania: Seven days, six nights
Dates:	*Victoria One* • January 14, 1991 • April 15, 1991 • April 13, 1992 • December 1, 1992 *Victoria Two* • March 11, 1991 • February 17, 1992 *Tasmania* • February 18, 1991 • December 2, 1991 • January 13, 1992 • March 9, 1992
Trips begin and end:	Motorcycle Adventures Australia base at Pearcedale, Victoria

Highlights, Victoria One and Two:
Victoria is quite a different state to those covered in our outback rides. It is a greener, more mountainous state and provides riders with excellent scenery and riding. You will travel the most popular stretch of road in Australia for motorcyclists, "The Great Ocean Road" on the southwest coast of Victoria. Visit the Mount Gambier area with its underground caverns, the mountainous Grampians, where grand prix star Kevin Magee learned to ride, various National Parks, and the great Victorian "High Country."

Highlights, Tasmania:
Tasmania is a large island off the south coast of Victoria and is reached by an overnight voyage from Melbourne aboard the ferry "Abel Tasman." It is here that Australia's convict heritage began. It is a mountainous state with hardly a stretch of straight road anywhere. The wildlife in Tasmania is different to that on the mainland and you will have the opportunity to see many species there. The seafood specialities of the island include lobster, shrimp, scallops, abalone, and sea trout.

Price (includes motorcycle rental):
Single rider, double occupancy
- Victoria One: .... U.S. $1,695
- Victoria Two: .... U.S. $1,295
- Tasmania: .... U.S. $1,530
- Extra mandatory cost for transfers, accomodations for first and last nights, with dinner and breakfast: .... U.S. $ 200

Note: All costs outside the duration of the tours must be met by participants. Motorcycle Adventures Australia can arrange additional accommodations, if desired.

Price includes:
All fuel, accommodations, meals, and entry fees, Dri-Rider wet weather suit, complimentary book about Australia, and a Motorcycle Adventures Australia tee shirt

Not included in price:
Personal accident and illness insurance (available through your travel agent), all drinks, and personal items

Motorcycle provisions:
An insured Honda NX 650 is included with the price.

Luggage provisions:
A Toyota 4WD accompanies each tour to carry luggage.

Special notes:
- Accommodations in Victoria and Tasmania are hotels, motels, and homestays
- A light aircraft flight is provided on each ride at the most scenic venues

[Tasmania tour duration (seven days) is actually from your arrival in Tasmania to your departure. You must allow an additional two days for the voyage to and from Tasmania. Included in the tour price is the transportation costs for the ferry, but no meals. You are responsible for costs outside the tour duration.]

QUEENSLAND

The Harley Flavour of Queensland

Tour operator:
Sarroy Enterprises

Length of tour:
Three, five, and seven days

Dates:
Three-, five- and seven-day tours depart once a month. Contact Sarroy Enterprises for exact dates.

Trip begins and ends:
Brisbane, Australia

Tsuguro and Keiko Asuma enjoy a day of riding.

Highlights:
Sarroy Enterprises has three-, five-, and seven-day tours of Queensland. Choose your own route and tour length or let Sarroy Enterprises plan your itinerary for you. All tours explore Queensland's beautiful and diverse landscape and many attractions.

The shorter tours remain within a 200 mile radius of Brisbane. Climb up Mount Tamborine to Tamborine National Mountain National Park, a lush subtropical rain forest, visit the "Old Caves Winery" in Stanthorpe and have a sample of some of the best wines in the area. Travel through farm country to the "outback" town of Texas, the center of the cattle district. On the seven-day tour journey to the Great Barrier Reef and Fraser Island, with its famous colored sand, shipwreck, and rain forests.

A twenty-one day tour, which can be arranged by special request, covers over 2,200 miles of Queensland's coast. Begin in Brisbane and travel along sweeping roads past isolated beaches and spectacular views. Visit Fraser Island, Wild World Nature Park, and the sport fishing village of Townsville. Take a day trip to the islands off the Great Barrier Reef and swim, sail, and boat at a national park reef. Head farther north to Cairns for a train ride through the local towns and sugar cane fields, and a tour of a sugar refinery. Depart Cairns and journey into the mountainous Atherton Tablelands and then ride west into the "outback" for Clermont, a mining town, and the precious gem fields at Emerald, Sapphire, and Anakie. Heading home you'll ride through sheep and cattle stations and stop at Bunya National Park, where you can pet wallabies or take a bush walk, and visit Byron Bay, Australia's most easterly point. After a stop on the Gold Coast, the tour ends in Brisbane.

Price:
- Per day: AUS $300 per person; AUS $375 per couple
- 3 days: AUS $900 per person; AUS $1,125 per couple
- 5 days: AUS $1,500 per person; AUS $1,875 per couple
- 7 days: AUS $2,100 per person; AUS $2,625 per couple
- (10 percent discount discount is available if you book directly with Sarroy Enterprises)

Price includes:
Harley-Davidson motorcycle complete with large saddle bags, pillion seat, and carry rack; all meals; fuel; oil; accommodations for each night of tour; entry fees to all attractions; and full repair service in the event of a breakdown.

Not included in price:
Personal/medical insurance, air fare, or helmets

Motorcycle provisions:
Harley-Davidson Sportsters and FXR Super-Glides are available for rent to tour participants; they are included in the price of the tour.

Luggage provisions:
A luggage van is provided on longer tours only. Otherwise, participants are expected to carry their own luggage.

Special notes:
- A deposit of 25 percent is required 30 days before the departure date.
- A limited number of helmets are available.

SOUTHERN AUSTRALIA	**High Country Tour**
Tour operator:	Trail Bike Tours
Length of tour:	Seven days
Dates:	• The High Country Tour is available November 1 through April 30, 1991. Tour dates are scheduled by reservation.
Trip begins and ends:	Melbourne, Australia

Highlights:

The High Country tour takes you through the mountain trails of Australia's Snowy Mountains. It uses only the best, most challenging trails, mountain passes, and river crossings that are available in Victoria, not just dirt trails. It is truly an off-road tour.

The tour starts from Melbourne and makes its way through Mansfield, Mt. Bueller, and Mt. Hotham. It then crosses the Murray river to Thredbo village. Here you leave the motorcycles behind for a walk up Mount Kosciusko, which at 2230 meters is Australia's highest mountain. Visit historic Harrietville and then continue through forests of mountain gums to Mount Stirling with its fantastic trails. Return to Melbourne for some shopping before returning home.

Price:

Per person, double occupancy .... AUS $1,750

Price includes:

Two tour guides, motorcycle rental, transfer from airport, accommodations for six nights, double occupancy, all meals, fuel, and admission to attractions

Not included in price:

Airfare, insurance, or drinks

Motorcycle provisions:

Yamaha motorcycles are provided for tour participants.

Luggage provisions:

A sevice van is available to carry excess luggage and anyone who is with the tour, but not riding a motorcycle.

Special notes:

- The High Country tour covers very mountainous terrain on difficult trails and is not suited for beginners.
- Tour reservations are confirmed on receipt of ten percent of the tour cost. Final tour payment must arrive at least 30 days prior to start of the tour.
- It is suggested that you bring comfortable riding gear with you on tour including heavy duty jacket, boots, pants, gloves, goggles, and a helmet, or request to hire these items when booking your tour.

AUSTRALIA SOUTHERN
Sunset Desert Tour

Rest stop at the Dargo Store

Tour operator:	Trail Bike Tours
Length of tour:	Seven days
Dates:	• The Sunset Desert Tour is available June 1 through September 30, 1991. Tour dates are scheduled by reservation.
Trip begins and ends:	Melbourne, Australia

Highlights:
The Sunset Desert tour travels through Victoria's desert lowlands. Start with a look at some gold mines at the historic Eureka Stockade in Ballarat and then move into the Big Desert and lonely Murrayville with its sand dunes and flora. From there you'll see the red of sunset country, Ouyen oasis, Hattah Lakes, and Desert National Park where kangaroos, emus and pelicans virtually surround the salt flats. Visit local wineries as you make your way back to Melbourne. Return in time for some shopping before departing home.

Price:
Per person double occupancy .... AUS $1,750

Price includes:
Two tour guides, motorcycle rental, transfer from airport, accommodations for six nights, double occupancy, all meals, fuel, and admission to attractions

Not included in price:
Airfare, insurance, or drinks

Motorcycle provisions:
Yamaha motorcycles are provided for tour participants.

Luggage provisions:
A service van is available to carry excess luggage and anyone who is with the tour, but not riding a motorcycle.

Special notes:
- Tour reservations are confirmed on receipt of ten percent of the tour cost. Final tour payment must arrive at least 30 days prior to tour start.
- It is suggested that you bring comfortable riding gear with you on tour including heavy duty jacket, boots, pants, gloves, goggles, and a helmet, or request to hire these items when booking your tour.

VICTORIA	**Victoria, Australia**
Tour operator:	Trail Bike Tours
Length of tour:	Two-, three-, and five-day tours
Dates:	• Tour dates are scheduled by reservation.
Trip begins and ends:	Tours begin and end at Nojee, Eildon and Mansfield depending on length of tour. A shuttle vehicle, however, is available to transfer you from Melbourne airport and back at tour's end.

Highlights:
Trail Bike Tours offers two-, three-, and five-day tours of Victoria's high country. All tours travel through the Snowy Mountains. However, Trail Bike Tours will design a trail route that is geared for your level of riding ability. Ride through the magnificent beauty of the Snowy Mountains, setting for "The Man From Snowy River", and see the house on top of Mount Stirling where this film was made. Climb Mount Kosciusko, Australia's highest mountain, cross rivers and travel along Victoria's rugged terrain. At night relax in the comfort of good accommodations, some of which have a pool or sauna.

Price:
Per person, per day, double occupancy ....AUS $250

Price includes:
Two tour guides, motorcycle rental, transfer from airport, accommodations (double occupancy), all meals, fuel, and admission to attractions

Not included in price:
Airfare, insurance, and drinks

Motorcycle provisions:
Yamaha motorcycles are provided for tour participants.

Luggage provisions:
On large group tours a service van is available to carry excess luggage. Small group tours, however, receive a backpack instead.

Special notes:
- Tour reservations are confirmed on receipt of ten percent of the tour cost. Final tour payment must arrive at least 30 days prior to tour start.
- It is suggested that you bring comfortable riding gear with you on tour including heavy duty jacket, boots, pants, gloves, goggles, and a helmet, or request to hire these items when booking your tour.

VICTORIA & NEW SOUTH WALES — The Oz Rider

Tour operator:	TransCyclist International
Length of tour:	Seven days, approximately 2,000 km (longer tour can be arranged)
Dates:	Monthly year round (dates subject to booking requests and minimum six participants)
Trip begins and ends:	Sydney, Australia

Highlights:
Oz is waiting with unlimited space and freedom. No boundaries other than its coastlines. Two-wheeling takes on a new dimension "down under" where highways retain their primary purpose: migratory lanes that keep the day's traveler "high" and blasting into the ever-expanding horizon. Be your own friendly Mad Max with sparse traffic and safety. TC

believes this tour will offer you "a truly pioneer-type bike adventure you will never forget." This tour is arranged out of Sydney, Australia's most scenic city, and routes up through New South Wales bush country to Queensland and back on beautiful Pacific coastal highway to Sydney.

Price (includes motorcycle rental):
- Single rider, double occupancy .... AUS $2,200
- Passenger (van or pillion), double occupancy .... AUS $1,600

Note: AUS $500 security deposit required on motorcycle (refundable)

Price includes:
All hotels, breakfasts, motorcycle rental and insurance, airport transfers, tour briefings, guide, and extras. Note: Add about AUS $40 to $50 per day for gasoline, lunch, dinner, etc.

Motorcycle provisions:
Yamaha 250/600/XJ750/900 and BMW 100 available

Luggage provisions:
A van will be provided for groups of ten or more participants.

Special notes:
International driver's license valid for motorcycle operation required by participants. You are advised to book at least three months in advance. This tour can also be offered self-guided. Prices range from AUS $1,300 per rider, double occupancy (all inclusive except for gas and meals). Send a self-addressed envelope and one international reply coupon (available from the post office) when inquiring about the tour.

QUEENSLAND	Longreach Tour
Tour operator:	Wild Bull Tours
Length of tour:	Eight days, covering approximately 1,500 miles
Dates:	Tours depart twice monthly between May and November. Contact Wild Bull Tours for detailed departure dates.
Trip begins and ends:	Tour begins in Maroochydore, Queensland, 62 miles north of Brisbane, and ends in Brisbane, Queensland.

Highlights:
The Longreach Tour uses public roadways of which 60 percent are dirt roads. Begin your tour with a ride through Southeast Queensland's citrus and cattle country. Then move into the gemfields of Sapphire and Rubyvale, where you'll visit the "Miner's Heritage" and go underground for a tour of a mine. As you cross the Great Dividing Range, you'll view some of Australia's most beautiful mountain scenery. Along the way you'll see a variety of wild life including kangaroos, emus, parrots, and reptiles. From Longreach, travel north to Lorraine Station, a 76,000-acre working sheep station (Aussie for "ranch") where you'll spend the night. Participate in station activities such as horse riding, sheep mustering, and shearing, or ride to Lark Quarry to see the dinosaur tracks. Your tour guides are very familiar with the outback communities and are able to introduce you to many of the locals. Finally, return to Longreach to catch a flight back to Brisbane where the tour ends.

Price:
Per person $2,950

Price includes:
Accommodations for seven nights, fuel and oil, motorcycle rental (fully registered and equipped with gear sack), all meals, service vehicle equipped with radio, airfare from Longreach to Brisbane, and transfer from Brisbane airport to tour start in Maroochydore

Not included in price:
Airfare to and from Australia, alcoholic beverages, and personal and medical insurance

Motorcycle provisions:
Wild Bull Tours has six Honda NX650s and two smaller Yamaha TT350s for rent to tour participants only.

Luggage provisions:
A service truck is available to carry excess luggage.

Special notes:
- A moderate level of physical fitness and some experience in off-road touring is necessary for this tour.
- A deposit of ten percent is required at least 21 days prior to tour start.
- Reservations are required at least 28 days prior to tour start.
- Riders must have an international or Australian motorcycle license.
- Each participant is responsible for providing his own helmet with full face mask or goggles.
- Wild Bull Tours recommends that each participant have adequate personal insurance coverage before leaving home.

ORGANIZED TOURS – NEW ZEALAND

288 ORGANIZED TOURS – NEW ZEALAND

NEW ZEALAND	**Beach's Maori Meander**
Tour operator:	Beach's Motorcycle Adventures, Ltd.
Length of tour:	22 days, approximately 2,600 miles

Dates:

1991
- February 16 – March 10
- March 9 through 31

1992
- February 1 through 23
- February 22 – March 15

1993
- February 6 through 28
- February 27 – March 21

Rob Beach, leader of Beach's New Zealand tours

Trip begins and ends:
Los Angeles (other cities on request)

Highlights:
The Beach Maori Meander tour kicks off in Christchurch and winds its way up to Auckland. Averaging 150 to 200 miles a day, each day allows plenty of time to sightsee, to relax, and to obtain an in-depth look at both of the islands that make up New Zealand. Four overnight stays on private farms allow participants a personal contact with the friendly New Zealanders.

A complete itinerary and a collection of excellent maps are provided, giving total freedom for riders to choose their own daily routes. Attractions included in the tour price are: a scenic flight over Fox Glacier and a sightseeing cruise in the fjords of the famous Milford Sound.

New Zealand is a fantastic area to tour by motorcycle. The traffic is very light, the roads are in excellent condition, and the Kiwis are always smiling. If you seek a relaxing vacation, there is no better destination than New Zealand.

As always, there will be a Beach on the tour. Both Rob and Bob spend the winter months staring out the windows at the piles of snow around western New York and dream of the Maori Meander.

Price (does not include motorcycle rental):
- Per person, double occupancy $3,750
- Supplement for single room occupancy .... $ 250

Price includes:
Round trip airfare from/to Los Angeles on Air New Zealand (departures from other gateway cities may be arranged), all hotels and overnight farm stays, all morning and evening meals, maps, tote bags, and additional surprises

Motorcycle provisions:
BMW R-series and Japanese motorcycles are available for rent. The rental rate, including insurance and with unlimited mileage, is $750. The insurance coverage has a $500 deductible.

Luggage provisions:
A van accompanies each tour to carry luggage.

NEW ZEALAND	**Three-Week Tour of New Zealand**
Tour operator:	Te Waipounamu Motorcycle Tours
Length of tour:	21 days, approximately 5,000 kilometers
Dates:	*1991* • March 14 through April 3, 1991 • November 20 through December 11, 1991 *1992* • February 14 through March 6, 1992 • March 13 through April 2, 1992 • November 20 through December 11, 1992
Trip begins and ends:	Begins in Christchurch, ends in Aukland, or vice versa

Highlights:
These tours either begin in the North Island and finish in the South Island, or vice versa, travelling as far South as Milford Sound and as far North as the Bay of Islands.

You'll stay in hotels, motor lodges, with New Zealand families, on farms and, for one night, in a Maori village. Detailed route plans allow tour participants to make their own riding plans, rather than travel in a convoy.

New Zealand has become a very popular "off-season" destination for Northern-hemisphere riders. The combination of quiet roads, mild climate, and the general friendliness of the local people provides an ideal balance for riders wanting a relaxing vacation with a good measure of excitement and surprises.

Price (includes motorcycle rental):
- Single rider, double occupancy .... NZ $3,995
- Passenger, double occupancy .... NZ $3,595

Note: A NZ $500 security deposit is required upon renting the motorcycle; the deposit is refunded when motorcycle is returned free of damage.

Price includes:
Accommodations for 19 nights in hotels, motels, and New Zealand farm stays with local people; breakfast each day; 17 dinners; ferry crossings; launch trip at Milford Sound; helicopter flight at Fox Glacier; transport from arrival airports; maps; route guides; luggage van; and tour guides. According to John Rains, the accommodations are "very good, not ostentatious or flashy." Price does not include gasoline.

Motorcycle provisions:
Choice of: BMW K-series, BMW R-series 800cc, and 1000cc models (with sidebags and fairings); Yamaha XJ750 and XJ900 (with fairings and soft luggage); or Honda 500 (with soft luggage)

Special notes:
- Tour participants must be at least 21 years of age (at least 25 for machines over 500cc).
- Rental price includes liability coverage
- Accessories are available. Helmet, gloves, and rain suits are available for rent at a nominal cost.

NEW ZEALAND	The Kiwi Rider
Tour operator:	TransCyclist International
Length of tour:	• Seven-days, covering approximately 1,200 km
Dates:	*1991* • January 13 through January 19 • March 17 through March 23 • April 28 through May 4 • September 8 through September 14 • November 3 through November 9 • November 24 through November 30

- December 15 through December 21
- December 29, 1991 through January 4, 1992
- Similar dates in 1992

Trip begins and ends: Christchurch, New Zealand

Highlights:
This tour reveals one of the great travel secrets left in the world. Enjoy New Zealand's amazing diversity of scenery still unspoiled by tourism. Experience the native Maori culture and the well-preserved Victorian towns. Meet people of genuine friendliness. Ride through a landscape of breathtaking fjords and volcanoes. Take a dip in a rejuvenating hot spring. Sample the rich food of New Zealand. On these tours, you'll travel a leisurely 300 kilometers per day, giving you plenty of time to meet the Kiwis and get to know them. Spend one morning on an operating sheep farm and another white-water rafting through rapids and gorges. Enjoy the Southern Alps with crystalline lakes, glaciers, and snowcapped peaks punctuating the Alpine settings. Return through awesome mountain scenery to the resort of Queenstown on the shores of Lake Wakatipu, and then fly back to Christchurch.

Price (includes motorcycle rental):
- Single rider or passenger, double occupancy .... NZ $1,550

Note: A NZ $500 security deposit is required for motorcycle (refundable).

Price includes:
All hotels, breakfast and dinner each day, motorcycle rental and insurance, Christchurch airport transfers, flight from Queenstown to Christchurch, maps, route guides, and tour guide

Not included in price:
Gasoline or lunches. You should add about NZ $30 to NZ $50 per day for gasoline, lunch, snacks, etc.

Motorcycle provisions:
Choice of BMW R65, R80, or R100 for riders over age 25; Japanese makes (Yamaha 440, 550, 650) for those under age 25. Motorcycle rental is included with the tour price.

Luggage provisions:
Travelers are expected to carry their luggage on their motorcycle. Pack lightly.

Special notes:
International driver's license valid for motorcycle operation required by participants. Tours include touristic extras (i.e., Cessna joy flight, white-river rafting, etc.). Tour prices are subject to change and based on mini-

mum of six participants. You are advised to book at least three months in advance. Tour participants must be at least 21 years of age (at least 25 for machines over 750cc). Send a self-addressed envelope and one international reply coupon (available from the post office) when inquiring about the tour.

NEW ZEALAND

New Zealand

Tongariro volcano, in Tongariro National Park

Tour operator:
Von Thielmann Tours

Length of tour:
19 days

Dates:
March, October, and November

Trip begins and ends:
Los Angeles

Highlights:
Experience South and North Island, a paradise for motorcyclists. The scenery ranges from Alpine country to tropical rain forests.

Price (includes motorcycle rental):
- Single rider, double occupancy $3,298
- Two people, double occupancy $6,204
- Single passenger, double occupancy $3,102
- Supplement for single room occupancy ....$ 530

Price includes:
Round trip airfare from Honolulu, hotel accommodations, breakfast daily (plus other meals), sightseeing, transfers, and inter-island ferry.

Motorcycle provisions:
Rental motorcycles are available (touring type).

Luggage provisions:
A support vehicle will carry the luggage.

MOTORCYCLE RENTAL AGENCIES

It is very convenient (and in many cases essential) for international motorcycle travelers to rent a machine at their destination. In fact, availability of motorcycle rental programs will be a key ingredient in the future growth of motorcycle touring. We applaud the rental programs of such organizations as Harley Owners Group, Moturis, Budget Rent-a-Car, and Scootabout Motorcycle Centre. Each of them is noteworthy for bringing a new perspective to motorcycle travel.

The Harley Owners Group has operated a rental program for its members for several years and offers rental locations at several points in the United States and in Frankfurt. Moturis operates several locations in the United States, and works with several tour operators to supply motorcycles to their guests. We are interested to see, with Budget Rent-a-Car, the first venture into motorcycle rentals by a major car rental company. Although Budget Rent-a-Car offers motorcycle rentals only in Germany, and offers only Harley-Davidson machines at this time, we will eagerly watch the progress of their program and hope it expands to include other locations and other types of motorcycles. Scootabout is a relatively small business, operating only in London, but has done an exceptional job serving the needs of international travelers. Their fleet has expanded steadily to its present size of over a hundred machines.

We would like to see more groups follow the lead of these companies. Since motorcycle rentals are more widely available in Europe and other areas than in the United States, we hope to have more U.S. entries in this section when we next go to press.

In planning your trip put yourself into a flexible frame of mind, since even the best plans do not always guarantee that you will get exactly what you want. We heard of one traveler who arrived at a rental agency to pick up his reserved CBR1000, only to discover that the previous renter had just totaled the bike. Since it was the only one of that kind in the agency's fleet, the vacationer had to settle for another kind of motorcycle. Not a disaster, but surely a disappointment.

You should discuss matters of insurance carefully with the rental agency or tour operator before you sign up. Many of the companies renting motorcycles provide only insurance that will pay for damage you cause to someone else's property, but not for damage to the rented machine (including theft). In those cases where "comprehensive" insurance is available, the deductible amount might be significant — up to $1,000. Be sure you understand the ground rules before you make your reservation.

If you are planning a long-distance trip you will probably want sizable side bags and possibly a top box and a tank bag. Discuss those options with the rental agency to be sure they can provide what you want. (In the case of tank bags, you might consider bringing your own, if it can be attached to the rental bike.)

In this section we have listed several companies who offer "buy-sellback" plans for motorcycles. Like rentals, buy-sellback plans allow a traveler to obtain a motorcycle on a temporary basis for a reasonable price. The main difference is that in the latter case the traveler must assume all risk of damage or loss of the machine. The way it works is that a traveler purchases a motorcycle outright from a provider, then registers and insures it. At the time of purchase, an agreement is reached for the price at which the provider will repurchase the machine after the trip — providing the bike is returned without major damage. While the administrative bother would probably make this idea unattractive for a short trip, it might be acceptable for a trip of a week or longer. In the United States, the high cost of insurance has inhibited the development of motorcycle rental plans. Buy-sellback arrangements offer a realistic alternative to pure rental plans.

If you would like to tour in a region where we have no listings for rental agencies or buy-sellback providers, try some of the local motorcycle dealers to see if they might be willing to arrange a buy-sellback deal for you. It is a low-risk way for the dealer to earn some money while satisfying your need for a short-term motorcycle. Finding motorcycle dealers is relatively easy since most public libraries keep yellow page directories for major cities of the United States.

RENTALS IN THE UNITED STATES

CALIFORNIA

American Motorcycle Rentals and Sales

10924 Portal Drive
Los Alamitos, CA 90720

Contact: Wayne Murphy
Phone: (213) 594-8901 or
  (714) 821-1590
FAX: (714) 821-8105

Wayne Murphy, traveling incognito

Hours:
Monday 8:00 a.m. to 5:00 p.m.; Tuesday through Saturday 9:00 a.m. to 6:00 p.m.; Sundays, by appointment

Motorcycles available:
Various types including Kawasaki KZ 440LTD, Yamaha XJ, ST, and Virago models; BMW K100; and Harley-Davidson FLT. Subject to change.

Rates:
- One day .... $55 to $125
- Two days .... $95 to $225
- Three days .... $120 to $300
- Four to seven days .... $150 to $450
- Eight to 14 days .... $275 to $850
- 15 to 21 days .... $375 to $1,200
- 22 to 28 days .... $450 to $1,500

Price includes:
Free 100 miles per day; add $.10 per mile thereafter, $.20 per mile for Harleys and BMWs. Free instructions for safe riding are available.

Deposit required:
Security deposit is $250 per unit, $1,000 for Harley or BMW. Major credit card (VISA, MC, AMEX) or cash required. Also, $50 cash or credit card imprint held to cover traffic tickets. Note $35 will be withheld from deposit if bike is not returned clean.

Insurance arrangements:
Collision and liability insurance are available for U.S. citizens and foreign nationals at extra cost. Contact American Motorcycle Rental for a quote.

Accessories:
Helmets are offered free to renters. Tank bags and soft saddle bags are available. Special clothing is not supplied; renter is responsible for providing his own.

Special requirements:
Primary renter must be at least 21 years of age and have a driver's license valid for motorcycle operation. Lerner's permit acceptable for California residents on half-day rentals only.

Reservations:
Reservations are recommended. With a limited supply, newest motorcycles are rented first. Deposits of $50 per vehicle required to confirm reservation (returnable with 14-day notice). Checks accepted if received 30 days in advance.

Other services:
- Tours to West Coast races. Write or call for rates and tour dates. Tour bookings must be made at least two months in advance. Deposit of 50 percent is required to hold your tour reservation.
- Motorcycle parts and accessories
- Service on all makes and models
- Motorcycle driving lessons, by appointment

UNITED STATES, CANADA, AND GERMANY

Harley Owners Group (H.O.G.) – Fly & Ride Program

Description:
H.O.G. operates a Fly & Ride program in ten different locations around the world to offer the opportunity for year-round motorcycling vacations. To make reservations, call the H.O.G. office listed below. From the rental location, you may travel anywhere you wish, except Mexico. Rental vehicles must be picked up and returned to the Harley-Davidson agent in that location. Pick-up and drop-off times must coincide with the operating hours of those businesses. Vehicle must be returned to the same location where it was picked up.

MOTORCYCLE RENTAL AGENCIES

H.O.G. office:	Harley Owners Group P.O. Box 453 Milwaukee, WI 53201 Contact: H.O.G. representatives Phone: 800-258-2464 (800-242-2464 in Wisconsin; 416-741-5510 in Canada; call collect at 414-935-4522 in Alaska and Hawaii) FAX: 414-935-4559
Frankfurt agent:	Harley-Davidson Motor Company Raunheim Industriestrasse 7 Frankfurt GERMANY
Boston agent:	Cycle Craft Co., Inc. 1813 Revere Beach Parkway Everett, MA 02149
Orlando agent:	Dick Farmer's Harley-Davidson of Orlando 46 North Orange Blossom Trail Orlando, FL 32805
Miami agent:	Harley-Davidson, Inc. of Miami 7701 NW Seventh Avenue Miami, FL 33150
Ft. Collins agent:	John's Harley-Davidson 2135 E. Mulberry Ft. Collins, CO 80524
Tempe agent:	Chosa's Harley-Davidson, Inc. 617 South Hayden Road Tempe, AZ 85281
Reno agent:	Harley-Davidson of Reno 3180 Mill Street Reno, NV 89502
Los Angeles agent:	Harley-Davidson of Glendale 3717 San Fernando Road Glendale, CA 91204

MOTORCYCLE RENTAL AGENCIES

Honolulu agent:	Cycle City Ltd. Honolulu Harley-Davidson Sales 2965 North Nimitz Highway Honolulu, HI 96819
Vancouver agent:	Trev Deeley Motorcycles, Ltd. 606 East Broadway Vancouver, B.C. V5T 1X6 CANADA
Hours:	These agents are open at various business hours. Contact the H.O.G. office for details.

Motorcycles available:
Several different models of Harley-Davidson motorcycles are available at each location. Models usually include: FLTs, FLHTs, and FXRTs. Preferences for specific models will be allowed on a first come, first served basis. The number of machines available is limited. Make your reservations early.

Rates:
Rates are $50 per day (for 24 hours), with $100 minimum; $250 per week (seven days). A 20 percent discount is given for rentals of four weeks or more.

Price includes:
Insurance (see below), free mileage, and state and local taxes.

Deposit required:
A 50 percent deposit is required to hold your reservation; the remaining 50 percent must be received at least three weeks before motorcycle is to be picked up.

Insurance arrangements:
H.O.G. provides liability insurance up to $10,000 per person, but not more than $20,000 per accident, and property damage up to $5,000. Renter is responsible for the first $250 of any physical damage to the rental vehicle, and the first $1,000 loss due to theft. A waiver of the $1,000 responsibility for theft loss can be purchased for $7 per day. Insurance limits may differ in various locations.

Methods of payment:
Motorcycle rent is payable by check, money order, Mastercard, or VISA.

Accessories:
Normal equipment found with each motorcycle. Each person must provide his own helmet.

Special requirements:
Fly & Ride is available only to H.O.G. members. Members must live 300 or more miles from the rental site. Motorcycle rider and passenger must wear a D.O.T. approved safety helmet at all times. You must have a valid motorcycle driver's license to rent a motorcycle. Vehicle will be provided with a full tank of gas and oil. Additional gas or oil needed en route must be provided by the renter.

Reservations:
All reservations are handled on a first come, first served basis and must be made through the Harley Owners Group office in Milwaukee at least three weeks in advance of the pickup date. The number of motorcycles in each location is limited. Make your reservations early. No reservation is confirmed until the deposit is received.

Other services:
The Harley Owners Group offers a number of other benefits to its members.

CALIFORNIA	**Kalman International Motorcycle Touring**
	534 Kelmore Street Moss Beach, CA 94038 Contact: David or Kathy Kalman Phone: 800-637-4337 or 415-728-3511 FAX: Same numbers as phone
Booking agent:	The Old Chapel North Street Leicester LE6 4EB ENGLAND Phone: (44) 530-811705 FAX: (44) 530-813410

Motorcycles available:
Kalman International owns seven Honda Gold Wings and three BMWs for rent to tour participants.

Rates:
- Per week, all models $500

Price includes:
Free mileage and insurance

Deposit required:
The security deposit is $1000 per motorcycle, payable by Major credit card (VISA, MC, AMEX) or cash. The security deposit is applied to the insurance deductible in the event of damage to the motorcycle, and is refundable if the motorcycle is returned without damage.

Insurance arrangements:
Liability insurance (with $1000 deductible) is included in the price of the rental. Collision, theft, personal liability, and personal damage insurance are included in the package.

Accessories:
All motorcycles are fully equipped for touring and have luggage bags, fairing, and windshield.

Special requirements:
Renter must be at least 28 years of age and have a driver's license valid for motorcycle operation.

Reservations:
Reservations are recommended. With a limited supply, newest motorcycles are rented first. Deposits of $250 per vehicle are required at least 60 days in advance to confirm reservation (returnable with 30-day notice). Checks accepted if received 30 days in advance.

Other services:
- Tours to United States West Coast
- Canadian tours (western Canada, Canadian Rockies)
- KIMT will design specific tours for groups of 5 or more participants
- Affiliated with tour operators in Alaska and Mexico
- KIMT's partner in the United Kingdom provides guided tours of Great Britain and France

UNITED STATES, GERMANY, AND SOUTH AFRICA

mhs Motorradtouren GmbH

Donnersbergerstr. 32
D-8000 Munich 19
GERMANY

Contact: Herbert Schellhorn
Phone: (49) 89/1684888
FAX: (49) 89/1665549

Hours:
Monday through Friday, 8:00 a.m. to 1:00 p.m.; Saturday, 9:00 a.m. to noon

Motorcycles available and rates:

In Johannesburg, South Africa
Prices include insurance (5 percent collision deductible, minimum R 250) and 400 km free per day, minimum rental time is four days, and international driver's license is required.
- BMW R80 G/S Paris-Dakar or K75, DM 155 per day plus R 0.20 per extra km; deposit R 1,000 (approximately U.S. $450)
- BMW R80 RT, DM 170 per day plus R 0.25 per extra km; deposit R 1,000

In Munich
Prices include insurance (DM 1,000 deductible) and 300 km are free per day.
- Several Suzukis from 250cc to 1100cc are available. Prices range from DM 90 per day to DM 225 per day. Extra km is DM 0.25 to DM 0.70. Deposit required is DM 1,000.

In the United States: Miami, New York, Los Angeles, or San Diego
Prices include insurance (with collision deductible) and 100 miles are free per day.
- Bikes from 400cc to 1200cc from several Japanese brands or BMW R80, K100, or Harley-Davidson are available. Prices range from DM 50 to DM 200 per day. Extra mileage is $.10 to $.30 per mile. Deposit is $250 to $1,000 depending on the motorcycle.
- "Drive USA" cross-country plan is available from Los Angeles to Miami or New York, or in the reverse direction.

Price includes:
See above.

Deposit required:
See above.

Insurance arrangements:
See above.

Accessories:
Rental bikes in South Africa and Germany are equipped with panniers; rental bikes in the United States have panniers or soft saddle bags.

Special requirements:
Renter must have driver's license validated for motorcycle operation. International driver's license should be validated for motorcycle operation.

Reservations:
Reservations in Germany must be made at least 21 days in advance; in the United States and South Africa reservations are required at least 40 days in advance. When bookings are made with shorter advance notice add DM 50 per booking and bike for express service.

Rental fees must be paid 40 days in advance. If the booking is made later than 40 days before the trip starts, payment must be made immediately upon receiving the bill.

Other services:
- Scheduled motorcycle tours
- Tour packages for individuals that include booked hotels, maps, and descriptions for any of the following countries: Germany, France, Switzerland, Austria, Italy, Northern Yugoslavia, Kenya, and South Africa. (Price is DM 40 to DM 60 plus DM 10 per day, plus DM 7 to DM 15 per booked hotel room. Each tour package is individually designed for each client.)
- Customized motorcycle trips for companies, clubs, and associations from five to 50 persons
- Various kinds of insurance packages
- Motorcycle Purchase Plan. Buy a new BMW (or a used one) in St. Louis and bring it back to Germany after your trip in the United States. mhs Motorradtouren will handle all the details, including: reservation of the bike, flight arrangements, insurance, air transportation of the bike to Germany, duty, taxes, and registration of the bike in Germany. Prices range from DM 14,000 to DM 25,000, all-inclusive. Reservations should be made early and must be accompanied by a deposit of DM 5,000. Balance is due within four weeks after all arrangements have been made.

UNITED STATES	**Moturis, Ltd.**
Moturis	P.O. Box 1294 CH 8058 Zurich Airport SWITZERLAND Office: Kirchgasse 22 CH 8302 Kloten SWITZERLAND Contact: Conny Miro Phone: (41) 1-814-09-61 FAX: (41) 01-814-14-79 Telex: 829 380 USAT CH
Hours:	• *Pickup hours:* Monday through Saturday 1:00 p.m. to 4:00 p.m. • *Drop-off hours:* Monday through Saturday 9:00 a.m. to 11:00 a.m. • Closed Sundays and holidays

Rental locations:
United States: Miami and Los Angeles

Motorcycles available and rates:
- Honda VT 800 C Shadow (800cc, two-cylinder, shaft-driven, liquid-cooled), two saddle bags, luggage rack, and windshield. Available in Los Angeles and Miami. Rates: $48 per day plus $.16 per mile over 100 miles; CDW insurance $10 per day
- BMW K 75 (750cc, five speed, three-cylinder, shaft-driven, liquid-cooled), two saddle bags, luggage rack, and windshield. Available in Los Angeles only. Rates: $68 per day plus $.18 per mile over 100 miles; CDW insurance $11 per day
- Suzuki GV 1400 Cavalcade (1400 cc, four-cylinder, shaft-driven, five speed, liquid-cooled) two saddle bags, top case, AM/FM radio, cassette, cruise control, auto level, windshield, and fairing. Available in Los Angeles only. Rates: $72 per day plus $.20 per mile over 100 miles; CDW insurance $12 per day
- Harley-Davidson Heritage Softail (1340 cc, two-cylinder, belt-driven, five speed, air-cooled), two saddle bags, luggage rack, and windshield. Available in Los Angeles only. Rates: $99 per day plus $.22 over 100 miles; CDW insurance $14 per day
- Prices do not include sales taxes (Los Angeles: 6.5 percent; Miami: six percent).

- Discounts of five percent for rentals over 28 days and ten percent for rentals over 42 days are available.
- All major credit cards are accepted (AMEX, VISA, Master/Eurocard, Diners card, and all U.S. travelers' checks). Eurochecks are not accepted.
- A preparation fee of $35 is charged for transfers to and from airport hotel. No transfers to or from downtown.
- Penalty for change in confirmed reservation: $25 for each change beyond the first.
- Penalty for cancellation of reservation: up to 31 days prior to rental date, $100; 30 days or less prior to rental date, 100 percent of rental price.
- Penalty for late drop-off: $30 per hour; $300 per day.
- Surcharge for cleaning the motorcycle, if it is returned dirty: $50.
- Surcharge for drop-off at different location: $300.

Price includes:
Free 100 miles per day; mileage charge thereafter. Free transfer from airport to rental location.

Deposit required:
Security deposit is $2,500 per unit without CDW. With CDW insurance, security deposit is $100. Major credit cards (VISA, MC, AMEX), cash, or traveler's checks required.

Insurance arrangements:
Rental price includes liability coverage ($300,000 in United States) and collision damage with $2,500 deductible. A Collision Damage Waiver (CDW) can be purchased to reduce the collision damage deductible to $100. United States residents, no matter what their nationality, must provide their own motorcycle liability insurance; they are not covered through the rental
insurance. U.S. residents should consult their own insurance agents for assistance.

Accessories:
Camping equipment is offered to renters at $50 per motorcycle. Neither helmets nor any special clothing are available from Moturis; renter is responsible for his own.

Special requirements:
Minimum rental is seven days. Renter must be at least 21 years of age and have driver's license valid for operating motorcycles over 125 cc. Motorcycles may not be taken into Mexico, Death Valley (between May 1 and September 30), logging roads, or other private roads.

Reservations:
Reservations must be made well in advance, as the supply of motorcycles is limited. Contact Zurich office.

Other services:
Moturis also offers campers and trailers for rent.

CALIFORNIA — S.F. Wheels

2715 Hyde St.
San Francisco, CA 94133

Contact: Jeff Sears
Phone: 415-931-0234
FAX: Not available

Hours:
Seven days per week, 9:00 a.m. to 7:00 p.m.

Background:
S.F. Wheels was founded by Jeff Sears in 1987 with ten motorscooters. He began renting large bikes in 1989 and expanded his fleet to its present size of 50 scooters and up to eight motorcycles during the summer months.

Motorcycles available:
Presently a small fleet, including a Kawasaki Concourse and Vulcan 750

Rates:
Both motorcycles cost $150 per day and $700 per week to rent.

Price includes:
Unlimited mileage, liability insurance, two helmets, and maps

Deposit required:
A $2,500 deposit is required on all rentals and is payable by cash, traveler's checks, or credit card.

Insurance arrangements:
Liability insurance is included in the price of rental. Comprehensive insurance is available at extra cost.

Accessories:

S.F. Wheels has a wide variety of accessories, including helmets, gloves, and leather jackets.

Special requirements:

Renters must have a valid motorcycle license. Minimum age to rent scooters is 18 and 21 for motorcycles.

Reservations:

Reservations are advised. A deposit of $50 per day per motorcycle will confirm your reservation with no advance time needed. S.F. Wheels accepts Mastercard, VISA and American Express.

Other services:

- Motor scooter and bicycle rentals
- Although S.F. Wheels does not have a formal buy-sellback program available, they are willing to purchase a motorcycle locally for you and then resell it for you after you have completed your trip. They would require two weeks notice to arrange the purchase and insurance documentation.

CALIFORNIA AND GERMANY

Von Thielmann Tours

P.O. Box 87764
San Diego, CA 92138

VON THIELMANN TOURS

Contact: Gina Guzzardo
Phone: 619-463-7788 or 619-234-1558
FAX: 619-234-1458

Motorcycles available:

Touring, sports, and chopper type motorcycles are available from approximately 400cc to 1200cc.

Rates:

Munich, Germany: prices range from approximately $65 per day and up, depending on size. Minimum rental is three days. Flat rates are available, including mileage.

California: prices range from approximately $48 per day plus $7 per day for insurance (includes 2,000 free miles per week). Minimum rental is two weeks.

Deposit required:
Germany, $600; California, $500.

Insurance arrangements:
Included is liability insurance and comprehensive insurance with a deductible.

Other services:
• Guided tours

SOUTHWESTERN UNITED STATES

Western States Motorcycle Tours

534 West Wilshire Dr.
Phoenix, Arizona 85003

Contact: Frank Del Monte
Phone: 602-258-9048
FAX: 602-274-2836

Motorcycles available:
One- to three-year-old Hondas, Harley-Davidsons, BMWs, and others are available for you to purchase and then sell back, using Western States Motorcycle Tours as your agent. In many cases the motorcycle can be resold at the end of your trip with less depreciation than comparable rental costs.

Rates:
Western States Motorcycle Tours charges a fee of $300 when you purchase the motorcycle initially, and $100 to sell it for you at the end of your trip.

Price includes:
A motorcycle that has been serviced, registered, licensed, and insured.

Deposit required:
Funds for motorcycle purchase are required 60 days in advance.

Insurance arrangements:
Western States Motorcycle Tours will arrange for motorcycles bought through them to be insured.

Accessories:
Western States Motorcycle will arrange for installation of requested accessories.

Reservations:
Ninety days notice is required to purchase, insure, license, and inspect motorcycle.

Other services:
- Guided motorcycle tours of the southwestern United States
- Trip planning services for motorcycle travelers

RENTALS IN SOUTH AMERICA

VENEZUELA   Tours, S.R.L.

VENEZUELA EN MOTOCICLETA
Venezuela on bike

Edif. Res. Los Sauces
Entrada A, Piso 8, Apto. 1
Valencia
VENEZUELA

Contact: Werner Glode
Phone: (58) 41-213007
FAX: (58) 41-342950
Telex: (58) 41-45116

Motorcycles available and rates:
- Yamaha RD350: $33 per day; $200 per week
- BMW R100: $70 per day; $450 per week

Security deposit:
A deposit is required: $1,400 for the RD350 and $3,000 for the R100. The deposit is refunded when the bike is returned free of damage.

Motorcycle insurance:
Liability insurance provided by Tours S.R.L.; insurance for the motorcycle itself is not available in Venezuela.

Helmets:
Riders are expected to bring their own

Reservations:
Must be made in advance as there is a limited number of machines

Other services:
- Guided tours of Venezuela

RENTALS IN GREAT BRITAIN

ENGLAND

H.G.B. Motorcycles

69-71 Park Way
Ruislip Manor, Middlesex HA4 8NS
UNITED KINGDOM

Contact: Sue Hale
Phone: (44) 895-676451
FAX: (44) 895-676822

Hours: Monday through Saturday, 9:00 a.m. to 6:00 p.m.

Motorcycles available:
H.G.B. Motorcycles is a Honda motorcycle retailer. Four models of Honda motorcycles are available for rent: H100, CB350, VT500, and NTV600.

Rates:

	Per day	Per weekend (Fri.-Mon.)	Per week
Honda H100 (min. age 17)	£20	N/A	£ 85
Honda CB350 (min. age 21)	£30	£60	£110
Honda VT500 (min. age 21)	£30	£75	£125
Honda NTV600 (min. age 21)	£30	£75	£125

Note: Prices exclude 15 percent Value Added Tax. H.G.B. Motorcycles accepts cash, traveler's checks, and any major credit card.

Price includes:
Insurance, luggage panniers and racks, and unlimited mileage

Deposit required:
A £100 deposit is required for rentals.

Insurance arrangements:
Insurance is included in the cost of rental and covers any damage in excess of £250. However, a damage waiver is available for £5 per day which would reduce the amount the renter would have to pay in the event of an accident to £50.

Accessories:
H.G.B. has a wide variety of accessories for sale.

Special requirements:
H.G.B. will accept any license providing that it is designated for motorcycle use.

Reservations:
For large groups during May through September it is advisable to make your reservations well in advance. A £100 deposit is required to reserve a motorcycle.

Other services:
- A buy-sellback plan is available which would allow you to buy a motorcycle from H.G.B. and sell it back, provided that it's in good condition, for 20 percent less than what you paid. Assistance is available in obtaining insurance.
- Honda sales and service.

ENGLAND

Raceways Rental

201/203 Lower Road
Rotherhithe, London SE16 2LW
UNITED KINGDOM

Contact: Greg Holland-Merten
Phone: (44) 71-252-3802 or
(44) 71-237-6494
FAX: Not available

Background:
Raceways Rental was founded ten years ago by Greg Holland-Merten as an extension of his Kawasaki dealership. He has been a motorcyclist all his life and a dealer for the past 22 years. His enterprise employs eight people. Raceways is conveniently located in central London 1.5 miles from the Tower of London, one-quarter mile from the Rotherhithe Tunnel, and 100 yards from the Surrey Quays underground station.

Hours:
Monday through Saturday,
9:00 a.m. to 5:00 p.m.

Motorcycles available:
Kawasaki motorcycles ranging from 50 cc to 750 cc. All are new machines (less than one year old).

Rates:
- Kawasaki 125 cc .... £ 95 per week
- Kawasaki 250 cc .... £ 95 per week
- Kawasaki 350 cc .... £125 per week
- Kawasaki 550 cc .... £155 per week
- Kawasaki 750 cc .... £185 per week

Price includes:
Insurance, 24-hour breakdown assistance, all government and sales taxes, and rear luggage rack and top cases

Not included in price:
Helmet or fuel

Deposit required:
A blank credit card voucher is required by Raceways to cover any damage to motorcycle.

Insurance arrangements:
Insurance is included in rental price and covers any damage to motorcycle and third party property worth more than £350. Renters are responsible for first £350 worth of damages. You must be at least 21 years old to receive insurance.

Accessories:
Raceways rents helmets (full face), rainsuits, gloves, throw-over panniers, etc., for £1 per day per item.

Special requirements:
A driver's license with proof of address and a passport are required to rent a motorcycle.

Reservations:
Reservations are recommended and may be made by telephone.

Other services:
New and used motorcycle sales, parts, servicing, and accessories

ENGLAND	**Scootabout Motorcycle Centre**
SCOOTABOUT motorcycle centre	59 Albert Embankment London SE1 7TP ENGLAND Contact: Charles S.C. Ram, Director Phone: (44) 71-582-0055 FAX: (44) 71-735-7818
U.S. agent:	International Motorcycle Touring Association 8119 North Calvert St. Baltimore, MD 21218 Phone: 301-889-6810 FAX: 301-235-1562

Background:

Scootabout is a resource touring enthusiasts should know about. It started back in 1974 when Charlie Ram, for the third time that month, had the pleasure of pushing his Triumph Bonnie two miles up the road to the shop. The prospect of his forthcoming two-week tour of Devon and Cornwall on foot with a sidecar as a backpack was rapidly losing its appeal. Upon his arrival back home, he was greeted by a flying "Yellow pages," dispatched by his brother with some terse advice: "Rent a bike if you really want to make that trip." However, Charlie soon discovered that no firms existed that would rent him a motorcycle. "Now, there's an idea," he thought. And so, his motorcycle rental business was conceived.

Since that precipitating event Scootabout has grown to its present inventory of more than 100 motorcycles, catering to the needs of a domestic and international motorcycling clientele. Charlie is well aware of the demands made by international travelers for dependability of his service and reliability of his machines. He supports his rental program with on-site mechanics to maintain his machines and a selection of accessories needed by touring riders.

Scootabout's location is ideal: In central London near the Vauxhall tube station, one over from Victoria station.

Hours:	Monday through Friday, 9:00 a.m. to 6:00 p.m.

Motorcycles available:

Various types from mopeds to 1000cc street touring machines. The larger machines are most suitable for touring and are maintained to high standards by Scootabout mechanics. In the event of a breakdown or tire puncture, the Automobile Association (AA) service (included in rental fee) provides for free assistance or transport of the machine anywhere in the

314 MOTORCYCLE RENTAL AGENCIES

United Kingdom. Not listed below are mopeds and small motorcycles. Contact Scootabout for more information about small machines.

Motorcycles available and rates:

	* Per day	Per week
Kawasaki GT550 (min. age 21)	£26.95	£134.75
Honda NTV600 (min. age 25)	£32.95	£164.75
Kawasaki GT750 (min. age 25)	£32.95	£164.75
Honda VFR750 (min. age 25)	£41.50	£207.50
Yamaha XJ900 (min. age 25)	£41.50	£207.50
Honda CBR1000 (min. age 25)	£47.50	£237.50
BMW 1000 (min. age 25)	£47.50	£237.50
Kawasaki GTR1000 Concours (min. age 25)	£47.50	£237.50

Monthly rate: 25 percent discount from weekly rate
All prices subject to 15 percent Valued Added Tax.
* Note: A surcharge of one third of the daily rate applies to all one-day rentals.

Price includes:
Insurance, unlimited mileage, open-faced helmet, luggage carrier, AA membership, security chain, top box, and oils. Rental fee payable in advance at the start of the rental period.

Not included in price:
Fuel

Deposit required:
A security deposit of £100 to £350 is required for those participants who are paying by cash or traveler's checks. No deposit is required for those who are paying by VISA, Access/Mastercard, or American Express.

Insurance arrangements:
Liability and collision insurance for driving in the United Kingdom included in the price. Renter is responsible for the first £350 of damage to the motorcycle in the event of an accident. If you want to take the motorcycle to Europe, you need "green card" insurance, which costs about £25 per week (or part). AA Continental Cover is also needed; price is £24.50 for one to five days, £31.95 for six to 12 days, and £39.95 for 13 to 31 days. Scootabout can arrange for the green card and for AA Continental Cover.

Accessories:
Open-faced helmets offered free to renters. A selection of full-face helmets, clothing, and accessories are available for rent at very reasonable rates.

Special requirements:
Renter must have driver's license validated for motorcycle operation and be of minimum age listed above. International driver's license should be validated for motorcycle operation.

Reservations:
Recommended. Even with over 100 motorcycles, it is desirable to reserve a machine early. Scootabout needs details of time, dates, and type of machine desired. Reservation requires money order or credit card in the sum of £50 (U.K. bookings) and £100 (overseas bookings) to secure a confirmed reservation. The deposit will be deducted to the rental charge. In the event of a cancellation, 14 days notice is required to ensure a full refund.

Other services:
- Motorcycle sales, service, repairs, and accessories
- Free storage for excess luggage
- Computerized U.K. route plans, ferry rates and schedules, and touring suggestions

RENTALS IN WESTERN EUROPE

AUSTRIA	InterCity
	Reinprechtsdorfer Strasse 17 A-1050 Wien AUSTRIA Contact: Karl Petrus Phone: (43) 1-55-29-39 or (43) 1-55-61-86 FAX: Not available

Hours:	Monday through Friday, 8:00 a.m. to 6:00 p.m.
Motorcycles available:	Honda and Kawasaki motorcycles

Rates (in Austrian schillings):

	Per day incl. 100km	Per weekend incl. 500km	Five days incl. 400km	Per week incl. 1,000km	Extra km
Honda 500	AS 700	AS 2,100	AS 2,400	AS 4,500	AS 2.10
Kawasaki 500	AS 700	AS 2,100	AS 2,400	AS 4,500	AS 2.10
Honda 750	AS 960	AS 2,860	AS 3,260	AS 6,120	AS 2.80
Kawasaki 750	AS 960	AS 2,860	AS 3,260	AS 6,120	AS 2.80

Special unlimited mileage rates are available. All prices are subject to a 20 percent local tax and a one percent contract tax

Price includes:
Insurance

Deposit required:
A minimum deposit of AS 5,000 is required for renters who do not have an accepted credit card.

Insurance arrangements:
Insurance is included in rental price and covers damage up to AS 20,000,000. All damage up to AS 5,000 is the responsibility of the renter.

Special requirements:
Renters must be at least 19 years old and must have had a valid motorcycle driver's license for at least one year.

Reservations:
Reservations are required

Other services:
- Automobile rentals

FRANCE	**Nicea Location Rent**
	9, Avenue Thiers Station Gare S.N.C.F. 06000 Nice FRANCE Contact: Finazzo Aldo Phone: (33) 93 82 42 71 FAX: (33) 93 87 76 36
Hours:	Every day, all year, 9:00 a.m. to 6:00 p.m.

Motorcycles available:
Nicea Location Rent has a variety of motorcycles ranging from 125 cc to 600 cc.

Rates:

	One day	Three days	One week	Two weeks	Deposit
Yamaha DT 125 cc	FR 385	FR 990	FR 1,855	FR 3,340	FR 10,000
Yamaha XR 125 cc	FR 385	FR 990	FR 1,855	FR 3,340	FR 10,000
Yamaha SR 125 cc	FR 425	FR 1,085	FR 2,000	FR 3,600	FR 10,000
Yamaha DTR 125 cc	FR 465	FR 1,185	FR 2,655	FR 4,780	FR 10,000
Yamaha Virago 240 cc	FR 465	FR 1,185	FR 2,655	FR 4,780	FR 10,000
Honda VT 500 cc	FR 725	FR 1,740	FR 3,555	FR 6,400	FR 20,000
Yamaha Tenere 600 cc	FR 785	FR 1,890	FR 3,890	FR 6,990	FR 20,000
Yamaha XTE 600 cc	FR 785	FR 1,890	FR 3,890	FR 6,990	FR 20,000

Note: Monthly rates are available. Payment must be made by cash or credit card.

Price includes:
Unlimited mileage, insurance, helmet, and security lock

Not included in price:
Fuel

Deposit required:
Deposit requirements are listed above. All deposits must be paid by credit card (AMEX, VISA, etc.).

Insurance arrangements:
Insurance is included in price of the tour, but only covers third party damage. Renter is responsible for any damage to himself, to the motorcycle, or for its theft.

Accessories:
None available

Special requirements:
An international driver's license is required to rent a motorcycle.

Reservations:
Reservations are recommended, as the number of vehicles is limited and the demand is high, especially during popular seasons.

Other services:
• Rental of bicycles, mopeds, motor scooters, and cars

GERMANY	**Bosenberg Motorcycle Excursions**
Bosenberg Motorcycle Excursions	Mainzerstrasse 54 D-6550 Bad Kreuznach GERMANY
	Contact: Leon A. Heindel Phone: (49) 671-67312 FAX: (49) 671-67153

Hours:
Motorcycles are available from May through early October. Rental center is open Monday through Friday from 9:00 a.m. to 1:00 p.m. and from 2:30 p.m. to 6:00 p.m.; and Saturdays from 9:00 a.m. to 1:00 p.m. On Sundays and German holidays rental center is closed (1991 dates: May 1, 9, and 30 and October 3); 1992 dates: May 1 and 28, June 8 and 18 and October 3).

Description:

BME offers individual BMW motorcycle rentals from a rental location near the Frankfurt International Airport. Model reservations are handled in the order received. Reserving your particular model four to six months in advance isn't too early to ensure you have your particular model(s) for the time frame you want. For the high demand periods of July through August, a second rental period and alternate model selections are also recommended. Only after receiving your rental application, deposit, and prepayment of any requested hotel rooms, can BME process your reservation. Final confirmation, detailed pick-up instructions, and your "European Travel" information packet is sent by return mail. If no motorcycles are available for your indicated choices and rental period, your entire deposit will be refunded promptly.

Motorcycles and rates:

Rental Daily Rates, in U.S. dollars

	1 to 6 days	7 to 14 days	15 to 45 days	Extra Km
BMW R80RT	$ 99	$ 88	$ 83	$0.45
BMW K75RT	$109	$ 98	$ 93	$0.50
BMW K100LT	$125	$110	$105	$0.60
BMW K100RS	$130	$115	$110	$0.65

Price Includes:

Each rental day includes 200 kilometers (122 miles) at the daily rental rate. Mileage over this average daily rate is charged at U.S. $0.45 to $0.65 per kilometer, depending on the rental model. Added value tax (14 percent), any required maintenance and services, liability insurance, and collision and comprehensive insurance (with deductible) are included in the listed rental rate. All motorcycles are 1991 models. All K-series models have ABS (anti-lock braking system).

- Coordination for a BMW motorcycle rental reservation based upon your model choices and rental time frame
- $300 rental deposit made in your name and fully credited against your total rental cost
- Confirmation letter and "European travel" information packet with detailed pick-up instructions are sent to you
- English language rental contract
- Two BMW travel cases, with tool pouch and first aid kit
- Owner's manual and BMW European service handbook in English
- Arrival packet with additional tourist information
- Luggage and suitcase storage space at your rental center

Deposit required:

Booking deposit of $300 required when applying for rental reservation (fully applied against listed daily rental rate). Upon arrival at the rental center, the full rental balance amount and a security deposit of DM 1,500 (approximately U.S. $950) must be paid. Upon return of the undamaged motorcycle, the security deposit is refunded.

Methods of payment:
Selected credit cards (American Express, MasterCard, and VISA), traveler's checks, or cash may be used for the required payments. A three percent rebate on the rental price can be made for cash payments in lieu of credit card use.

Insurance arrangements:
International motor insurance card (i.e., green card) providing third party liability insurance with Deutsche Mark (DM) 2,000,000 ceiling (approximately U.S. $1,100,000) and for the motorcycle itself, collision and comprehensive insurance with a self-insured deductible of DM 1,500 (approximately U.S. $950)

Accessories:
You can rent BMW System III helmets, tank bags, sidecase inner bags, and roll bag at the rental center.

Special arrangements:
- Five or more motorcycles rented at the same time receive a five percent group discount.
- Hotel reservations near your rental center can be made by BME for your arrival and departure dates upon prepayment.

Special requirements:
Motorcycles can only be picked up the day after an international flight.

Other services:
- Guided tours in Europe

GERMANY   **Budget Rent-a-Car**

Dr.-Carl-V.-Linde-Str. 2
8023 Pullach
GERMANY

═Budget

Contact: Kathrin Fromling
Phone: (49) 89-79107-225
FAX: (49) 89-79107-282

Locations: In addition to the address above, motorcycles can be rented in any of the following locations:

Budget Rent-a-Car
Budapester Str. 16
1000 Berlin 30
Contact: Mrs. Schafer
Phone: (49) 30-2611357
FAX: (49) 30-2628857

Budget Rent-a-Car
Allerheiligen Str. 52
6000 Frankfurt/M.1
Contact: Mr. Zeller
Phone: (49) 69-290066
FAX: (49) 69-296328

Budget Rent-a-Car
Spalding Str. 110
2000 Hamburg 1
Contact: Mr. Voller
Phone: (49) 40-232393
FAX: (49) 40-234028

Budget Rent-a-Car
Amalienburgstr. 25
8000 Munich 60
Contact: Mr. Reither
Phone: (49) 89-8119292
FAX: (49) 89-79107311

Budget Rent-a-Car
Am Wehrhahn 77
4000 Dusseldorf 1
Contact: Mrs. Markowski
Phone: (49) 211-360401
FAX: (49) 211-161949

Hours:
Rental motorcycles are available April 1 to October 31.
Berlin: Monday through Friday 7:00 a.m. to 6:00 p.m., Saturday 8:00 a.m. to 1:00 p.m.
Frankfurt: Monday through Friday 7:00 a.m. to 6:30 p.m., Saturday 8:00 a.m. to 1:00 p.m.

Hamburg: Monday through Friday 7:00 a.m. to 7:00 p.m., Saturday 7:30 a.m. to 3:00 p.m., Sunday 11:00 a.m. to 7:00 p.m.
Munich: Monday through Friday 7:00 a.m. to 6:00 p.m., Saturday 8:00 a.m. to 12:00 p.m.
Dusseldorf: Monday through Friday 7:30 a.m. to 7:30 p.m., Saturday 8:00 a.m. to 1:00 p.m.

Motorcycles available and rates:

	Per day (70km)	Per weekend (140km)	Per week (400km)	Per month (1,500km)	Extra km
Low Rider Custom	DM 77	DM 118	DM 498	DM 1,980	DM 0.77
Heritage Softail Classic	DM 86	DM 139	DM 598	DM 2,450	DM 0.88
Electra Glide Classic	DM 99	DM 159	DM 698	DM 2,980	DM 0.99

Price includes:
Limited free kilometers as indicated above

Not included in price:
Fuel or insurance

Deposit required:
You must have a major credit card to leave as a deposit.

Insurance arrangements:
Insurance is available at extra cost. Weekly rates range from DM 95 to DM 135 (monthly rates range from DM 190 to DM 290). All motorcycle insurance has a deductible ranging from DM 500 to DM 1,000.

Accessories:
Helmets and kidney belts are available for rent for DM 15 and DM 5 per day, respectively.

Special requirements:
Renters must be at least 26 years old and have five years of licensed driving experience.

Reservations:
Reservations can be made via FAX. Reservations must be confirmed 48 hours prior to rental.

Other services:
- Car rentals

GERMANY   Harley Owners Group

See United States rentals section

GERMANY   K & K Fahrzeug Center Berkheim

Oberwiesenweg 22/1
7300 Esslingen-Berkheim
GERMANY

Contact: Peter & Michael Ksiazek
Phone: (49) 711-345-1081
FAX: (49) 711-345-4111

Hours:	Monday through Friday, 9 a.m to 6:00 p.m.; Saturday, 9:00 a.m. to 2:00 p.m.; Sunday 10:00 a.m. to 11:00 a.m. and 6:00 p.m. to 7:00 p.m.

Motorcycles available:
The Ksiazeks have a wide range of Kawasaki, Honda, Suzuki, and Yamaha motorcycles, including the following: Honda XBR500, CBX650E, VFR750F, and CBR1000F; Kawasaki EL250, GPZ500S, 550GT, GPX600R, ZZ-R600, GPX750R, ZXR750, GPZ900R, GTR1000, ZL1000, and ZZ-R1100; and Suzuki GS500E and GSX600F.

Rates:
Ranges from DM 135 per day to DM 270 per day, and DM 450 per week to DM 900 per week

Price includes:
German taxes, unlimited mileage, general insurance, and unlimited third party insurance

Not included in price:
Gasoline or additional insurance for damage to motorcycles

Deposit required:
A deposit is required ranging from DM 500 to DM 1000 per motorcycle and is payable by credit card or check.

Insurance arrangements:
Insurance is available at extra cost. Contact K & K for quotes.

Accessories:
Helmets, kidney belts, topcases, and trailers

Other services:
- Buys and sells motorcycle spare parts
- Automobile rentals

GERMANY AND TURKEY

Motorrad Spaett, KG

Rüdesheimerstrasse, 9
8000 Munich 21
GERMANY

Contact: Peter Spaett or
  Tommy Wagner or office
Phone: (49) 89-579370
FAX: (49) 89-5701769

Motorcycles available:
In Munich
Various types from 50cc city bikes to 1200cc street touring bikes, including Honda ST 1100, CBR 1000, NTV 650, CBR 600, NX 250, NX 650, VFR 750, and XL 600V (Transalp); Yamaha XTZ 660, XT 600, FZR 1000, FJ 1200, XJ 900, and XV 535. All motorcycles are 1990/1991 models.
In Antalya, Turkey
Yamaha XT600Z (Ténéré), XJ650, XJ550, and Honda CM400T

Rates:
- One day: DM 59 to DM 319, depending upon model chosen
- One week: Five times daily rate
- Two weeks: Nine times daily rate
- Three weeks: 13 times daily rate
- Four weeks: 17 times daily rate
- Five weeks: 21 times daily rate
- Six weeks: 25 times daily rate

Price includes:
Unlimited mileage

Deposit required:
Security deposit of DM 1,500 per unit. Major credit cards (Diners, American Express) or cash are accepted.

Insurance arrangements:
All vehicles are fully insured for comprehensive damage, with deductible of DM 1,500 (that is, you pay the first DM 1,500 of any damage caused by you; the insurance pays above that). An exclusion to the deductible amount is not possible. It is possible to travel to other European countries, but in case of damage you will have to arrange and pay for transport youself and the motorcycle back to the rental location.

Accessories:
Tank bags and clothing can be rented. Windshields are available only on touring bikes. A limited supply of helmets can be rented for a small charge.

Special requirements:
Primary renter must be at least 18 years of age for motorcycle under 50hp, and at least 21 years of age for motorcycle over 50hp. Renters need a passport and driver's license validated for motorcycle operation. German or American driver's license is acceptable, as is international driver's license validated for motorcycle operation.

Reservations:
Reservations must be made at least four weeks in advance. Inventory of motorcycles is limited.

Other services:
- Motorcycle parts, service, and accessories
- Guided tours to Turkey, the Alps, Austria, Italy, Switzerland, and Yugoslavia
- Training on GP courses in Rijeka, Yugoslavia; Brno, Czechoslovakia; Budapest, and Hungary

326 MOTORCYCLE RENTAL AGENCIES

GERMANY	Von Thielmann Tours

See United States rentals section

SWITZERLAND	Desmond Adventures, Inc.

DESMOND ADVENTURES, INC.

1280 South Williams Street
Denver, CO 80210

Contact: Thomas E. Desmond or Randall B. Harmon
Phone: 303-733-9248
FAX: 303-733-9601

Hours (in Denver):	Monday through Friday, 9:00 a.m. to 5:00 p.m. (Central time)
Rental locations:	Los Angeles and Zurich

Prices (motorcycles):
Starting at about $90 per day for a 750, a wide variety of motorcycles are available, averaging less than one year old, from BMW (K75S, K75C, K100RT, K100RS); Honda (CBR 600 and 1000, TransAlp, Shadow, VFR 750, ST1100); Suzuki (Katana 600, 750 and 1100); and Kawasaki (Concours 1000). Contact Desmond Adventures for complete information.

Price includes:
Unlimited mileage, limited liability insurance, van pickup and return, and directions and maps

Deposit required:
Security of $1,000 cash required for all motorcycles. Must be paid to Desmond prior to release of motorcycle.

Insurance arrangements:
Insurance is included in the rental price. The insurance has a deductible of $1,000, making the renter liable for the first $1,000 of damage to the motorcycle or to third parties. No medical insurance is provided to renters by Desmond Adventures, Inc.

Accessories:
All models have fairings, windshields, and saddlebags.

Special requirements:
Renter must be at least 25 years of age, have driver's license valid for motorcycle operation, and demonstrate driving ability to Desmond Adventures. Drivers and passengers must wear helmets and proper clothing.

Reservations:
Reservations are essential. Desmond has a good supply of motorcycles, but many of them are committed to scheduled tours.

Other services:
- Organized motorcycle tours through the European Alps and through the Southwest United States
- Shipping service to transport motorcycles anywhere in the contiguous United States and most of Canada

RENTALS IN THE MEDITERRANEAN AREA

CYPRUS — Prima Klima Reisen GmbH

Hohenstaufenstrasse 69
1000 Berlin 30
GERMANY

Contact: Peter Schmidt, Klaus Brass
Phone: (49) 30 216 10 82/83
FAX: (49) 30 216 10 80
Telex: 186381 pkr d

Location:	Polis, Cyprus

Motorcycles and rates:

Rental Daily Rates, in Cyprus pounds

	1 to 2 days	3 to 6 days	7 to 14 days	15 or more days
Yamaha 50cc	C£3.00	C£2.50	C£2.50	C£2.25
Suzuki 125cc	C£6.00	C£5.00	C£4.50	C£4.50
Yamaha 175cc	C£7.50	C£6.00	C£5.00	C£5.00
Honda 200cc XR	C£8.50	C£7.00	C£6.50	C£6.00
Honda 250cc HR	C£9.00	C£8.00	C£7.00	C£6.50
Yamaha 350cc or Cagiva 350cc	C£10.00	C£9.00	C£8.00	C£7.50

Price includes:
Maintenance, oil, unlimited mileage, and substitute vehicle in case of a breakdown. Fuel is not included in the price.

Insurance arrangements:
Liability insurance is included, with a deductible of C£300 which is the responsibility of the renter. A collision damage excess waiver is available at C£3 per day. Damage to tires is not included.

Helmets:
Riders are expected to bring their own helmet.

Reservations:
Must be made in advance as there is a limited number of machines.

Special notes:
All current foreign driving licenses are valid in Cyprus. Minimum age for renting a motorcycle is 25 years. Minimum rental is two days.

Other services:
- Scheduled motorcycle tours to Cyprus and India
- Surfboard and equipment rental, all watersports (diving, water skiing)
- Self-catering guest houses
- Informal hotels
- Coach tours through Europe and India
- Jeep tours through Venezuela and Morocco
- Guided walks
- Mountain bike tours and rentals in Cyprus

TURKEY — Motorrad Spaett, KG

See Western European rentals section

RENTALS IN AFRICA & MIDDLE EAST

SOUTH AFRICA	mhs Motorradtouren GmbH
See United States rentals section	

RENTALS IN AUSTRALIA

AUSTRALIA	Bike Tours Australia
	Einsiedeleiweg 16 D-5942 Kirchhundem 4 GERMANY Contact: Eveline Veenkamp Phone: (49) 2764-7824 FAX: (49) 2764-7938
Motorcycles available:	Yamaha XT 600
Location:	Motorcycle must be picked up and returned to Melbourne, Australia.

Rates:
You can buy the Yamaha XT 600 on a sell-back basis for AUS $2,950. It will be one to two years old, in good condition, and ready to drive away. Bike Tours Australia will guarantee to buy it back up to six months later for AUS $1,500, if the motorcycle is returned to the premises with no severe damage or severely worn parts. Repurchase is made in cash.

Price includes:
Maps, travel information and advice, transfers between airport and Bike Tours Australia, and limited liability insurance (personal injury)

Price does not include:
Insurance (see below)

Deposit required:
A deposit of DM 500 is required at time of making reservation. The balance of payment is due in Melbourne in Australian dollars at the time of pickup.

Insurance arrangements:
All-risk insurance (fire, theft, and property damage) available at the Melbourne location for AUS $35 per week (the first AUS $500 damage must be paid by the owner), or AUS $60 per week (with no deductible).

Accessories:
Camping equipment (tent, mattress, cooking gear, and cook stove) can be provided by Bike Tours Australia on a rental basis for AUS $250.

Special requirements:
Renter must be at least 21 years of age and have driver's license valid for motorcycle operation.

Reservations:
Reservation must be made in writing to Bike Tours Australia's German office at least 30 days in advance.

Other services:
- Bike Tours Australia also operates organized tours of Australia, the United States, and Canada.
- Bike Tours Australia will also sell a motorcycle without a commitment to repurchase it, at the same price given above. The motorcycle must then be registered in the name of the new owner. The total extra costs are AUS $120 for Australian sales tax, and AUS $230 for registration and insurance. The owner can resell the motorcycle anywhere and anytime he wishes.

AUSTRALIA — Hawthorn Motorcycles

163 Camberwell Rd.
East Hawthorn, Victoria 3123
AUSTRALIA

Contact: Ed Garner
Phone: (61) 3-882-5973
FAX: (61) 3-882-7467

Hours: Monday through Friday, 9:00 a.m. to 6:00 p.m.; Saturday, 9:00 a.m. to 1:00 p.m.

Motorcycles available:
Hawthorn Motorcycles has 60 motorcycles for hire, ranging from 250cc license test bikes to 1100cc touring motorcycles. Listed below is a sampling of their larger machines.

Motorcycles and rates:

Rental Rates, in Australian dollars

	Per Day	Two-day Weekend	Per Week	Deposit
BMW R100	$95	$190	$490	$300
BMW R65L/S	$95	$190	$490	$300
Harley-Davidson XLX883 Sportster	$125	$250	$600	$1000
Harley-Davidson FXR Superglide	$150	$300	$800	$1000
Harley-Davidson FXRS Low Rider	$150	$300	$800	$1000
Harley-Davidson FXSTC Softail Custom	$175	$350	$900	$1000
Honda CB750F	$85	$170	$450	$300
Honda FT500	$80	$160	$420	$300
Kawasaki GPZ900R	$110	$220	$600	$500
Kawasaki GPZ750	$100	$200	$560	$300
Kawasaki GT550	$80	$160	$420	$300
Suzuki GS1100	$90	$180	$450	$300
Suzuki GS650G	$85	$170	$420	$300
Suzuki GR650	$80	$160	$420	$300
Yamaha XJ900	$90	$180	$450	$300
Yamaha XJ750	$85	$170	$450	$300

Note: Mini bikes, unregistered trail bikes, registered trail bikes and 250cc road bikes are also available at lower prices. All purchases subject to four percent tax. All major credit cards accepted (AMEX, VISA, Bankcard, or Diners Club).

Price includes:
Insurance, unlimited mileage

Not included in price:
Fuel, accessories

Deposit required:
See price list above

Insurance arrangements:
Insurance is included in the price of rental. If the motorcycle is damaged, the renter must pay the first AUS $500 of the cost (AUS $1,000 for Harleys).

Accessories:
Hawthorn Motorcycles has a wide range of accessories available for rent including trailers, jackets, gloves, gearsacks and helmets. Helmets can be rented for AUS $5 per day or AUS $20 per week; trailers for AUS $15 per day or AUS $50 per week.

Special requirements:
Renters must be at least 21 years of age.

Reservations:
Hawthorn Motorcycles recommends that you make reservations in advance.

Other services:
- Buy-sellback arrangements are available
- License tests available for AUS $60
- Monthly rates available upon request

AUSTRALIA

Sarroy Enterprises

P.O. Box 660
Capalaba, Queensland
AUSTRALIA 4157

Contact: George Cunningham
Phone: (61) 7-207-4267
FAX: (61) 7-245-6184

Background:
Sarroy Enterprises was formed in January 1989 by David Wells and George and Linda Cunningham after six months of research on motorcycle tours in Queensland. They began their motorcycle touring business with the idea of offering organized sightseeing tours to Australia's East Coast and later expanded the scope of their business to include motorcycle rentals to independent travelers.

Motorcycles available:
Well-equipped BMW and Japanese touring bikes

Rates:
- Per day .... AUS $120
- Per week .... AUS $720

Price includes:
Unlimited mileage, liability insurance, two helmets, touring information, extras. One-way rental with drop-off in another city is possible at extra charge.

Deposit required:
The estimated amount of the rental fee along with a security deposit of AUS $1,000 is required on all rentals and is payable by cash, travelers checks or credit card. The deposit is refundable when the bike is returned in good order and on time. If damage to the bike occurs, the deposit is used to cover the insurance deductible.

Insurance arrangements:
Liability insurance is included in the price of rental.

Accessories:
Sarroy can supply helmets to renters, although it is better to bring your own.

Special requirements:
Renters must have a valid motorcycle license.

Reservations:
Reservations are required. The estimated rental fee and security deposit are required to confirm your reservation.

Other services:
- Guided motorcycle tours of Australia's East Coast

RENTALS IN NEW ZEALAND

NEW ZEALAND	**Graeme Crosby Motorcycles**
	299 Great North Road P.O. Box 78-015 Grey Lynn, Auckland NEW ZEALAND Contact: Bruce Pollard Phone: (64) 9-763-320 or (64) 9 762 711 FAX: (64) 9-765-033
Booking agents:	Von Thielman Tours P.O. Box 87764 San Diego, CA 92138 Phone: 619-463-7788 FAX: 619-234-1458 Select Destination Resources, Costa Mesa, CA Phone: 714-722-6406

Motorcycle bookings can be made through a computerized booking service at any New Zealand Embassy or Consulate, or through one of Graeme Crosby's many booking agents worldwide. Contact Graeme Crosby for the agent nearest you. Above are booking agents for the United States.

Hours:	• Monday through Wednesday and Friday, 8:00 a.m. to 5:30 p.m. • Thursday, 8:00 a.m. to 8:30 p.m. • Saturday, 9:00 a.m. to 12:30 p.m.

Motorcycles available:
Yamaha and Kawasaki motorcycles

Rates:
- Yamaha XV500 NZ $75 per day
- Yamaha XJ600 NZ $85 per day
- Kawasaki 750 NZ $95 per day

Note: A discount of 10 percent is available to group tours and long term rentals. Prices are subject to change.

Price includes:
Insurance, taxes, and unlimited mileage

Not included in price:
Fuel and oil, helmets, or tire punctures

Deposit required:
A $500 deposit/bond is required for all motorcycle rentals. Any damage to motorcycle or third party's property will deducted from deposit.

Insurance arrangements:
Insurance is included in the price of rental and covers any damage over NZ $500. Renter is responsible for any damage to motorcycle, accessories, and third party property damage up to NZ $500.

Accessories:
Helmets and packs are available for hire at NZ $20 for the term of hire.

Special requirements:
- Most foreign/domestic driver's licenses are accepted provided they are valid for motorcycle use and cover the motorcycle to which the rental is applicable.
- Renters must be at least 18 years old.

Reservations:
Required. You should make them at least a month in advance.

Other services:
- Yamaha, Kawasaki, and Harley-Davidson retailer
- Airport transfers available with prior arrangement at a cost of NZ $30 per person
- Motorcycle repairs and parts

NEW ZEALAND — Te Waipounamu Motorcycle Tours

P.O. Box 673
Christchurch
NEW ZEALAND

Contact: John Rains
Phone: (64) 3 523 541
FAX: (64) 3 652 155

Booking agent:	Beach's Motorcycle Adventures 2763 West River Parkway Grand Island, NY 14072-2087 USA Phone: 716-773-4960 FAX: 716-773-5227
Booking agent:	Schnieder Reisen Schomburgstrasse 120 2000 Hamburg 50 GERMANY Phone: (49) 403 802 0633 FAX: (49) 403 88965
Booking agent:	Volker Lenzner TransCyclist International CPO Box 2064 Tokyo, 100-91 JAPAN Phone: (81) 3-402-5385 FAX: (81) 3-402-5358

Motorcycles available:
- BMW K-series and BMW R-series models, side bags, fairing, and windshield
- Yamaha XJ750 and XJ900, fairings, and soft luggage
- Honda 500 models and soft luggage

Rates (in New Zealand dollars, for one-week period):
- BMW K-series: NZ $645 plus NZ $.10 per km
- BMW R-series (late models): NZ $545 plus NZ $.10 per km
- BMW R-series (early models): NZ $475 plus NZ $.10 per km
- Yamaha XJ750 or XJ900: NZ $475 plus NZ $.10 per km
- Honda 500cc models: NZ $375 plus NZ $.10 per km

Deposit required:
Security deposit is NZ $500 per unit; will be refunded if motorcycle is returned without damage

Insurance arrangements:
Rental price includes liability coverage.

Accessories:
Helmet, gloves, and rain suits are available for rent at a nominal cost.

Special requirements:
Renter must be at least 21 years of age (25 years of age for larger motorcycles) and have driver's license valid for motorcycle operation. Te Waipounamu reserves the right to decline to rent to anyone for any reason.

Reservations:
Should be made in advance, as the supply of motorcycles is limited.

Other services:
Te Waipounamu also runs guided tours of New Zealand and can offer considerable assistance in planning your trip, arranging accommodations, and suggesting routes in New Zealand. Motorcycles must be rented from and returned to Christchurch.

MOTORCYCLE TRANSPORT FACILITIES

In response to inquiries from several travel agencies and prospective overseas travelers, we have identified three companies that will help you ship motorcycles. Of course, most ships and ferries that carry automobiles will also carry motorcycles if they are properly secured. Some tour operators will arrange for shipment of motorcycles as part of their total service menu for clients. See the Tour Operator section for details. Please let us know if you find other companies that offer motorcycle shipping services.

UNITED STATES AND CANADA

Desmond Adventures, Inc.

1280 South Williams Street
Denver, CO 80210

Contact: Thomas E. Desmond
   or Randall B. Harmon
Phone: 303-733-9248
FAX: 303-733-9601

| Hours: | Monday through Friday, 9:00 a.m. to 5:00 p.m. (Central time) |

Description:
Desmond Adventures will transport your motorcycle between points in the contiguous United States and most of Canada. There is no need for disassembly or crating of your motorcycle for the Desmond service. You can use the service to attend distant rallies or to tour far places.

As the prices and details are dependent upon the destination of your trip and other factors, contact Desmond Adventures for more specific information.

WORLDWIDE

mhs Motorradtouren GmbH

Donnersbergerstr. 32
D-8000 Munich 19
GERMANY

Contact: Herbert Schellhorn
Phone: (49) 89/1684888
FAX: (49) 89/1665549

Description:
mhs Motorradtouren's "Fly and Ride" program is a new and easy way to take your own motorcycle to one of 18 different cities on five continents. The procedure is easy: you bring your motorcycle to the airport one day prior to departure, put it onto a provided pallet, and the bike will travel on the same airplane in which you are flying.

Locations:
The "Fly and Ride" program is available from the following airports to Frankfurt, or vice versa: Los Angeles, San Francisco, Dallas, Miami, Atlanta, Boston, Newark (New York), Toronto, Vancouver, Rio de Janeiro, Buenos Aires, Cairo, Johannesburg, Tel Aviv, Sanaa (Jemen), Sydney (Australia), Nice, and Malaga. It is also possible to book flights between any two cities on the list, but Frankfurt must be the "hub" for those trips. For example, to fly from Los Angeles to Sydney, you would book two legs: Los Angeles to Frankfurt, and Frankfurt to Sydney.

Price:
Tariffs are determined according to the German Holiday tariff on Lufthansa Airlines. Passengers pay the normal holiday rate (plus airport fees); the motorcycle tariff is equal to the tariff for one passenger, plus DM 395 (round trip).

UNITED STATES **World Motorcycle Tours**

14 Forest Avenue
Caldwell, NJ 07006

Contact: Warren Goodman
Phone: 201-226-9107 or 800-443-7519
FAX: 201-226-8106

Description:
Over the years Warren Goodman has shipped many motorcycles, all *uncrated*, both for participation in his organized tours and for those travelers going "on their own." He continues to offer his services to one and all for the transport of uncrated motorcycles, with gateways at New York, Chicago, and Los Angeles. Warren is continually working on expanding the number of departure points.

As the prices and details are dependent upon the destination of your trip and other factors, contact World Motorcycle Tours for more specific information. As a guide, the cost to ship a motorcycle to Yugoslavia is about $.90 per pound from New York City, $1.05 from Chicago, and $1.20 from Los Angeles. Liability insurance in Europe will cost about $101.

RIDES AND RALLIES IN THE UNITED STATES

Motorcyclists love to get together. Indeed, the cameraderie of motorcycling is one of its strongest appeals. Anyone whose motorcycle has ever broken down on the road has probably learned that you don't have to wait long before a passing motorcyclist stops to help. It's one of the phenomena that has drawn many of us into the sport and kept us interested. In spite of the many opportunities for solo exploring and "getting away from it all", motorcycling is very much a people- oriented activity.

There are a great many organized activities for motorcyclists throughout the year and throughout the world. You only have to purchase one of the enthusiast magazines to learn of the many events held in your area. *Rider* and *Road Rider* magazines are good sources of information about touring activities. For those interested in more local events, participation in clubs and associations provide excellent opportunities to network.

In this section we have listed only rallies of national scope that have attracted at least 5,000 attendees in the past. At least three of these rallies are endorsed by local civic organizations such as the Chamber of Commerce, showing that motorcycle touring enthusiasts can be desirable visitors and important to the economy of an area.

NEW YORK STATE — Americade East 1991

Americade '91
P.O. Box 2205R
Glens Falls, NY 12801
Phone: 518-656-3696
FAX: 518-656-9207

Dates:	June 4 through June 8, 1991
Location:	Lake George, NY
Price:	• Per person, $45; per passenger, $40 • Children 3–11, $20; children under 3, free Payable by check, money order, VISA, or Mastercard

Description:
The Americade rally has a variety of events and tours including a championship rodeo, a scenic boat cruise, and minitours to Ausable Chasm, Vermont and the waterfalls of the Adirondacks. Activities include safety clinics, field events, contests, picnics, parades, barbecues, music, and dancing, and the crowning of King and Queen for 1991. Charity events such as a poker run and picnics are planned. All events and tours cost extra ranging in price from $6 to $11.

COLORADO — Americade West 1991

Americade '91
P.O. Box 2205R
Glens Falls, NY 12801
Phone: 518-656-3696
FAX: 518-656-9207

Dates:	September 2 through September 6, 1991
Location:	Estes Park, CO
Price:	• Per person, $40; per passenger, $35 • Children 3–11, $15; children under 3, free Payable by check, money order, VISA, or Mastercard

Description:
The Americade West rally includes a host of events such as a special barbecue, concert, entertainment, and contests (with over 100 trophies for motorcycles, clubs, and riders). In addition, there will be $10,000 in prizes given away. Various seminars and clinics will be offered, as well as demo rides from major manufacturers. Take one of the optional minitours such as the Canyon Tour, Peak to Peak Tour, or Horseback Tour. Explore the beautiful Rocky Mountains on a self-guided tour. By nightfall, join in the light parade, or sit on the sidelines and simply watch the spectacular show.

SOUTH DAKOTA	**Black Hills Classic**
	Jackpine Gypsies Motorcycle Club P.O. Box 627 Sturgis, SD 57785 Phone: 605-347-3418
Dates:	August 5 through August 11, 1991 and August 3 through August 9, 1992
Location:	Sturgis, South Dakota
Price:	$12 per person per event; you have choice of two events: tour of Mt. Rushmore National Park or tour of Devil's Tower.

Description:
Events include Hill Climb, Annual Big Daddy Rat Custom Chopper Trike and Motorcycle Show. Races include 600cc National Championship Short Track Race, the U.S. Western Regional Half Mile Championship Race, the Pro-Am Short Track Race, the Vintage TT, and Half Mile Races for pre-1972 motorcycles, the Sturgis Fifth Annual Harley National Dragstrip Finals, and the Harley-Davidson National Championship Half Mile Race. A wide range of vendors will be set up along Main Street during rally week.

ARIZONA	**1991 Grand Canyon International**
	1991 Grand Canyon International BMW Motorcycle Owners of America P.O. Box 489 Chesterfield, MO 63006-0489 Contact: Mr. D. N. Douglass, Managing Director Phone: 314-537-5511
Dates:	July 18 through July 21, 1991
Location:	Flagstaff, Arizona
Price:	• For registration by June 7, $18 per adult • For registration at the gate, $22 per adult

Description:
The 1991 International Classic will be at the Fort Tuthill County Fairgrounds which is situated in the middle of the Coconino National Forest. This area is laced with breathtaking, well-kept roads for touring. The Grand Canyon is within a lazy day's ride round-trip and the three county area is steeped in the history of the closing West.

Some of the highlights of the week include factory technical seminars, motorcycle safety, education and skills classes, a maintenance seminar, tours of historic sites, vintage BMW motorcycle judging, field events (non-competitive) for rider, two km Fun Run (foot race), 10 km Serious Run, kite flying contest, volley ball, music, and dancing.

This year's rally will draw about 4,500 from as far away as Great Britain, Europe, Canada, Japan, and Australia.

IOWA	**13th Annual Davis Rally**
	13th Annual Davis Rally Gene and Luci Davis 713 East Hamilton New Hampton, IA 50659 Phone: 515-394-2311
Dates:	September 6 through September 8, 1991 (Friday morning through Sunday afternoon)
Location:	New Hampton, Iowa

Price:	• $13 per person, with a discount available to AMA members • Children under 15 may attend for free

Description:
The Davis family celebrated the 12th anniversary of their rally in 1990 with an attendance of 3,500 touring enthusiasts from 28 states. Gene Davis, rally founder, began motorcycling at the young age of 52. He enjoyed attending rallies, but felt that there weren't enough of them so he started one of his own; his rally has become an annual event!

The Davis rally is for all motorcycle touring enthusiasts and does not cater to any particular type of motorcycle. Some of the planned events include breakfast and dinners rides, motorcycle stunt groups exhibition, Night Lights parade, and a poker run with 1,200 to 1,500 expected participants. Five bands are scheduled to perform and $15,000 in prizes will be awarded during the weekend. About 40 vendors with be there to offer you a variety of riding wear, souvenirs, and motorcycle accessories. Contact the Davises for a list of motels and campgrounds within the area.

FLORIDA	**Daytona Bike Week**
	Destination Daytona Information Services Dept. P.O. Box 910 Daytona Beach, FL 32115-0910 Phone: 800-854-1234
Dates:	March 1 through March 10, 1991
Location:	Daytona Beach, Florida

Description:
Daytona Bike Week, which celebrates its 50th year in 1991, is the largest motorcycle event in the world. Each year about 400,000 motorcycle enthusiasts from around the world come together for a ten-day festival that features both motorcycle races at the Daytona International Speedway and numerous motorcycle related activities and exhibits.

The city's Main Street is bustling with activity during Bike Week, and many other events are scheduled throughout the area including product expos, motorcycle tours, the "Big Daddy Rat Custom Chopper Show," Harley-Davidson exhibits, the world's largest motorcycle swap meet, the American Motorcycle Auction, the Great American Motorcycle Rodeo, and the 3rd Annual Malcolm Forbes Motorcycle Parade, with an estimated 5,000 motorcycle participating.

The centerpiece of Bike Week is the annual Daytona 200 motorcycle race, but a variety of other competitions including Supercross, sprint, enduro, and dirt track races are schedules to occur throughout the week.

NEW MEXICO — Golden Aspen Rally

Golden Aspen Rally Association
P.O. Box 2427
Ruidoso, NM 88345
Contact: Ron Andrews
Phone: 800-772-5597

Dates: September 25 through September 29, 1991

Location: Ruidoso, New Mexico

Description:
The Golden Aspen Rally began 22 years ago as part of a city-wide festival celebrating the foliage of the fall. The rally is part of Ruidoso's four-week Aspenweek event. There were 1,700 registered attendees in 1990, with 6,000 people attending the trade show. The 1991 rally is expected to draw at least 2,500, as it is scheduled at the same time of the Southwest Regional Road Riding Convention.

Daily events include a night light display contest, poker runs, tours, seminars, custom motorcycle contests, field event competition, the Iron Butt Run, and a Saturday parade. Thousands of dollars in prizes, including a motorcycle, will be awarded. Attend a Chuck Wagon dinner show and other entertainment events. Visit the large trade show (over 85 vendors and dealers) and browse through the motorcycles, riding gear, and accessories.

KENTUCKY — Harley Owners Group Rally

Harley Owners Group
3700 West Juneau
P.O. Box 453
Milwaukee, WI 53201
Contact: Vicki Lake
Phone: 800-258-2464
FAX: 414-935-4559

Dates: June 7 through June 9, 1991

Location:	Louisville, Kentucky

Description:
Preparation for the H.O.G. starts one to two years before the rally occurs. A prerequisite for the rally location is that a place must have beautiful scenery, good surrounding roads, and accommodations to take care of all H.O.G. participants (like the nearly 6,000 members who attended the 1990 rally in Sturgis, South Dakota).

Highlights for this year's rally include field events, seminars, demo rides, a poker run, and a ride-in show. Exhibitors are Harley-Davidson dealers or licensees representing motorcycle-related apparel and accessories. A Harley Owners Group hop is scheduled for one evening. Contact H.O.G. for information concerning lodging arrangements.

KENTUCKY — Rider Rally Kentucky

Rally Sponsor:	*Rider* Magazine P.O. Box 4000 Agoura, CA 91301 Contact: Rider Rally Staff Phone: 800-234-3450 or 818-991-4980
Location:	Richmond, Kentucky
Dates:	May 22 through May 25, 1991
Main theme:	Tour the Blue Grass country

Description:
This will be the fifth year of motorcycle rallies sponsored by *Rider* magazine. Their previous events have been so popular that Rider Rallies have now become a regular summer event for thousands of motorcyclists. The Rider Rally East returns to Richmond, Kentucky for its third straight year. Richmond has proven to be very hospitable to motorcyclists. The accommodations are plentiful and reasonably priced and the surrounding countryside is beautiful. Events will include a trade fair; guided scenic and historic tours; CMA services; bike judging; seminars; field events; barbecue; entertainment; touring bike prize drawing; factory demonstration rides; and much more. Hosting the ceremonies will be Beau Allen Pacheco; columnist, singer, and humorist.

Once you've registered for the rally, *Rider* will furnish you with a list of nearby motels and accommodations.

Price:
$50 per person

WYOMING — Rider Rally Wyoming

Rally Sponsor:	*Rider* Magazine P.O. Box 4000 Agoura, CA 91301 Contact: Rider Rally Staff Phone: 800-234-3450 or 818-991-4980
Location:	Cody, Wyoming
Dates:	July 17 through 20, 1991
Main theme:	Tour the wild west

Description:
Being held again by popular demand is the Rider Rally in Cody Wyoming. In Cody you'll see one of the most beautiful parts of the United States, including Yellowstone Park and the boundless buffalo country nearby. Events include a trade fair; seminars; motorcycle judging; field events; entertainment; great mini tours; Buffalo Bill Historical Museum tickets; touring bike giveaway, a Honda Pacific Coast; and much more. Hosting the ceremonies will be Beau Allen Pacheco: columnist, singer, and humorist.

Once you've registered for the rally, *Rider* will furnish you with a list of nearby motels and accommodations.

Price:
$55 per person

MICHIGAN — V-Daze

	Venture Touring Society 1615 South Eastern Ave. Las Vegas, NV 89104 Contact: Joe Schaerer, Executive Director Phone: 702-457-6657
Dates:	June 25 through June 29, 1991
Location:	Sault Ste. Marie, Michigan
Price:	• VTS members: rider, $42; passenger, $38 • AMA/VTS Booster: rider, $45; passenger, $40 • Other delegates: rider, $47; passenger, $43

- Children (12 and under): no charge
- When registering after June 1, 1991, add $5 to all fees

Description:
V-Daze is an annual convention for VTS members and friends to get together. The event, which is in its seventh year, is open to the public. Some of its highlights include poker runs, minitours, seminars, clinics, demos, field events, motorcycle contests, and a motorcycle parade and light show. Over 50 vendors will be exhibiting products ranging from accessories to insurance. Special events include attempting a world record for the longest parade of motorcycles crossing an international border and a grand prize drawing of a 1991 Venture Royale.

OKLAHOMA	**Wing Ding XIII**
	Gold Wing Road Riders Association, Inc. 3035 West Thomas Road Phoenix, AZ 85017 Contact: Neal Dushane, Executive Director Phone: 602-269-1403
Dates:	July 29 through August 1, 1991
Location:	Tulsa, Oklahoma Expo Center
Price:	• For GWRRA members: $45 per person on-site; lower rates for early registration • For nonmembers: $60 per person on-site; lower rates for early registration

Description:
Wing Ding is an opportunity for members of the Gold Wing Road Riders Association (GWRRA) to share, on a national level, the camaraderie and fellowship for which the organization is known. Over the past years 12 years a number of cities have hosted the event, and it has grown to the point where this year 10,000 members and associates are expected to attend.

Many events are planned for the convention including seminars, field events, door prizes, parade, poker run, talent show, bike judging, and a grand prize drawing of a 1991 Honda Gold Wing. Over 230 vendors are expected to attend with a wide variety of products. Take a demo ride in a new Honda, or a side car. Visit the sights of Tulsa including the Will Rodgers Museum, Indian shows, Oral Roberts University, and the beauty of the surrounding countryside.

INTERNATIONAL WEATHER CHART

To give you a sense of what kind of weather to expect on your travels we've listed several cities throughout the world with their average high and low seasonal temperatures, and relative humidity. It is always possible to find a place to ride your motorcycle. If the weather doesn't suit you, move on down the road.

Table entries are:
Average high temperature/Average low temperature, Relative humidity
  (Temperature is given in degrees Fahrenheit)
  (Relative humidity is in percent)

City	Jan–Mar	April–June	July–Sept	Oct–Dec
Arctic Bay, Canada	-14/-28, 0%	27/12, 80%	47/35, 81%	2/-10, 82%
Vancouver, B.C.	44/34, 78%	64/46, 63%	73/54, 62%	48/39, 84%
New York, NY	38/24, 58%	68/53, 54%	80/66, 60%	51/37, 60%
San Francisco, CA	59/47, 66%	63/51, 62%	65/53, 70%	63/51, 60%
Monterrey, Mexico	72/52, 59%	87/68, 51%	92/72, 57%	71/55, 60%
Buenos Aires, Arg.	83/63, 63%	64/47, 74%	60/43, 74%	76/56, 60%
Caracas, Venezuela	77/56, 62%	80/62, 71%	79/61, 75%	77/60, 66%
London, England	44/36, 72%	62/47, 57%	71/56, 62%	50/42, 78%
Innsbruck, Austria	40/24, 58%	68/46, 43%	75/54, 52%	46/ 0, 65%
Lugano, Switz.	48/31, 52%	69/50, 53%	80/60, 51%	51/38, 59%
Belgrade, Yug.	42/29, 67%	73/54, 51%	83/62, 46%	51/39, 71%
Moscow, U.S.S.R.	22/ 8, 66%	66/46, 43%	72/53, 55%	35/26, 79%
Oslo, Norway	30/19, 74%	61/43, 52%	70/53, 61%	38/31, 83%
Rome, Italy	55/42, 64%	74/56, 54%	86/67, 43%	61/49, 66%
Madrid, Spain	52/36, 62%	70/50, 49%	85/63, 35%	55/42, 65%
Bordeaux, France	51/36, 73%	69/48, 60%	78/56, 60%	55/40, 80%
Ankara, Turkey	42/26, 67%	73/49, 38%	87/59, 25%	57/37, 52%
Cameron Highlands, Malaysia	72/55, 73%	74/58, 79%	72/56, 76%	71/57, 81%
Beijing, China	39/18, 50%	81/55, 49%	86/68, 74%	48/28, 56%
Katmandu, Nepal	67/39, 68%	86/61, 61%	83/68, 84%	74/45, 78%
Bangkok, Thailand	91/72, 55%	93/77, 64%	90/76, 66%	87/72, 65%
Darwin, Australia	90/77, 72%	91/73, 47%	89/70, 45%	94/78, 58%
Melbourne, Australia	78/57, 50%	62/47, 62%	59/43, 60%	71/51, 52%
Christchurch, NZ	69/53, 60%	56/40, 69%	52/36, 66%	66/47, 64%
In Salah, Algeria	75/47, 34%	99/69, 23%	111/82,19%	80/53, 38%
Douala, Cameroon	86/74, 75%	86/73, 79%	80/71, 84%	84/73, 80%

INDEX

A

Acapulco, 127
Adriatic Sea, 204
Adventure Center, 14
Aegean Sea, 214
Alander, Carl, 10
Alaska Motorcycle Tours, Inc., 8, 66
Alcatraz, 86
Aldo, Finazzo, 317
Algeria, 216–217, 220, 222
Alps, 150, 153, 158, 162, 164, 179, 186, 189–191, 207, 209
American Motorcycle Rentals and Sales, 295
American Motorcyclist Association, 9, 60, 142–143
American Sportbike Tours, 10
Andes, 134
Andrews, Ron, 348
Apel, Peter, 56
Apennines, 205
Argentina, 140
Armonk Travel, 27
Aushina Tours, 11, 234
Australia, 261
    Eastern, 267
    Gold Coast, 258
    New South Wales, 259, 262, 264, 268, 273–274, 284
    Northern Australia, 271
    Northern Territory, 266, 270
    Queensland, 258, 268, 279, 285
    South Australia, 264, 269–270, 274
    Southern, 280, 282
    Tasmania, 277
    Victoria, 262, 264, 266, 268, 270, 273, 277, 283–284
    Western Australia, 269
Australia, Tasmania, 277
Australia, Victoria, 277
Australian Motorcycle Adventures, 13, 261
Australian Motorcycle Touring, 14, 262, 264
Australian-American Mototours, 12, 258–259
Austria, 150, 158, 162, 164, 170, 180, 185–186, 189–191, 197
Ayers Rock, 266, 275

B

Badanjilin Desert, 253
Baja, 115–116
Baja Expeditions, 15, 104
Bali, 236
Banff National Park, 69
Beach's Motorcycle Adventures, Ltd., 16, 53, 144, 150, 288, 337
Beach, Elizabeth L., 16
Beach, Rob, 16
Beach, Robert D., 16
Beijing, 235
Big Bike Tours, 17, 78, 80, 152
Big Sur, 90
Bike Tours Australia, 19, 67–68, 81, 236, 266–267, 269–271, 330
Bivak International, 20, 237
Black Forest, 152, 187
Black Sea, 213
Blackwood, David, 48
Blue Ridge Mountains, 96
Bodenburg, Elke, 37
Bosenberg Motorcycle Excursions, 21, 153–154, 156, 194, 318
Brass, Klaus, 47, 328
Brazil, 135, 137–138
Bryant, Jan, 36
Bryant, Terry, 36
Bryce Canyon, 78, 91
Bryce Canyon National Park, 100
Bryce National Park, 95
Budget Rent-a-Car, 320
Bunya National Park, 279

C

Cameroon, 219, 222
Canada
    Alberta, 71–72
    British Columbia, 67–68, 70–72, 74–75, 81
    Yukon Territory, 67–68
Cancun, 127
Caribbean, 110, 125–126, 130
Cascade Range, 82
Central African Republic, 218, 221
Chiang Mai Motorcycle Touring Club, 22, 238
China, 234, 253, 255
Chinatown, 86
Chocolate Mountains, 86
Chosa's Harley-Davidson, Inc., 297
Claude Kidd, 70

354 INDEX

Coat, Geoff, 14
Colorado, 88
Comerford Tours, 23, 146
Comerford, Paul, 23
Cook, Colin, 49
Copper Canyon, 106, 115, 121–122
Corbett National Park, 250
Corsica, 202
Costa Rica, 119
Crosby, Graeme, 335
Cunningham, George, 50, 333
Cunningham, Linda, 50
Custom tours, 35, 51
Cycle City Ltd. Honolulu, 298
Cycle Craft Co., Inc., 297
Cycle-East Adventures, 24, 240
Cyprus, 208–210
Czechoslovakia, 167, 180, 194, 199

D

Dagiel, Gary, 51
Dahl, Ms. Vonnie, 8
Death Valley, 78, 86, 90–91, 95
Death Valley National Monument, 82, 92
del Bondio, Christoph, 52
Del Monte, Frank, 60
Denali National Park, 66
Deroeux, Francois, 51
Desert National Park, 282
Desmond Adventures, Inc., 25, 83, 158, 160, 326, 340
Desmond, Thomas E., 25, 326, 340
Dick Farmer's Harley-Davison of Orlando, Inc., 297
Dolomites, 151, 158, 162, 164, 183, 206
Douglas, D.N., 346
Drescher, Jim, 26
Dushane, Neal, 351
Dutchcountry Motorcycle Tours, 26, 85

E

Edelweiss Bike Travel, 27, 86, 162, 164, 195, 273
Egypt, 226–228
El-Mahdy, Karim, 40
El-Mahdy, Tarek, 41
England, 143–144, 146, 148, 313
European Adventures, 28, 165–166, 168–173
European Alps, 165, 175–176, 182–183, 190–192
Explo-Tours, 29, 216–218, 220–222
Explorer, 269

F

FIM Rally, 142
Finland, 196

Fish, Jean, 41
Fisherman's Wharf, 86
France, 150, 154, 160–161, 164, 175–177, 182, 187, 190, 202
Frank Del Monte, 307
Freedom Tours, 30, 88
French, Les "Gringo", 31
Fromling, Kathrin, 320

G

Garner, Ed, 332
Geltl, Josef, 29
General Travel America, 13
Gennargentu Mountains, 202
Geoff Coat, 273
Germany, 150, 153–154, 156, 158, 162, 164, 166, 168–173, 177, 182–183, 185, 187, 189–191, 194–195, 197, 199, 205
Germany, Munich, 306
Glode, Werner, 54, 309
Golden Gate Bridge, 86
Goodman, Flori, 62
Goodman, Warren, 62, 341
Graeme Crosby Motorcycles, 335
Graham, Alyce, 13
Grand Canyon, 78, 82, 86, 90–92, 95, 98, 100–101, 346
Great Barrier Reef, 258, 268, 279
Great Britain, 146
Great Motorcycle Adventures, 31, 106–107, 109–110
Great Smoky Mountains, 96
Greece, 211
Greif, Jürgen, 49
Gulf of Mexico, 125
Guzzardo, Gina, 59, 306

H

H.G.B. Motorcycles, 310
Hale, Sue, 310
Halpern, Jed, 32
Harley Owners Group, 296
Harley-Davidson Motor Company, 297
Harley-Davidson of Glendale, 297
Harley-Davidson of Reno, 297
Harley-Davidson, Inc. of Miami, 297
Harmon, Randall B., 25, 326, 340
Harrison, Greg, 9
Hawthorn Motorcycles, 332
Heindel, Leon A., 21, 318
Hell's Gate, 75
Hluhluwe National Park, 224
Hoggar Mountains, 220
Holland, 188
Holland-Merten, Greg, 311
Holzberger, Bernd, 56

INDEX 355

Holzberger, Helmut, 56
Hong Kong, 234
Hosgood, Mike, 28
Hosgood, Renate, 28
Huasteca Canyon, 109
Hungary, 177

I

India, 241, 243–244, 246–247, 249, 251
Indonesia, 236
Indsun Adventure Tours, 33, 241, 243–244, 246–247, 249
InterCity, 316
Ireland, 142, 146, 148
Ireland, Republic of, 148
Isle of Man, 143
Isle of Skye, 143
Italy, 150, 158, 160, 164, 175–176, 179, 183, 190–191, 202–203, 205–206

J

Jamaica, 126
Japan, 252
Jasper National Park, 69
Jones, Mark, 61
Jureia National Park, 136, 138

K

K & K Fahrzeug Center Berkheim, 323
Kalman International Motorcycle Touring, 34, 89, 299
Kalman, David, 34, 299
Kalman, Kathy, 34, 299
Kenny, Robert, 30
Kenya, 218, 221
Keown, Craig, 12
Keown, Kerry, 12
Kidd, Claude, 40
Kiefer, Werner, 17
Kimmel, Sandy, 9
Klein, Hans-Joachim, 33
Kruger National Park, 224
Ksiazek, Michael, 323
Ksiazek, Peter, 323
Kumaon Mountains, 250

L

Lake, Vicki, 348
Lang, Warren, 13
Las Vegas, 95
Lenzner, Volker, 53, 57, 337
Liechtenstein, 150, 158, 162, 164, 191
Loch Ness, 143, 145
Loef, Alex, 43
London, 144

Los Alercos National Park, 140
Lotus Consulting Services, 35

M

Malaysia, 240
Mali, 217
Markowski, Mrs., 321
Martinique, 112
Mascorro, Skip, 46
May, Stephen, 45
McCamey, Marv, 45
McDonnell, Duke, 8
Mediterranean, 176, 182, 202, 205, 220, 222
Meier's Weltreisen, 91
Meier's Weltreisen GmbH, 37
Mexico, 106–107, 109, 113, 115–117, 120, 122–123, 125, 127
    Baja California, 104
    Yucatan Peninsula, 110
Mexico City, 127
mhs Motorradtouren GmbH, 38, 175–177, 179–180, 197, 202–203, 205, 224, 301, 340
Midwestern United States, 80
Mikumi National Park, 221
Miro, Conny, 303
Moar, Nicholas, 48
Mojave Desert, 90
Monaco, 160
Monte Carlo, 176, 182
Monte Pellegrino, 203
Motorcycle Adventures Australia, 36, 274, 277
Motorcycle buy and sellback plan
    Arizona, Phoenix, 307
    Australia, Melbourne, 330, 332
    California, San Francisco, 305
    England, 310
Motorcycle rental
    Arizona, 297
    Arizona, Tempe, 296
    Australia, Capalba-Queensland, 333
    Australia, Melbourne, 330, 332
    Austria, Vienna, 316
    British Colombia, 298
    British Columbia, Vancouver, 296
    California, 297
    California, Los Alamitos, 295
    California, Los Angeles, 296, 301, 303
    California, San Diego, 301, 306
    California, San Francisco, 299, 305
    Colorado, 297
    Colorado, Ft. Collins, 296
    Cyprus, Polis, 328
    England, London, 311, 313
    England, Middlesex, 310
    Florida, 297

356 INDEX

Florida, Miami, 296, 301, 303
Florida, Orlando, 296
France, Nice, 317
Germany, 297
Germany, Berlin, 320
Germany, Dusseldorf, 320
Germany, Esslingen-Berkheim, 323
Germany, Frankfurt, 296, 318, 320
Germany, Hamburg, 320
Germany, Munich, 301, 306, 320, 324
Germany, Pullach, 320
Hawaii, 298
Hawaii, Honolulu, 296
Massachusetts, 297
Massachusetts, Boston, 296
Nevada, 297
Nevada, Reno, 296
New York, New York, 301
New Zealand, Auckland, 335
New Zealand, Christchurch, 337
South Africa, Johannesburg, 301
Switzerland, Zurich, 326
Turkey, Antalya, 324
Venezuela, Valencia, 309
Motorcycle Tours North, 40, 70
Motorcycle transport
   Atlanta, 340
   Boston, 340
   Buenos Aires, 340
   Cairo, 340
   Canada, 340
   Chicago, 341
   Dallas, 340
   Frankfurt, 340
   Johannesburg, 340
   Los Angeles, 340–341
   Malaga, 340
   Miami, 340
   New York, 341
   Nice, France, 340
   Rio de Janeiro, 340
   San Francisco, 340
   Sanaa, Jemen, 340
   Sydney, 340
   Tel Aviv, 340
   Toronto, 340
   United States, 340
   Vancouver, 340
Motorrad Expedition Sahara, 40, 226
Motorrad Spaett, KG, 42, 207–208, 324
Motorrad-Reisen, 41, 92, 112, 182–183, 185, 187, 199, 206
Motorsportvereniging Ophemert, 43, 188
Moturis, Ltd., 303
Mount Fuji, 252
Mount Gambier, 265
Mount McKinley, 66–67
Mount Olympus, 210

Mount Sinai, 230
MSV Ophemert, 43, 188
Mt. Kilamanjaro, 219
Mueller, Barbara, 55
Mueller, Klaus, 55

N

Nakata, Kaz, 10
Napa Valley, 83
National Park of Calábria, 204
Nepal, 246
the Netherlands, 166, 168–169, 171–172, 188
New South Wales, 260, 285
New Zealand, 288–290, 292
New Zealand Embassies and Consulates, 335
Nicea Location Rent, 317
Nicholson, Martha, 21
Niger, 216, 222
Nigeria, 222
Nile River, 228
Nile Valley, 227
North Africa, 230

O

O'Brien, Suki, 58
Ortega, Brad, 45
Overland Tours, 44, 113

P

Pacific Northwest Motorcycle Adventures, 45, 93
Panama, 119
Pancho Villa Moto-Tours, 46, 95, 115–117, 119–120, 122–123, 125
Pantanal, 137
Peeples, Bruce, 44
Pennsylvania, 85
Peterborough Rally, 143
Petrus, Karl, 316
Pollard, Bruce, 335
Prima Klima Reisen GmbH, 47, 210, 251, 328
Pueblo National Park, 140

Q

Queensland, 258, 285

R

Raceways Rental, 311
Raedisch, Karl, 54
Rains, John, 53, 337
Rains, Maria, 53
Rallies
   13th Annual Davis Rally, 346
   1991 Grand Canyon International, 346
   Americade East 1991, 344

INDEX 357

Americade West 1991, 344
Black Hills Classic, 345
Daytona Bike Week, 347
Golden Aspen Rally, 348
Harley Owners Group Rally, 348
Rider Rally Kentucky, 349
Rider Rally Wyoming, 350
Sturgis, 345
V-Daze, 350
Wing Ding XIII, 351
Rallies in Arizona, 346
Rallies in Colorado, 344
Rallies in Florida, 347
Rallies in Iowa, 346
Rallies in Kentucky, 348–349
Rallies in Michigan, 350
Rallies in New Mexico, 348
Rallies in New York State, 344
Rallies in Oklahoma, 351
Rallies in South Dakota, 345
Rallies in Wyoming, 350
Ram, Charles S.C., 313
Reither, Mr., 321
Rentals, 17, 42, 47, 57
Richmond, Burt, 35
Rider Magazine, 349–350
Rio De Janeiro, 139
Rocky Mountain Moto Tours Ltd., 48, 71–72
Rocky Mountain Motorcycle Touring, 49, 74
Rocky Mountains, 69, 71, 82
Rosenbaum, Linda, 27

S

S.A.P. Tour, 32, 174
S.F. Wheels, 305
Sahara, 220, 222
Sahara Cross, 49, 227–228, 230
Sahara Desert, 226
San Bernardino Mountains, 86
Sardinia, 202
Sarroy Enterprises, 50, 279, 333
Schaerer, Joe, 350
Schafer, Mrs., 321
Schellhorn, Herbert, 38, 301, 340
Schellhorn, Wolfgang, 38
Schmidt, Peter, 47, 328
Schnieder Reisen, 53, 337
Scootabout Motorcycle Centre, 313
Scotland, 143–146, 148
Scottish Highlands, 143
Sears, Jeff, 305
Senegal, 217
Seymour Mountains, 75
Shipping, 42, 57, 62
Sicily, 203
Sierra Madre Mountains, 106, 109, 115, 121, 124

Sierra Mountains, 90
Sierra Nevada Mountains, 86
Singapore, 240
Singh, Himmat, 33
Smoky Mountain Motorcycle Vacations, 51, 96
Snowy Mountains, 263, 283
South Africa, 221, 224, 231
Southeast Asia, 237
Soviet Union, 195
    Russia, 200
Spaett, Josef, 42
Spaett, Paul, 42, 324
Spaett, Peter, 42
Spencer, David, 15
St. Catarina, 135
Stonehenge, 142, 144
Sunset Off-Road, 51
Sunshine Travel, 21
Switzerland, 150, 152, 158, 160–162, 164, 170, 174, 176, 182, 190–191

T

Tamborine National Mountain National Park, 279
Tanzania, 218, 221
Tassili Mountains, 220
Te Waipounamu Motorcycle Tours, 53, 289, 337
Team Aventura, 52
Tengri Desert, 253
Thailand, 238, 256
Tobler, Urs, 152
Tours
    Affordable Alps, 162
    Alaska, 66
    Algeria and Niger (Explo-Tours #TEN), 216
    AlpenTour™ East, 158
    AlpenTour™ West, 160
    Alpine and Dolomites Excursion, 153
    Alpine Countries, 192
    Alps and Southern France, 182
    AMA's EuroTour to Ireland and FIM Rally, 142
    AMA's EuroTour to Isle of Man, 143
    American Southwest, 95
    Argentina, 140
    Athens and The Cyclades, 211
    Aussie Tour, 273
    Austrian Tyrol, 165
    Ayers Rock – Alice Springs, 274
    Baja & Copper Canyon, 115
    Baja Expedition, 104, 116
    Bavaria and Bohemia Excursion, 194
    Bayerischer Wald, 166
    Beach's Alpine Adventures, 150
    Beach's British Bat, 144

358 INDEX

Beach's Maori Meander, 288
Best from the West, 78
Best of the Alps, 164
Best of the West, 86
Bike Tours Special '91, 266
Bikes and Buddies, 152
The Black Forest, 187
Boomerang Tour, 262
British Isles, 148
Castles and Grapes Excursion, 154
Chiang Mai Tour, 238
China, 255
China Motorcycle Expedition 1991, 234
Colonial Tour, 117
Colorado, 88
Copper Canyon Tour, 113
Copper Canyon Trail Ride, 106
Corsica and Sardinia, 202
Costa Rica, 119
Custom designed, 35, 51
Cyprus, 210
Dakar to Tunis (Explo-Tours #M7), 217
Desert Tour, 241
Destination High Alps, 190
Destination Moscow, 200
Dikes Tour, 188
The Dolomites, 179
Douala to Mombasa (Explo-Tours #MOM), 218
East Coast Australia, 261
East Coast Tour, 267
East Turkey, 213
Egypt Short Tour, 227
Egypt Tour, 228
Eifel Mountains, 168
Eifel Mountains, Black Forest and the Mosel, 169
Enduro High Alps Tour, 175
Fairbanks to Vancouver, 67
Four Nations Vacation, 146
Freedom Rider USA, 98
Garwhal Mountain Tour, 243
Goa, South Indian Coasts and Jungle by Royal Enfield, 251
Gold Coast to Cairns: Amazing Queensland, 258
Grand Alpine Tour, 191
The Grand Circle, 91
Grand India Tour, 244
Great Northern Tour, 70
High Alpine Circular Trip, 183
High Country Tour, 280
High Dunes and Deep Valleys: Algeria (#M4), 220
Himalaya Tour, 246
The Indian Badlands Rider, 99
Istra — a gourmet tour, 197
Jamaica, 126

The Kiwi Rider, 290
Longreach Tour, 285
Lykien on Motorcycle, 207
M'am Butterfly Tour Riders, 252
Magic Austria, 185
Mark Twain Tour, 80
Martinique, 112
Mazatlan Winter Get-Away, 120
Mexico, 127
Mombasa to Capetown (Explo-Tours #CAP), 221
Monterrey Sierra Madre Road Tour, 107
Monterrey Trail Ride, 109
Motorcycle Vacation in Bali, 236
Motorrad Expedition Sahara, 226
Mulga Tour, 264
New Zealand, 292
Nilgiri Tour, 247
Outback Tour One, 274
Outback Tour Three, 274
Outback Tour Two, 274
Outbacker, 270
Pancho Villa Motorcycle Campaign, 122
Pennsylvania Dutch Country, 85
Ride the West, 89
S.A.P. Tour, 174
The Safari Rider, 231
San Francisco to Vancouver, 81
Sicily and Southern Italy (a gourmet tour), 203
Sierra Madre Expedition, 123
The Silk Road Rider, 253
Sinai Tour, 230
Singapore–Malaysia Motorcycle Tour, 240
Smoky Mountains, 96
South Africa, 224
South Turkey and Cyprus, 208
Southern Bavaria, 170
Southern France, 176
Southwest United States, 100
Soviet Union '91, 195
Sport-Bike Tour, 177
Sunset Desert Tour, 282
Tasmania, 277
Temple Tour, 249
Thailand, 256
Thailand Tour, 237
The Best of the Canadian Rockies, 71
The Grand Tour, 101
The Harley Flavour of Queensland, 279 The Mountains of British Columbia, 72
The Oz Rider, 284
The Search for Bigfoot™, 93
The Wonders of New South Wales, 259
Three-Week Tour of New Zealand, 289
Tour Florianopolis, 135
Tour Pantanal, 137
Tour Parati, 138

INDEX 359

Tunis to Douala (Explo-Tours #DLA), 222
Tuscany (a gourmet tour), 205
Tuscany: The Magic Spell of Italy, 206
U.S.A. The Great American Dream: The New World, 92
United Germany Excursion, 156
Upper Austria, 180
Vancouver Island & Sunshine Coast Tour, 74
Vancouver Road Rider, 75
Vancouver to Fairbanks, 68
Vancouver to San Francisco, 81
Venezuela: East, West and the Andes, 134
Venezuela: The Andes, 131
Venezuela: The Northeast, 130
Venezuela: The West and the Andes, 132
Victoria One, 277
Victoria Two, 277
Victoria, Australia, 283
Vogelsberg, Sauerland and the Harz Mountains, 171
The Wandervogel Rider, 189
West Turkey, 213
Westerwald, 172
Westerwald and Mosel, 173
Wild West Tour, 83
Yucatan Peninsula Road Tour, 110
Yucatan Tour, 125
Tours, S.R.L., 54, 130–132, 134, 309
Trafalgar Square, 144
Trail Bike Tours, 55, 280, 282–283
Trans America Tours, 56, 135, 137–138
TransCyclist International, 53, 57, 75, 98–99, 189, 231, 252–253, 284, 290, 337
Travel Star, 58
Trev Deeley Motorcycles, Ltd., 298
Troost, Sjon, 20
Tropicana, 271
Tunisia, 217, 220, 222
Turkey, 207–209, 213
Turner, Andrew, 49
Tuscany, 205–206
Twickers World, 14

U

Uganda, 219
United States
  Alaska, 66–68, 70
  Arizona, 100
  California, 81, 100, 306
  Colorado, 99
  Nevada, 81, 92, 100
  New Mexico, 99
  North Carolina, 96
  Northwest, 93
  Southeast, 96
  Southwest, 78, 83, 86, 89, 91–92, 95, 98–101
  Utah, 81, 92, 100

Wyoming, 82
Unkovich, David, 22

V

van Bentum, Trudi, 20
Veenkamp, Eveline, 19, 330
Venezuela, 130–132, 134, 309
Victorian Tour Operators Association, 55
Villa Velha National Park, 135
Vogt, Lorne, 49
Voller, Mr., 321
Von Thielmann Tours, 59, 100, 126–127, 140, 148, 190–191, 200, 211, 213, 255–256, 292, 306
Von Thielmann, Michael, 59
Vosges Mountains, 187

W

Wachter, Werner, 27
Wagner, Tommy, 42
Wales, 142–143, 146
Warren, Randy, 58
Washington, 82
Wayne Murphy, 295
Weather chart, 352
Weidner, Kurt, 19
Weil, Hermann, 41
Western States Motorcycle Tours, 60, 101, 307
Wild Bull Tours, 61, 285
World Motorcycle Tours, 62, 192, 341
Wu, Michael, 11

Y

Yellowstone National Park, 82
Yeo, Rodney, 24
Yosemite National Park, 78, 92, 100
Yucatan Peninsula, 110, 125
Yugoslavia, 191–192, 197

Z

Zaire, 219
Zborschil, Judith, 41
Zeller, Mr., 321
Zion Canyon, 78
Zion National Park, 86, 91, 95, 98

ORDER FORM — POPULAR BOOKS ON MOTORCYCLE TOURING

Whitehorse Press
154 West Brookline Street
Boston, MA 02118

(UPS will not deliver to a P.O. box)

SOLD TO:

Name: _____

Street: _____

City: _____

State: _____ Zip: _____

Daytime Phone: (____) _____

UPS SHIPPING ADDRESS: *(If different):*

Name: _____

Street: _____

City: _____

State: _____ Zip: _____

(Speeds orders if we have a question.)

How Many	Item Code	Description	Price Each	Total Price Dollars	Cents
	B-B	Wageck: Motorcycle Bed & Breakfast	$15.00		
	BLNK	Blankenship: Best Roads of California	$13.95		
	COOP	Cooper: The Rider's Guidebook	$ 4.95		
	CULB	Culberson: Obsessions Die Hard	$11.95		
	DIR	Motorcycle Touring: International Directory – 91/92	$19.95		
	HD50	H-D: America's 50 Best Touring Roads	$12.95		
	JACDT	Jacobs: Ultimate Motorcycle Detailing	$16.95		
	PHIL	Philcox: How to Tour Europe by Motorcycle	$ 9.95		
	STER	Stermer: Motorcycle Touring and Travel	$24.95		
	SUN	Richmond: Run to the Sun	$24.95		
	THOEM	Thoeming: Motorcycle Touring	$24.95		
	ZEN	Pirsig: Zen and the Art of Motorcycle Maintenance	$ 5.95		
		Catalog of all our motorcycling books	free		
		Prices subject to change without notice.	Subtotal		
			MA Residents Add 5%		
			Shipping & Handling		
			Total Payment		

Order Toll-Free: 800-842-7077
(617-241-5241 in Massachusetts)
Order by FAX: 617-241-5247

Shipping and Handling:

U.S.: Add 10% of the total order, but not less than $1.00.
On request, we will ship by overnight delivery;
call us for shipping rates.

Canada and Mexico:
Add 15% of the total order, but not less than $1.50 U.S.

Australia, New Zealand, Asia & the Far East:
Shipped by air mail; $10.00 U.S. for FIRST BOOK,
plus $6.00 for each additional book

Other Countries:
Shipped by air mail; $8.00 U.S. for FIRST BOOK,
plus $5.00 for each additional book

PAYMENT: *(payment required before shipment)*

Credit card: ( ) Master Card ( ) VISA ( ) Amex ( ) Check ( ) Money Order (U.S. dollars only, please)

__ __ __ __ __ __ __ __ __ __ __ __ __ __ __ __ .
Credit Card Number *(please show spaces used in number)*

Expiration Date _____ / _____

Name on Card: _____

Signature: _____

Thanks for your order!

dirins91